PERIOD DETAILS SOURCEBOOK

MITCHELL BEAZLEY

PERIOD DETAILS SOURCEBOOK

JUDITH MILLER

First published in Great Britain in 1999
by Mitchell Beazley, an imprint of
Octopus Publishing Group Ltd
2–4 Heron Quays, London E14 4JP

Chief Contributor **John Wainwright**
Contributor **Suzanne Woloszynska**

Executive Editor **Judith More**
Executive Art Editor **Janis Utton**
Project Editor **Julia North**
Editor **Arlene Sobel**
Designer **Christopher Sparks**
Production Controller **Karen Farquhar**

A CIP record for this book is available from the
British Library.

ISBN 1 84000 137 2

Printed in China by Toppan Printing Co Ltd

CONTENTS

FOREWORD

We produced the first *Period Details* in 1987 and, judging from our readers' comments and subsequent sales, it proved a major success as a source of reference and inspiration for homeowners wishing to restore their period houses or re-create period interiors. Much, of course, has happened since its initial publication.

First, and foremost, the substantial growth of interest in period architecture and ornament that began in the 1970s has continued unabated, as more and more people have come to recognize the decorative (and, indeed, financial) potential of their homes. Second, in response to the considerable demand, numerous designers and manufacturers have been making an evermore extensive and diverse range of high-quality reproduction architectural fixtures and fittings. As demand for salvaged original components has often outstripped supply, this has been a welcome development, and one that has made restoration not only easier, but also, generally, more affordable.

Third, and equally significantly, ongoing historical research has continued to unearth new examples of period styles and period details – mostly adding to our knowledge, but sometimes requiring a reassessment of previously held beliefs.

Because of these developments we feel the time is right for a totally new *Period Details Sourcebook*. Among the many improvements on the original title, you will find a comprehensive style guide to the prevailing fashions in architecture and ornament from the Middle Ages to the end of the First World War. This should make it much easier to match particular fixtures and fittings to their original historical context. In addition, all the illustrations are new, technically superior to their predecessors and accompanied by far more detailed and useful descriptions. Empowered with all this information, I believe that you will find restoring and improving your home much easier, and also, as I have, even more rewarding.

Judith Miller

7

MEDIEVAL

During the Middle Ages – the period that began in the 5th century A.D., following the fall of the Roman Empire, and lasted until the Renaissance (*see* pp.10–11) – architecture and interior decoration were the preserve of the seigneurial classes, who alone had the time and money to indulge in these "artistic" preoccupations. Consequently, what is now referred to as "Medieval style" was confined to their sparsely furnished stone-built or timber-framed castles and manor houses, rather than the primitive and often impermanent dwellings of the poor.

The prevailing vocabulary of architecture and ornament in the Middle Ages was Gothic. While exhibiting various regional variations, Gothic style was characterized by the use of architectural elements such as lancets (pointed arches); foils (lobed forms shaped like the outlines of grapevine, ivy or strawberry leaves); cusping (decorative projections, mainly in the form of heads, animals or leaves); tracery (decorative ribs applied to the upper sections of arched windows, and often consisting of foils and cusps); and arcading (linked arches supported by piers or columns). These forms were also applied (carved or painted) to furniture and artefacts, and were augmented with a rich canon of decorative motifs and imagery, much of which was derived from illustrated medieval manuscripts or, simply, the architect's or artist's imagination. Notable examples included naturalistic representations of flora and fauna; the seasons; human figures, such as clerics, masons and patrons of the arts; chevron and chequer patterns; and heraldic emblems, such as cyphers, coats-of-arms, mythical beasts and the "Tree of Life".

While the Middle Ages ended in the 14th century, with the flowering of the Renaissance and its revival of the classical Graeco-Roman vocabulary of architecture and ornament, medieval style lingered on, especially in England, where Gothic and heraldic forms and motifs were, until the 17th century, often combined with their classical equivalents. Moreover, like its eventual successor, the style was to enjoy a revival during the 19th century (*see* pp.24–5).

1 In many single-storey medieval houses, and in the upper rooms of two-storey houses, ceilings consisted of the exposed skeletal structure – the wooden beams, trusses, purlins (horizontal timbers) and rafters – of the roof, and the underside of the roof covering, made of woven straw matting, wattled hazel twigs or wooden boards. Ceilings in the ground-floor rooms of two-storey houses were the supporting beams and joists of the upper floors, the spaces in between being either the undersides of the floorboards or, as here, plaster panels. Decoration of the beams and joists ranged from simple chamfering to elaborate carvings, usually of organic motifs. Plaster infills were limewashed, either white or, as here, in earth tones, and sometimes hand-painted or stencilled with heraldic motifs.

2 Plastered wall surfaces above wainscotting (see 4) often featured heavy tapestry hangings, which provided pictorial decoration and insulated against the cold. These were usually suspended from metal or wooden rods, now used here to hang paintings, sculptures and a mirror above the fireplace.

3 Internal door surrounds in medieval houses were often more elaborate than their external counterparts. They could be made of either wood or stone, and either flat-topped or "four-centred" (in the form of a shallow arch rising to a central point). Many were unornamented. However, some were carved with foliate and heraldic motifs. Most doors were battened planks, usually oak or elm, and occasionally the securing nailheads were left exposed as decoration. During the late Middle Ages, lighter panelled doors were sometimes installed in lieu of heavier battened ones.

4 Many timber-framed medieval houses had half-timbered walls. These consisted of an exposed framework of vertical wooden studs and horizontal cross-rails, filled in between with lath-and-plaster or wattle-and-daub. However, in stone-built and some grander timber-framed houses, the walls were uniformly plastered. As with the plaster infills

on ceilings (see 1), basic decoration took the form of limewashing, in either in white, "natural" stone or earth colours. Stencilled motifs, such as flowers and heraldic devices, were often applied over the limewash in contrasting colours, including gold. In the most flamboyant interiors, large murals of landscapes, or hunting, biblical or mythological scenes, could also be applied.

5 In the wealthiest medieval households, plastered walls (see 4) were often lined with wainscotting – usually half-height, as here, but sometimes full-height. The panelling, mostly of oak or elm, but sometimes painted fir, was constructed in simple geometric patterns. The finest also featured decorative carvings and roundel paintings.

6 For most of the Middle Ages, open fires (from which the smoke drifted up through a hole in the roof) were universal. However, late in the period, the enclosed wall fireplace was gradually adopted. In many cases, as here, there was no fire surround – just an open hearth – although some hearths were topped with a carved wooden or stone lintel, usually in the shape of a four-centred arch. The painted chequer pattern applied here to match the flooring (see 8) is a rather elaborate, but not untypical, form of decoration.

7 The hearth itself was either made of stone or brick, the rear of which was often protected by a wrought-iron fireback. Logs were the primary source of fuel, and burned on a pair of small brick walls, or on wrought-iron firedogs or, very occasionally, in an iron firebasket.

8 While oak or elm boards were used in upper storeys, at ground level beaten earth, bricks laid on edge, stone slabs or tiles laid in geometric patterns were the most common types of flooring. Some floors were embellished with stencilled patterns. However, carpets were only laid on tabletops. Floor coverings, if used, were either strewn rushes or plaited rush matting – the latter loose-laid, or fused to a thin plaster screed before it dried.

ℛENAISSANCE

Classical Graeco-Roman architecture and ornament, largely dormant during the Middle Ages (*see* pp.8–9), was revived during the 14th, 15th and 16th centuries – a period known as the Renaissance. Beginning in Italy, following archaeological excavations of buildings and artefacts that had survived from ancient Rome, and thereafter spreading across Europe, the Renaissance saw the reintroduction of the columns, pilasters, pedestals, capitals and entablatures of the Classical Orders of architecture, as well as classical forms such as temple-front porticoes, curved arches and rusticated masonry. Equally significant was the readoption of classical Roman motifs, such as acanthus leaves, scrolling foliage, swags and festoons, *pateras* and scallop shells, which were applied not only as architectural ornament, but also to furniture, textiles and decorative artefacts.

The impact of the Renaissance on subsequent styles of architecture and ornament was substantial. For example, the High Renaissance classicism of architects such as Andrea Palladio, who strove to preserve the integrity and purity of original Roman forms, provided the inspiration for early 18th-century Palladianism (*see* pp.12–5), while the Renaissance Mannerism of architects such as Michelangelo, who elaborated on Roman forms in a highly sculptural way, gave rise to the flamboyant, 17th-century Baroque style (*see* right). Interestingly, however, the influence of Renaissance classicism on contemporary 16th-century Elizabethan, and early 17th-century Jacobean, houses in England wasn't all-embracing. As this room (*see* left) at Parham House reveals, the inherent symmetry and proportion of classical forms is evident in the rectilinear configuration of the wall panelling and the panelled doors, in the scrolling arms and stretchers of the upholstered chairs and in the gilt picture frames with their bands of bead and foliage mouldings. However, in this example these features are characteristically and eclectically combined with lingering elements of Medieval style, notably the rush matting on the floor, the stretchered stool and the barley-twist table legs.

1 *Medieval-style, battened-plank oak doors were still hung in most Renaissance interiors. However, in the grandest houses they were increasingly supplanted by lighter panelled oak doors – the oak either a natural honey colour, or limed. Carved, linenfold panels were very fashionable, although plain geometric panels defined by simple mouldings were more prevalent. Most doors were secured with a simple wooden or iron latch; iron or brass box locks were the preserve of the wealthy.*

2 *The most common interior wall surface was limewashed flat plaster. However, full-height oak panelling, or dado-height panelling surmounted by tapestry hangings, were installed in the best houses. The configuration of the panels generally echoed those on the doors, with the most opulent featuring carved arabesques, strapwork or foliate forms.*

3 *Where full-height panelling was used, ornate, gilt-framed paintings provided pictorial decoration previously supplied by tapestries.*

4 *Except in the poorest households, which were lit by rushes dipped in fat, and fire from the hearth, wax candles were the source of artificial illumination in Renaissance houses. Some were housed in lanterns, wall sconces and, in the finest reception rooms, centrally hung chandeliers. However, most were fixed in candlestands made of, as here, turned and carved wood, or brass or pewter.*

5 *Stone slab floors were often laid on ground floors in Renaissance houses, sometimes in illusionistic, geometric patterns. However, as methods of damp-proofing improved, wide butt-jointed oak or elm boards were increasingly used, having once been confined to the upper storeys. Where a floor covering was employed, as here, the near-universal choice was woven rush matting.*

6 *Imported oriental carpets were considered too expensive to walk on, and thus only used as table coverings or, as here, placed under the best pieces of furniture.*

BAROQUE

Emerging from the late-16th-century Mannerist interpretation of classical Roman architecture and ornament (*see* left), the flamboyant Baroque style swept across Europe during the 17th century, and lasted until the Palladian Revival of the early 18th century (*see* pp.12–3). This English Baroque fireplace exhibits many of the fundamental characteristics of this style, in which architectural fixtures and fittings – pediments, cornices, arches, columns, corbels, fire surrounds – and furniture, were voluptuously carved and, in some cases, embellished with figural ornaments (especially cupids and angels). When combined with an extensive use of exotically coloured marbles, mirror-glass, extravagantly painted *trompe l'oeil* decorations and, as here, displays of oriental ceramics, the overriding effect was one of exuberant and grandiose theatricality.

GEORGIAN

Historically, the Georgian period began with the accession of George I to the English throne and ended with the death of George IV. However, the description "Georgian style" is more usually applied to the architecture and interior decoration fashionable during the reigns of George I and II (1714–60) – the reigns of George III and IV (1760–1830) being dominated by the neo-classical Adam and Regency styles (*see* pp.16–17 and 20–1).

Chiefly promoted by the influential Scottish architect, Colen Campbell, and the leading patron of the arts, Lord Burlington, Georgian style emerged as a reaction to the grandiose excesses of the 17th-century Baroque style (*see* p.11), and was based primarily on the buildings and republished observations of the 16th-century Italian architect, Andrea Palladio (*see* pp.10–11). Essentially classical Roman, rather than Greek, in origin, Palladianism in its purest form, and particularly when applied to the grandest exteriors, was characterized by bold, austere and massive architectural elements, such as temple-front porticoes; giant Roman columns; rusticated masonry; tripartite, arch-topped Venetian windows; and coffered ceilings. In the finest interiors, it manifested itself in heavily sculptured Roman motifs, such as herms, eagles, dolphins and masks, which were applied to both architectural fixtures and fittings and furniture.

Ultimately, however, Georgian style – which was widely adopted in Russia, Prussia and America (*see* pp.14–15 and 18–19) – relied for effect not upon sheer scale, but instead on harmony of proportion and detail, and it was these fundamental characteristics which underpinned the more understated modelling and ornamentation of most Georgian houses. The Georgian drawing room (*see* left) exemplifies a style in which architectural columns, fire surrounds, linear mouldings and built-in display cabinets are positioned, scaled and painted to establish an aesthetically pleasing symmetry – a quality that also extends to the construction and arrangement of the fine Georgian furniture.

1 The ornamentation of Georgian ceilings usually reflected the status of the house. The most elaborate were divided into geometrical compartments by plaster mouldings. Further embellishment – either trompe l'oeil *painted or plastered – typically took the form of scrolling foliage, husks and other classical motifs. However, many ceilings consisted of an expanse of flat plaster, painted white or in "sky" tones (such as gray, yellow or pink) and bordered with a plaster cornice bearing bands of foliate, coin, wavescroll or dentil motifs.*

2 Full-height wooden wall panelling was used in many Georgian reception rooms up until c.1740, and usually flat-painted – the most fashionable colour being "drab" (a mixture of gray, blue and green) – or, in some cases, painted faux marbre. *However, flat-plastered walls topped with a cornice (see 1), divided by a dado rail (see 8) and bottomed with a skirting board, were more prevalent, especially from the 1740s onward. Favoured finishes for the field above the dado included flat paint, as here, silk damask or brocade (stretched over a series of thin wooden battens nailed to the plaster) or wallpaper. Fashionable wallpaper patterns were mostly based on stylized or naturalistic depictions of flowers and foliage.*

3 Columns derived from the classical Roman Orders of architecture – Doric, Ionic, Corinthian, Composite and Tuscan – were often installed in larger Georgian houses, either to provide structural support or, when that was not required, as here, for architectural effect. This fluted column – one of a pair used to define the division between two reception rooms – is carved and turned from wood.

4 The best Georgian fire surrounds were made from white statuary marble, while the most exotic featured inlays of multi-coloured marbles or porphyries. Cheaper scagliola or wooden surrounds were also installed – the latter flat-painted, or painted faux marbre. *All surrounds had a narrow mantelshelf supported by simple brackets, architectural jambs or pairs of carved caryatid figures. The "earred" egg-*

and-dart moulding that borders the jambs and divides the frieze of this surround is a typical embellishment, as are the blue-and-white delftware tiles lining the hearth.

5 The cast-iron dog grate, incorporating a raised basket well-suited to burning coals, became increasingly popular during the first half of the 18th century as coal gradually superseded logs as the primary source of fuel in Europe. Fenders, which defined the perimeter of the hearth and protected adjacent floor coverings from hot coals, were mainly brass, and often ornamented with classical details, such as urn-shaped finials.

6 Many fire surrounds had an architectural overmantel which echoed the form and ornamentation of the surround itself, and often incorporated a picture panel or a mirror-glass. The alternative was to hang a picture above the surround, or stand a gilt-framed mirror on the mantelshelf – the latter was an increasingly fashionable option in later Georgian interiors.

7 Built-in bookcases and cupboards were installed in most Georgian houses, usually flanking fireplaces. Their frames and doors were often defined by mouldings that matched those employed elsewhere in the room. The best were oak or mahogany, but most were painted pine. Where glazed doors were used, the configuration of the glass panels invariably corresponded to that of the windows.

8 The profiles of wooden and plaster dado rails, like the tops of skirting boards, were derived from the mouldings used in the Classical Orders of architecture. Favoured profiles included torus, scotia, ovolo, astragal, ogee, cyma reversa and cyma recta.

9 While the oriental rug in front of the fireplace is an authentic Georgian floor covering, the fitted ivory-coloured carpet is a much later addition. Most rooms had oak, elm, fir or pine floorboards, either left untreated or stained and polished at the edges to provide a border for a centrally placed rug.

AMERICAN COLONIAL

The term "American Colonial" is applied to all permanent buildings constructed in the American Colonies, from their initial settlement in 1607, to their gaining independence from Britain in 1783. Covering virtually a 200-year span, the description is thus very broad, and really embraces two distinct architectural phases: the settlement period, up to the 1720s, and the Georgian (or Palladian, or classical) period thereafter.

Except in the southern Colonies, where some of the finest houses were constructed of brick, the majority of dwellings during the settlement period were of timber-frame construction and modelled on late-medieval post-and-beam houses (see pp.8–9) – although toward the end of the 17th century many had developed the symmetry of plan and fenestration, and architectural features, notably jettied overhangs, of provincial Renaissance town houses (see pp.10–11). However, a fundamental difference between these American houses and their European counterparts lay in the treatment of the structural wall system: in Europe, the vertical studs and the wattle-and-daub panels in between were usually left exposed – an effect known as half-timbering – whereas in most Colonial houses they were sheathed in clapboards (outside) and wooden panelling (inside). The interior (see left) of an early 18th-century house in New Hampshire, is typical of the American approach, which provided better insulation against the rigours of the climate, and was made possible by the considerable resources of locally available timber.

Introduced by wealthy merchants and planters, and largely inspired by English architectural pattern books, the Georgian period witnessed the gradual establishment of Palladian-inspired housing in the Colonies – a classical style of architecture and ornament described on pages 12–13. Again, however, there was a basic difference between the English and Colonial models: while the former were constructed of brick and stone, the latter were mostly made of wood.

1 The earliest American Colonial houses had low ceilings with exposed joists and beams, between which the wooden floorboards of the floor above were left clearly visible. In the simplest dwellings the joists and beams were sometimes left with the bark intact, while in grander houses they were smoothly planed and squared and sometimes embellished with chamfering and decorative stops. However, by the late 17th century, plain lath-and-plaster ceilings, as here, began to be installed in new houses; sometimes these displayed slightly undulating surfaces owing to the unevenness of the joists to which the laths were attached. The favoured finish was flat-painted limewash – usually white or pale off-white colours. Toward the end of the Colonial period, more flamboyant plaster ceilings appeared in grander houses. The configuration of their elaborate plaster mouldings was mainly based on either English Georgian (see pp.12–13) or German Baroque (see p.11) precedents. It is interesting to note that as the Colonies moved closer to establishing independence, native North American motifs, such as the tobacco leaf, were increasingly incorporated into these designs.

2 A variety of wall treatments was employed in Colonial houses. Plain plaster, and lath-and-plaster infills with the studs left exposed, appeared early on in the Colonial period, while in the 18th century plaster fields were sometimes combined with dado wainscotting. However, given the abundance of timber in the Colonies, full-height wall panelling was particularly prevalent in larger and smaller houses alike – although the grander the house, the more elaborate the panelling. Here, unpretentious, chamfered, tongue-and-groove planks are used, bordered at the ceiling with a simple cornice moulding. Made of softwood, they are characteristically flat-painted in green – a favourite colour from the Colonial palette that also included earth tones of red, brown, almond and yellow, and slightly brighter blues. Fashionable and more decorative paint finishes included marbling and grained simulations of expensive hardwoods.

3 Panelled doors, typically with two panels in low relief, began to appear in better Colonial houses in the late 17th century, and more elaborate Georgian-style raised-panel doors with classical surrounds (see pp.12–13) became increasingly common from the 1730s onward. However, most 17th- and many early 18th-century houses had simpler battened doors, constructed of vertical boards nailed together with two or more horizontal boards at the rear. Most were made of softwood, and painted in one of the darker colours from the Colonial palette, notably earthy browns, reds or greens. Where better-quality hardwoods were used, these were usually stained a natural wood colour.

4 Chandeliers and pendant lamps were very rare in Colonial houses prior to the 1750s, and were mainly made of wood, iron or tinned sheet iron, rather than glass or crystal. Thus the primary sources of lighting for most of the Colonial period were the glow from the fireplace, rush candles, oil lamps, Betty lamps (boat- or saucer-shaped lamps filled with grease or oil) and, as here, candle sconces. The simplest were made of tinned sheet iron; more elaborate versions incorporated small, concave mirrors to enhance the illumination.

5 Although the earliest Colonial houses had compacted earth floors, this butt-jointed pine floorboard, unstained and unvarnished, is typical of most houses. Marginally more sophisticated variations included tongue-and-groove and spline-jointed boards – the latter consisting of grooved boards joined by thin strips of wood. In the late 18th century, some wooden floors were painted in imitation of stone. Real stone floors were rare, and were usually confined to halls and porches.

6 While European or oriental carpets were laid in the finest houses from the early 18th century onward, rush matting, rag rugs or, as here, painted canvas floorcloths were the staple floor covering of Colonial houses. The diagonal check pattern, which was sometimes marbled, was particularly popular.

Adam

The interior (*see* left) is in Home House, in London, England, and was designed *c.*1775 by the Scottish architect Robert Adam (1728–92). It is one of the grander examples of the neo-classical style of architecture, decoration and ornament known as Adam style that was established by Robert Adam, and his less influential brothers James and John, during the second half of the 18th century. The inspiration lay in the buildings and artefacts of Roman antiquity, the Italian Renaissance (*see* pp.10–11) and ancient Greek and Etruscan civilizations, and was fuelled by new information on the Graeco-Roman vocabulary of architecture and ornament that had come to light as a result of the archaeological excavations of classical Greek and Roman cities and towns – notably Herculaneum (beginning in 1738) and Pompeii (starting in 1755), in southern Italy. The inspirational reference material unearthed at these sites was widely disseminated throughout Europe and America by architects, designers, craftsmen and patrons of the arts, who either personally visited them on the Grand Tour, or studied the writings and pattern books of architects such as Giovanni Battista Piranesi (1720–78), who promoted the richness and diversity of Greek, Roman, Etruscan and ancient Egyptian architecture and ornament.

Robert Adam – who undertook the Grand Tour and was strongly influenced by the works of Piranesi – drew on this wealth of information to create the eclectic and highly distinctive Adam style that became widely admired for its grandeur and elegance, the subtlety of its deployment of classical motifs and imagery and its integration of architectural structure and interior design of the buildings. First fashionable in Britain, Adam style provided much of the inspiration for the emergence of neo-classicism in France during the reign of Louis XVI, which, in turn, influenced English Regency style (*see* pp.20–1). Adam style also made a significant impact in Italy, Germany and Russia and, toward the late 18th century, formed the basis of early Federal style in America (*see* pp.18–19).

1 *During the second half of the 18th century, most ordinary houses had plain plaster ceilings augmented with relatively simple dentil or egg-and-dart plaster cornices. However, in grander Adam-style houses, and especially in their reception rooms, plasterwork ceilings were divided by decorative panels or bands of stylized flower or leaf motifs derived from the classical vocabulary of ornament. The panels or bands were usually arranged around a central medallion or roundel, and were either painted or gilded plaster mouldings, painted onto flat plaster, or painted on canvas or paper, and then fixed to the ceiling. In the grandest reception rooms, Adam often employed artists such as Biagio Rebecca and Angelica Kaufmann to paint some of the panels or roundels with figures or scenes from classical Greek or Roman mythology.*

2 *The ornamentation of the deep frieze below the cornice is typical of Adam style. Here, radiating bands of anthemia – stylized representations of the acanthus flower and one of the most regularly employed motifs in classical ornament – are flanked by figurative plaster roundels. The latter are encompassed by strings of stylized bud-like motifs known as husks. As on the ceiling above and the walls below, the use of gilded ornament set against various shades of green is typically Adam.*

3 *On the entablature that runs along the top of the lower section of the walls, Adam has applied painted and gilded plaster urns above the pilasters (see 5). Urns, which were usually distinguished from vases by their lids, were originally employed in Greek and Roman architecture as a symbol of death, loss or mourning. However, in late-18th-century neo-classical interiors this funerary connection was rarely intended, and urns were used interchangeably with vases – the latter being probably the most enduringly popular of all classical architectural motifs.*

4 *Husks also feature on the entablature, and here they are hung from ribbons and strung as gilded-plaster festoons – the latter inspired*

by the fruit-and-floral garlands that were hung in Greek and Roman temples. Positioned within the swags of the festoons are plaster pateras. Based on the fluted dishes or wine holders used in classical Greek religious ceremonies, these circular (and sometimes oval) forms have the appearance of stylized flowers, and thus, from the 18th century onward, were also known as rosettes.*

5 *Adam has flanked the pair of double-doors with ornate pilasters. These flat, rectangular, column-like forms are linked by the entablature (see 3 and 4) and are derived from classical architecture. As well as being decorated with acanthus-leaf capitals, figurative roundels and bucrania (the skulls of rams or goats originally hung within festoons in Greek and Roman temples), the pilasters also frame mirrored panels. The purpose of the mirrors is to increase the sense of space and to enhance the candlelight from wall-mounted girandoles (branched, wall-mounted candleholders) (see 6).*

6 *Gilded or painted girandoles were a popular source of lighting in neo-classical interiors. Here they are mounted above candelabra-like tiers of gilded wreaths – a form of decoration inspired by Roman wall paintings.*

7 *Six-panelled doors, either singles or pairs, were almost standard in Neo-classical houses of the late 18th century. The grandest examples were made from polished hardwood, such as mahogany, and the most exotic were inlaid with finely figured woods such as ebony, holly or cherry. However, softwood doors, wood-grained in imitation of expensive hardwoods as here, or painted with motifs and imagery, from the classical vocabulary of ornament, were perfectly acceptable alternatives.*

8 *Butt-jointed boards of oak, fir or pine were the most common type of flooring during the late 18th century. However, in many Adam-style reception rooms, rugs – either geometrically patterned or with floral designs of oriental origin – were laid on top.*

AMERICAN FEDERAL AND EMPIRE

Neo-classical styles of architecture and decoration began to cross the Atlantic from Britain and mainland Europe through émigré architects and pattern books just prior to the Declaration of Independence in 1776. Generally referred to as Federal style, American neo-classicism was initially based on Adam style (*see* pp.16–17), with exteriors characterized by delicate columns, arch-top windows and fanlights, and interiors richly decorated with classical motifs such as festoons, *pateras*, rosettes, urns and scrolling foliage. However, early Federal style also embraced a purer, sterner, Roman-based neo-classicism which, by the end of the 18th century, had largely superseded Adam style. Promoted by Thomas Jefferson, third President of the United States, as an appropriate architectural language for the new republic, this "Roman Revival" was partly inspired by English Palladian models (*see* Georgian style, pp.12–13), partly by French neo-classicism during the reign of Louis XVI (*see* Regency style, pp.20–1) and partly by original Roman buildings that had recently been discovered in southern France.

During the first three decades of the 19th century, until the emergence of the Greek Revival style (*see* pp.22–3), French neo-classical taste continued to exert a considerable influence, especially in the adoption of Empire style for the interior decoration and ornament of finer American houses – represented by the dining room (*see* left) of Richard Jenrette's early 19th-century American Empire-style house on the Hudson River, in New York State. Empire style originated in France in the late 1790s under the patronage of Napoleon Bonaparte and his Empress Josephine, and through designers Charles Percier and Pierre Fontaine's post-revolutionary restorations of French palaces. Inherently opulent, the style was characterized by the use of Imperial Roman ornament and decoration, augmented with Etruscan, ancient Egyptian and military motifs, and applied not only to architectural fixtures and fittings, but also to furniture, wallpapers, carpets, curtains, light fittings and decorative artefacts.

1 Federal ceilings ranged from wooden boards (usually whitewashed) in the simplest houses, through flat plaster in larger dwellings, to flat plaster embellished with decorative mouldings in the grandest houses. This dining room has a flat-plaster field and a central rose featuring rings of acanthus leaves. More flamboyant ceilings were also bordered or segmented with bands of neo-classical motifs, such as guilloche or scrolling foliage, sometimes highlighted with gilding.

2 This relatively plain cornice is derived from the concave cyma recta mouldings used in the Classical Orders of architecture. Deeper and more elaborate cornices featured rows of other classical motifs, such as anthemia, swags-and-tails, vases and beading.

3 The most notable development in wall treatments during the Federal period was the gradual elimination of the full-height wainscotting favoured during the Colonial era. Instead, many walls were divided horizontally into a dado, field and frieze. Some typical configurations included a wainscot or papered dado (above a wooden skirting board), a flat-painted or wallpapered field and a plaster or papered frieze. Whatever the material, in the finer houses the dado and frieze were usually embellished with neo-classical motifs; popular wallpaper patterns for the field were florals, stripes and pictorials of either classical or contemporary scenes. The alternative, and more austerely classical arrangement, as here, was to divide the walls vertically into panels – the divisions marked by paper cutout or paint mouldings. Flat paint or painted faux marbre, were usual finishes for the areas between the divisions.

4 Federal windows were distinguished from their Colonial counterparts by thinner glazing bars and larger panes of glass. As here, the windows in grander houses often extended from near the ceiling to the floor, and featured architrave embellished with neo-classical detailing, such as fluting and corner pateras; some were also set in recessed arches.

5 While most Federal houses were lit by oil-burning lamps or candles, fine glass or bronze chandeliers (mainly from England and France) were often employed in the reception rooms of more opulent houses from the early 1800s. As here, these were often supplemented with brass, bronze or crystal candle sconces.

6 Although pictures were often hung above the fireplace in Federal houses, overmantel mirrors became increasingly popular from the early 19th century onward. As in Regency interiors, oval mirrors (either with flat or convex glass) were very fashionable, the most elaborate bordered with bead or dentil mouldings, flanked by candle sconces and crested with fishes or birds, notably eagles.

7 The best Federal fire surrounds were made of marble, although painted wooden ones (with marble slips) were also in widespread use. This example is relatively plain; more decorative surrounds featured neo-classical motifs such as vases, swags, garlands, pateras and mythological scenes.

8 While stoves and imported hob grates were in widespread use by the 1780s, most Federal hearths burned logs on firedogs. Iron firedogs were most common, but in grander houses brass firedogs embellished with neo-classical urns or spherical finials were more usual.

9 Six-panelled doors featured in most Federal houses, although four- and even eight-panelled versions were also used. Most were made of pine, maple, poplar or cypress, and often grained in imitation of mahogany – real mahogany doors were confined to the wealthiest households. Door surrounds invariably echoed their counterparts around windows.

10 Pine boards were the standard flooring in Federal houses, and often stencilled with neo-classical motifs or diamond patterns. Floor coverings included straw matting, stencilled or marbled floorcloths and, in the grandest houses, carpets with floral or neo-classical motifs set in geometric patterns.

REGENCY

The English Regency was the period from 1811 to 1820 when George, Prince of Wales, ruled England as Prince Regent during the illness of his father, George III. However, what became known as Regency style emerged through the patronage of Prince George as early as the late 1780s, and remained in vogue until the end of his reign as George IV in 1830. The style was initially inspired by Prince George's admiration for French architecture and interior decoration during the reign of Louis XVI (1774–92) – a style characterized by rectilinear neo-classical fixtures and fittings, such as columns, pilasters, friezes and architraves, providing a perfect foil for precise arrangements of mirror-glass, crystal chandeliers and fine furniture. The resulting elegance, space, symmetry and proportion – evident in the South Drawing Room (*see* left) of the house built 1792–1824, in London, by the architect Sir John Soane – remained essential characteristics of Regency interiors. The style did not remain static, and around the turn of the 19th century it began to evolve in response to the emergence of French Empire style which, under the patronage of Napoleon Bonaparte, swept first across Europe and later America. English architects and designers did not simply copy Empire style, and so while French interiors were dominated by replications and adaptations of the architectural ornament of ancient Rome, many Regency interiors combined these with classical Greek equivalents and elements of *Le Style Etrusque* (*see* pp.16–17).

Further differences between English Regency and French Empire lay in the former's adoption of some architectural features, such as pointed arches, window tracery, castellated parapets and fan vaulting, derived from the medieval vocabulary of ornament. Also, exotic *chinoiserie*-based schemes, absent from French interiors, appeared in some grander Regency buildings, although they were generally confined to one room. Common, however, to both French Empire and English Regency was the use of ancient Egyptian motifs, such as palm trees and sphinxes – inspired by the military campaigns in Egypt during the Napoleonic wars.

1 *In comparison with the highly elaborate decoration of late-18th-century Adam-style ceilings (see pp.16–17), the ceiling in Sir John Soane's South Drawing Room displays the more austere ornamentation favoured by 19th-century Regency architects. Here, a series of recessed, slightly concave compartments, or coffers (only one shown), is linked by pairs of relatively plain linear plaster mouldings. Each compartment features a central pendant medallion encompassed by bead moulding and, in the four corners, by classical Greek anthemia. Bead mouldings also help to define the perimeters of compartments.*

2 *Relatively restrained ornamentation of the cornice is also characteristic of most 19th-century Regency interiors. Here, the plaster moulding is a simple string of plaster husks – a favourite neo-classical motif.*

3 *Most Regency architects maintained the classical tripartite division of walls. However, in the South Drawing Room, Soane has dispensed with the usual demarcation between the three sections by applying the same decorative treatment – flat paint over plaster – to all of them. The sulphurous yellow finish is typical Regency; other fashionable colours include lilac, emerald green, crimson, deep shades of pink, strong blues and gold. Note how the yellow paint on the walls matches both the yellow-silk pelmets and tied-back curtains framing the doorways, and the top cover and bolster on the classic Regency settee. En-suite wall finishes and soft furnishings were the height of fashion in grander Regency interiors.*

4 *In Soane's initial modelling of the room, full-length windows opened out onto a loggia (a pillared gallery open to the outside). In 1832, however, he enclosed the loggia with glass, removed the windows, replaced the latter with pelmeted and draped doorways, but retained the original arch-topped pier glass – its purpose, as before, being to enhance the level of lighting in the room and to increase the sense of space.*

5 *Built-in bookcases were commonly installed in Regency houses, often in reception rooms as well as libraries. Usually made of hardwood, notably mahogany, or rosewood veneer, and sometimes fitted with glass-panelled doors, they were frequently employed to display artefacts from classical antiquity, as well as books.*

6 *The candlelit, glass, metal or, as here, crystal chandelier was the primary source of artificial lighting in Regency reception rooms, with oil-burning pendant lamps favoured in halls. Oil-burning table lamps also came into general use. However, gas-fuelled equivalents (available toward the end of the period) were considered something of a dangerous novelty.*

7 *Overmantel mirrors were standard in Regency drawing rooms. This one has a very plain frame, although ornamentation rarely extended beyond reeding, corner roundels or repeats of ancient Greek or Egyptian motifs.*

8 *In its simplicity of outline and profile, this fireplace is quintessentially Regency. Characteristic elements include reeded flat jambs, a plain lintel and a narrow mantelshelf – the latter growing deeper toward the end of the Regency as changing fashions dictated the display of an ever-greater number of decorative artefacts. This example is made of lightly veined gray-white marble, but white statuary marble, exotic coloured marbles and porphyry were also popular, while wooden surrounds, painted in imitation of marble, were acceptable for lesser rooms. The copper and iron firedogs were old-fashioned for the period – coal-burning hob grates and, by the late 1820s, register grates, were more usual.*

9 *The butt-jointed floorboards of the most fashionable Regency interiors were laid with wall-to-wall carpets, stitched together from narrow widths cut around the perimeter to fit the shape of the room. Favoured all-over patterns included naturalistic floral designs and verdure patterns of ferns, foliage and palms.*

AMERICAN GREEK REVIVAL

The Greek Revival was a strand of neo-classicism that had made a major impact on European architecture and interior design from the 1780s onward, and was then enthusiastically taken up in America during the late 1820s, notably by influential architects William Strickland, Ithiel Town and Thomas Walter. There is no doubt that the widespread commitment to the Greek Revival style in the country, which endured until the 1850s, lay in the often-expressed sentiment that America, with its democratic ideals, was the spiritual successor to the birthplace of democracy: ancient Greece.

The primary sources of inspiration for the revival were the temple buildings and artefacts of ancient Greece, many of which had been unearthed from the mid-18th century in archaeological digs on mainland Greece and in southern Italy. During the earlier Adam-inspired Federal period (*see* pp.18–19), the Greek vocabulary of architecture and ornament had been combined eclectically with classical Roman forms and motifs. However, in the "full-blown" Greek Revival, the vast majority of Roman elements, such as arched entrances and fanlight windows, were abandoned and replaced by purer Greek forms from the Greek Doric and Ionic Orders of architecture.

Characteristic features of the American Greek Revival houses included temple-front facades, rectangular windows, columnar door surrounds and the embellishment of architectural fixtures and fittings, as well as furniture and soft furnishings, with Greek motifs such as anthemia, key frets, lyres and bands of egg-and-dart. Above all, however, as the front parlour (*see* left) of Andrew Low House (built in Savannah, Georgia, in 1848) demonstrates, Greek Revival houses were also distinguished from their earlier Federal counterparts by a greater austerity of ornament and decoration. Nevertheless, as the upholstered furniture (attributed to American cabinet-maker, Duncan Phyfe) reveals, this was a purist aesthetic rarely allowed to undermine domestic comfort.

1 In many Greek Revival houses, the classic tripartite division of walls into frieze, field and dado was abandoned. Instead, walls were either vertically panelled in a manner similar to earlier Federal and Empire houses (see pp.18–19) or, more usually, bordered at floor level with a skirting board (see 8) and topped with a deep cornice-frieze of either plain moulding or decorated with Greek anthemia or key patterns. The prevalent treatment for the large field in between was either flat paint or wallpaper in terracotta, deep pink or, as here, stone colours.

2 Window surrounds were characterized by the simplicity of their mouldings, with interior ornamentation rarely exceeding reeding or fluting – although squared corner blocks were sometimes incorporated. In contrast to many earlier Federal and Empire houses, Greek Revival windows were not set in arches – these never having been employed in classical Greek architecture. However, thin glazing bars, large panes of glass and floor-to-ceiling casement windows (sometimes in the form of French doors) remained in vogue – the latter often fitted with internal wooden shutters. On upper floors, sliding six-over-six pane sash windows were also prevalent.

3 As in many Federal and Empire interiors, window hangings were often elaborate and, with the exception of light-diffusing lace sheers, purely ornamental. These red-and-gold, geometric-pattern lampas pelmets are swagged-and-tailed from concealed rods and, the centres, prominent gilt-metal rosettes. Also employed here on the sides of the window surrounds (as tie-backs for the lace sheers), rosettes were very fashionable in Greek Revival interiors, and were derived from the circular, formalized floral ornaments much used in classical Greek architecture.

4 Elaborate crystal chandeliers, which had first appeared in America in the reception rooms of earlier 19th-century Federal and Empire houses, became more commonplace during the Greek Revival period, although they remained the preserve of the wealthy. Most were still imported from England or France. However, by the 1840s they were also being produced by American craftsmen.

5 As in many grander late-18th- and early 19th-century interiors, pier glasses were often installed between the windows of Greek Revival reception rooms. This example has a particularly ornate architectural frame, consisting of pilasters and an entablature gilded and decorated with Greek fluting, tiers of wreaths and theatrical masks.

6 Brass or silver Argand lamps were often used in Greek Revival houses in lieu of candles. Generally fuelled by whale or lard oil, they incorporated a hollow wick which fed substantial levels of oxygen to the flames. The flames, burning within glass "chimneys", thus gave off a light brighter and cleaner than that produced by candles or Betty lamps (see p.15).

7 Marble and painted wooden fire surrounds were generally more austere in appearance than their earlier Federal counterparts, especially those made of black and white marbles. Decoration was often confined to the figuring of the marble. However, it sometimes also took the form of fluting on pilaster jambs and Greek key patterns along the frieze.

8 Heavily moulded skirting boards replaced dado panels in most Greek Revival houses. Some were made of marble. Most, however, were wooden and either flat-painted (usually white or black), or painted faux marbre.

9 Except in entrance halls, where stone or marble was often used, pine floorboards remained the standard flooring. If uncovered, they were usually bordered with stencilled Greek motifs, such as rows of anthemia or Greek keys. Favoured floor coverings included similarly stencilled, or faux marbled, floor-cloths. However, fitted carpets – displaying Greek (rather than Roman) motifs set in geometric patterns – remained the preferred choice in the reception rooms of the wealthy.

GOTHIC REVIVAL

A revival of interest in Gothic architecture and ornament gradually emerged in Europe during the second half of the 18th century, and was partly fuelled by a reaction to the prevailing preoccupation with classicism (*see* pp.12–23). Initially, this gave rise to a style of architectural detailing and interior decoration known as "Gothick", which was based on a rather romanticized view of medieval precedents (*see* pp.8–9). However, during the early years of the 19th century the publication of diligent archaeological research into medieval ruins resulted in a far more historically accurate Gothic Revival – a movement that was given additional impetus and prestige by the decision in Britain in 1836 to rebuild the Houses of Parliament in the Gothic style.

Led by influential architects and designers such as A.W.N. Pugin, George Gilbert Scott and William Burges, the British Gothic Revival lasted until the 1870s and left its mark not only on civic, ecclesiastical and college buildings, but also on many country houses, villas and entire suburbs. In the United States the Gothic Revival was similarly influential, but lasted longer – the fundamental perpendicularity of the architectural style proved well-suited to the modelling and ornamentation of some of the 20th-century skyscrapers.

The drawing room (*see* left) is in a five-storey house in Greenwich Village, New York, and displays many of the hallmarks of a mid-19th-century Gothic Revival interior. The stone fire surround, the patterns of the wallpaper and the floor covering, the overall colour scheme and the subdued lighting are all highly characteristic (*see* right). However, as was often the case, it is the ecclesiastical-style, dark-brown mahogany furniture, more than the decorations and the architectural fixtures and fittings, which best encapsulate and instantly confirm the style – the distinctive ogee-arched and pinnacled backs of the sturdy upholstered chairs (echoed in the carved tabletop cornice) being derived from the authentic medieval Gothic vocabulary of ornament.

1 The walls in residential Gothic Revival rooms were invariably defined with a skirting board along the bottom and a cornice along the top. The latter, made of wood, plaster or sometimes stone, was often highly elaborate, and usually in the style of rows of Gothic ogee arches or openwork pendant forms. The large field in between the skirting and cornice was usually undivided, although chair rails or dado-height carved wooden panelling were occasionally installed, notably from the 1860s onward. Favoured finishes on the field include flat paint (stone colours were very popular) and, especially, wallpaper. This wallpaper pattern, displaying a profusion of naturalistically depicted flowers and foliage, is typically Gothic. Even more popular, however, were the Gothic Revival papers with stencilled lattice- or trelliswork, or chevron, ground patterns embellished with heraldic emblems, such as coats-of-arms and fleurs-de-lis, or stylized fruit and foliage inspired by medieval manuscripts and textiles.

2 Arched recesses (or "niches") were a popular architectural motif in both classical and Gothic architecture, and were traditionally used to display sculptures or decorative artefacts, such as vases and urns. This wall niche is defined by a simple, painted wooden moulding which, in the Gothic tradition, rises to a point at the apex of the arch. In an original twist to its traditional purpose, it has been filled with a large mirror-glass which serves as a light- and space-enhancing background for a display of gilt-framed fine art.

3 While some Gothic Revival interiors were illuminated almost exclusively with candles (like their medieval prototypes), most were lit with contemporary oil- or gas-fuelled fittings. In reception rooms, centrally hung chandeliers were often employed, and were usually made of carved wood or wrought iron, with glass "chimneys". This chandelier is particularly flamboyant – its S-shape scrolled branches inspired more by the often-exaggerated forms of the 18th-century "Gothick" style than by the more restrained medieval Gothic originals.

4 Overmantel mirrors, rather than pictures, were invariably hung above Gothic Revival fire surrounds. As with this gilt-wood example, their frames were usually fashioned in the shape of ogee-arched Gothic windows – the upper sections embellished with elaborate tracery (a series of C- and S-shaped curved ribs). Additional ornament often took the form of fleur-de-lis or cross-shaped finials, and crockets (small, hook-shaped ornaments, carved or moulded in the form of buds, curled leaves or animals).

5 The best Gothic Revival fire surrounds were made of stone (especially limestone), although softwood surrounds painted in imitation of stone were an acceptable alternative. Many had a pointed (four-centred) arch around the hearth, although this example is curved. Most had clearly defined spandrels (the two triangular-shaped sections flanking the apex of the arch) and jambs (the uprights that form the sides of the surround). In terms of decoration, this surround is rather plain. The spandrels and friezes of more elaborate versions featured Gothic motifs, such as rosettes, fleurs-de-lis, coats-of-arms and quatrefoils (four-lobed motifs similar in appearance to four-leaf clovers).

6 Candelabra and, as here, oil-burning lamps provided supplementary illumination for centrally hung chandeliers (see 3) in Gothic Revival houses. Free-standing or wall-mounted, most lamps were forged iron or brass (with glass "chimneys"), and bore Gothic motifs, such as pendants and crockets.

7 Apart from encaustic tiles or stone slabs in hallways, most Gothic Revival rooms were floored with dark-stained oak parquet or, more commonly, butt-jointed pine boards. The latter were usually dark-stained, but sometimes painted faux stone, and bordered with stencil-painted decoration, or covered with pile rugs, canvas floorcloths or, from c.1860, linoleum – each displaying geometric, foliate or heraldic patterns and motifs derived from the Gothic vocabulary of ornament.

VICTORIAN

The period from $c.1850$ to $c.1870$ was marked by the adoption of an eclectic mixture of architectural and decorative styles on both sides of the Atlantic. For instance, while a Gothic Revival (*see* pp.24–5) captured the imagination of many, it faced strong competition from various classical revivals. Notable examples of the latter included the last stages of the Greek Revival (*see* pp.22–3); Renaissance and Baroque Revivals (*see* pp.10–11) – the latter known as Second Empire style in the United States; and often rather heavy-handed reworkings of late-18th- and early 19th-century neo-classical styles (*see* Adam, Federal and Regency, pp.16–21). In addition to these various historical revivals, styles that were derived from the Chinese, Persian, Indian, Arabian and African vocabularies of architecture and ornament were also assimilated following increased trade with, and travel to, these regions.

In some Victorian houses, one particular decorative style prevailed. However, in other houses it was not unusual to find, for example, a neo-classical hallway, a Gothic Revival dining room and library, a Moorish-style boudoir and a Baroque Revival drawing room. But such stylistic eclecticism often went further than that, as many architects, designers and builders pilfered and adapted forms, motifs and imagery from numerous and diverse historical sources, and creatively combined them in a single room.

While the architectural fixtures and fittings and furnishings of such rooms may have been eclectic, the overall style invariably had a coherence that became instantly recognizable as "Victorian". However, the distinctiveness of the style – as Jonathan Hudson's re-creation of a typical Victorian drawing room (*see* left) illustrates – resides not only in the eclecticism of its component parts, but also in the combination of rich colours, intricate patterns, multi-layered drapery, heavy furniture, overstuffed and deep-buttoned upholstery, and displays of numerous decorative artefacts, all of which are uniquely Victorian.

1 *A plaster ceiling rose was a fairly standard fixture in Victorian rooms, the intricacy of its ornamentation reflecting the status of both the room and the house. This one features boldly carved acanthus leaves radiating from a gilded rosette and bordered by a ring of small palmettes – all foliate motifs derived from the classical vocabulary of ornament. In the finest reception rooms, the flat plaster around the rose could be embellished with Baroque- or 18th-century-style plaster ribs, swags and festoons (or embossed paper simulations of them, in lesser houses). Here, however, the flat plaster is papered with a realistically coloured willow pattern. Equally fashionable mid-19th-century alternatives included oak leaf, ivy and grapevine patterns.*

2 *Regardless of the type of decoration on the field of the Victorian ceiling, the border with the walls was always defined by a cornice. This example is highly characteristic of the period, its bands of rosettes, scrolling foliage and other foliate motifs typically echoing the classically inspired motifs on the central rose.*

3 *Most Victorian walls were papered, rather than panelled, although some were flat-painted and then stencilled at dado and frieze level. A wide and diverse range of patterns was popular. These included the geometric designs favoured in Gothic Revival houses (see pp.24–5), naturalistic willow and acanthus leaves, and stylized fruits and lotus and bamboo leaves. Most popular, however – as here – were intricate patterns of realistically represented large, coarse flowers, such as dahlias, hollyhocks and hydrangeas.*

4 *This window treatment is typically Victorian. Lace sheers are employed to diffuse incoming sunlight (they also serve as an insect barrier in hotter climates). Over these, multi-layered, heavy, tassel-edged drapes, which hang from a substantial brass pole, provide insulation and establish a sense of comfort and opulence. The valance and the outer, tied-back drapes are swagged-and-tailed – a configuration inspired by neo-classical drapery.*

5 *Enclosed glass or crystal pendant lights vied for popularity with chandeliers in Victorian reception rooms. In dining rooms, pendant lights sited over tables were often attached to pulleys, so that they could be raised and lowered, depending on whether the table was out of, or in, use.*

6 *Overmantel mirrors were sited above most Victorian fire surrounds, and in some cases were built into an overmantel unit which sat on the mantelshelf and incorporated shelving for the display of decorative artefacts. This wall-hung oval mirror has an ornate, gilded wooden frame, like many of the chain-hung pictures that proliferated on Victorian walls. However, polished hardwood frames, usually of mahogany, were also popular.*

7 *Fire surrounds in Victorian rooms were modelled on a wide range of historical precedents, notably Gothic, Renaissance, Baroque and Georgian. Favoured materials included intricately veined and colourful marbles; black and gray slate; finely figured hardwoods (often mahogany and rosewood); flat-painted, faux marbre or wood-grained pine; and cast iron – the latter mass-produced in large quantities from the mid-century onward. Characteristic of most types were patterned tile slips, and a deep mantelshelf often covered, as here, with a tour de cheminée – a fabric mantel frill or pelmet.*

8 *In keeping with the extensive use of fabrics for windows and as floor coverings, Victorian table lamps were, as here, often dressed with fabric shades, although glass "chimneys" were also employed, as in previous eras.*

9 *Apart from in hallways and kitchens, where patterned encaustic or plain quarry tiles, or patterned linoleum, were usually laid, most Victorian rooms had a central carpet or floorcloth, displaying patterns of oriental or European origin. These were bordered with either dark-stained or stencilled pine boards or, in grander interiors, more expensive hardwood parquet laid in geometric patterns.*

AMERICAN VICTORIAN

In terms of architecture and design, the second half of the 19th century saw a significant movement away from the Graeco-Roman classicism that had previously dominated (*see* Federal style, pp.18–19, and American Greek Revival, pp.22–3). Diverse styles were adopted and developed, mainly from historical and contemporary European models, and were often categorized under the heading American Victorian. Such examples included a Gothic Revival, similar to the British version (*see* pp.24–5); Italianate, loosely based on English Regency (*see* pp.20–1); Second Empire style, inspired by a French revival of Renaissance and Baroque ornamentation (*see* pp.10–11); a Colonial Revival (*see* pp.14–15); and a very eclectic style similar to British High Victorian (*see* pp.26–7). However, one of the most distinctive styles – Eastlake – was inspired by the English architect and designer Charles Eastlake (1836–1906), and provided an important link between the Gothic Revival and the emerging Arts and Crafts movement (*see* pp.30–1).

The interior (*see* left) is in Durfee House, built *c.*1880 in Los Angeles, California. It is typical Eastlake style, which became fashionable following the publication of his *Hints on Household Taste in Furniture, Upholstery and other Details* (1872), and after Clarence Cook's *The House Beautiful* (1877) and the Philadelphia Centennial Exhibition (1876) promoted his work and ideas. Underpinning the style was a rejection of the over-elaborate eclecticism of many Victorian interiors, and a return to the clarity and simplicity of design typical of medieval Gothic and early English Renaissance architecture, decoration and furniture. This approach was also evident in the work of Arts and Crafts designers. Unlike many of them, however, Eastlake preferred less expensive machine-made equivalents to hand-crafted fixtures and furnishings, believing them perfectly acceptable in an age of industrial mass production – provided attention was paid to quality control. This not only endeared Eastlake to the manufacturers, but also meant that most Eastlake-style products were affordable to the public at large.

1 While tongue-and-groove wooden boards or tin sheeting were often used for ceilings in the less important rooms of American Victorian houses, reception-room ceilings were usually made of plaster and tended to be highly decorative. Flat plaster embellished with elaborate cornices and central roses, and plaster panelling, were much in evidence, and were painted either plain white or polychrome. Colourful paper-panelled and stencilled ceilings were also fashionable. However, in many houses, especially those which were designed in Eastlake style, coffered (compartmented) ceilings similar to those found in late-medieval and early Renaissance European dwellings enjoyed a revival. Some of the grandest examples boasted moulded wooden bosses or pendants sited on the intersections between the wooden straps, while others carried repeat motifs – either inlaid or painted on the straps. In most cases the sections of flat plaster between the straps were finished with patterned papers.

2 The division between adjoining reception rooms in larger Eastlake-style houses was sometimes marked by arcading – a series of linked arches supported by piers, columns or colonettes. Stone or wooden arcading had featured in many medieval Gothic and early Renaissance buildings. In Victorian houses, the arcading was invariably hardwood, such as oak or mahogany, or softwood, such as pine or fir, grained with paint in imitation of hardwood. The best examples boasted highly intricate pierced and carved arches.

3 On walls (usually above the dado), as on ceilings, paper patterns tended to be either geometrical or based on plant forms. The latter were either naturalistically depicted, like the medieval-style millefleurs pattern to the left of the arcading, or botanically correct but highly stylized, as on the right of the arcading.

4 Complementary coloured but contrastingly patterned border papers were also often applied above the dado or, as in the entrance hall beyond, above the picture rail.

5 From the early 1880s, the walls below the dado rail in hallways and many reception rooms were often covered with Lincrusta – a type of wallpaper made from linseed oil, gum, resins and wood pulp spread over a canvas backing. Deeply embossed with patterns (often stylized fruit and flowers) in imitation of traditional and more expensive relief mouldings made of wood or plaster, Lincrusta could be painted, stained or gilded, and provided a durable finish well-suited to these busy areas of the house.

6 In many Victorian houses, the staircase was often sited asymmetrically, rather than centrally, in the hallway, and usually ran in single flights from floor to floor. Made from hardwood, or sometimes painted softwood, most staircases had elaborate, rounded balusters and turned, faceted and chamfered newel posts.

7 Most interior doors in American Victorian houses were panelled. Four or six panels were usual, in various configurations, and sometimes the panels were raised and fielded. Some doors were also embellished with decorative carvings which, in Eastlake-style houses, often took the form of linenfold panelling derived from 15th- and 16th-century models. The best doors were made of hardwood, notably mahogany and rosewood. However, pine doors grained in imitation of finely figured hardwoods were acceptable.

8 In urban areas, gas lighting had been in use since the 1850s, although it was usually augmented with oil-burning lamps. However, during the 1890s, cleaner and brighter electric lighting became available. Brass fittings with glass shades were especially popular during this period.

9 Although wall-to-wall carpets were laid in many reception rooms, there was a notable revival in the use of stained and polished, butt-jointed wooden boards and parquet flooring in many houses – with the flooring embellished with oriental-style rugs.

ARTS AND CRAFTS

The Arts and Crafts movement emerged in Britain in the late 1860s, and soon after in the United States, as a reaction to the stylistic eclecticism, the clutter of ornament and the often poorly made, mass-produced furnishings prevalent in Victorian houses during the third quarter of the 19th century (*see* pp.26–7). Initiated by English commentators, architects, designers and craftsman, such as John Ruskin, William Morris and Philip Webb, and taken up in America by, notably, William Eyre, Elbert Hubbard, Gustav Stickley, and Charles and Henry Greene, the movement's members advocated not only a simpler, more coherent style, but also the re-establishment of traditional materials and pre-industrial standards of craftsmanship for the manufacture of furniture, textiles, wallpapers, and architectural fixtures and fittings.

The primary sources of inspiration to the movement were the medieval vocabulary of architecture and ornament (*see* pp.8–9), and the related, but simpler, vernacular architecture of old English cottages and farmhouses. However, Renaissance, Middle Eastern, oriental and Art Nouveau (*see* p.33) forms and imagery were also, to varying degrees, accommodated to enrich the style. The early 20th-century American interior (*see* left) embraces most of these essential ingredients, and displays throughout the qualities of craftsmanship and design that characterize Arts and Crafts houses. The latter are evident in the medieval-style pictorial wallpaper frieze, the Art Nouveau-style lights and the oriental-style rugs. However, they are most clearly represented by the joinery and the wooden furniture. The door, the window, the wall panelling, the floor and the table and chairs are all exceptionally well made, and, above all, "honest" in the manner in which they emphasize, rather than disguise, the traditional methods of construction (with pegging, and dove-tail and mortise-and-tenon joints), and also enhance the inherent aesthetic qualities of the material (in this case oak) from which they are assembled.

1 *Most ceilings in Arts and Crafts houses were modelled on late-medieval architectural forms. The simplest had exposed wooden beams and ribs infilled with lath-and-plaster, or, as here, plain wooden boards. In larger houses the beams and ribs were invariably embellished with chamfering, pendants and bosses, and in many cases the ceiling was barrel-vaulted (curved). Flat or barrel-vaulted plaster ceilings were also employed in some houses, the grandest compartmented with low-relief plaster mouldings. Favoured finishes for plaster surfaces included flat-painting (often white or beige), and stencilled, or hand-painted, or papered patterns (mostly depicting medieval or oriental motifs and imagery).*

2 *Most Arts and Crafts architects retained the classic tripartite division of walls into frieze, field and dado, although the field and dado were often effectively combined where wall panelling was used (see 4)). While stencil-painted decoration was commonly used on the frieze, wallpapers were equally popular. Fashionable designs included simple flowers, such a poppies, daisies, marigolds and jasmine, set within formal pattern structure, and, as here, pictorials. Medieval imagery was often favoured for the latter – notably beasts and birds among stylized or naturalistic plant forms, and heraldic motifs such as emblems and coats-of-arms. (This paper frieze,* The Lion and the Dove, *is by Bradbury & Bradbury – see Directory of Suppliers, pp.174–87).*

3 *English medieval, Georgian and Victorian precedents provided the inspiration for Arts and Crafts doors. This door, with elongated wooden panels set beneath two rows of small, glazed panels, is based on a design in the English vernacular tradition by C.F.A. Voysey. Much imitated, it became the standard American Arts and Crafts door of the early 20th century. Alternatives included the Georgian six-panelled door, often modified by widening the panels to create a sense of horizontality, and Victorian four-panelled doors, painted or papered with plant motifs.*

4 *Three-quarter-height wainscotting was very common in Arts and Crafts rooms, with full-height panelling sometimes used in halls and dining rooms. Stained, indigenous hardwoods, notably oak, as here, was preferred. However, cheaper pine or fir were also used, and often flat-painted – ivory white and sage and olive green being fashionable colours. The alternative to wainscotting was wallpaper, depicting floral, medieval or oriental imagery.*

5 *Wooden casement windows were also common to Arts and Crafts houses, and either uniformly divided by rows of leaded lights, or, as here, made up of a large single pane topped by smaller panes. Bay windows, consisting of a series of casements, were also widely employed (see pp.32–3). However, sliding sash windows were also used, usually an upper sash of small rectangular lights over a single-paned lower sash, as were stone mullions in the grandest houses.*

6 *Fitted furniture played a crucial role in Arts and Crafts houses. Window seats and settles built into inglenooks (both with integral storage space), and fitted sideboards, bookcases and kitchen cabinets, symbolized the craftsmanship inherent in Arts and Crafts interiors, and helped to minimize unnecessary clutter.*

7 *While candlelight and gas lamps remained the common sources of lighting during the late 19th century, electric lights did appear in Arts and Crafts houses as early as the 1880s. Art Nouveau-style, electric table lamps by makers such as Tiffany found favour around the turn of the century, although copper, brass and, as to the right of the window here, wrought-iron wall lamps (oil or electric) were more in keeping with the Arts and Crafts look.*

8 *Apart from in halls, where stone flags were favoured, wooden flooring was almost universal in Arts and Crafts houses and, as here, was invariably chosen to match the wall panelling. Favoured floor coverings included Turkish, Indian and Persian rugs, and European carpets with floral or simple geometric patterns.*

EDWARDIAN

The era that began with the death of Queen Victoria and the coronation of Edward VII in 1901, and endured until the outbreak of the First World War in 1914, was characterized by a widespread acceptance of eclecticism in architecture and interior design. Thus, an early Renaissance (Tudor) Revival (*see* pp.10–11), late-18th- and early 19th-century French and English neo-classicism (*see* pp.16–17 and 20–1), Arts and Crafts (*see* pp.30–1) and Art Nouveau (*see* below right) all proved fashionable during this period. As in the Victorian era, these various historical-revival styles were rarely fastidious replications of the originals. Indeed, elements of more than one style were still sometimes incorporated in the same interior. However, they were distinguished from their Victorian counterparts by a greater clarity of line and a notable reduction of clutter in the architectural fixtures and fittings and in the furnishings.

The Arts and Crafts-influenced drawing room of a large house in Yorkshire, England (*see* left) is a good example of this Edwardian "thinning out" or "watering down" of the late-Victorian look. For example, the ceiling, although still ornate, is painted a subtle monochrome (a fashionable cream colour), rather than a more intense and busy polychrome, and there is a characteristic absence of "distracting" pattern in the pine-panelled walls (equally restrained but popular painted panelling, woodwork and wallpapers included off-white, oyster, lilac, stone gray, pale blue or green and dusty pink). Also significant is the disappearance of over-stuffed late-Victorian upholstery, the employment of a relatively simple pelmet and drapes in the bay window, and the installation of a built-in window seat. The plain wooden floorboards (augmented with rugs) and the considerable reduction in the quantity of decorative bric-a-brac contributed to the creation of a lighter and more spacious look. However, despite these embryonic moves toward later 20th-century minimalism, the emphasis remained firmly rooted in practicality of use and, above all, in comfort.

1 While Edwardian ceilings were generally plainer than their Victorian counterparts, a variety of ornate historical styles was adopted in many grander houses. Typical examples included Renaissance ceilings with exposed oak beams, and Baroque, Georgian and Adam styles with elaborate applied mouldings made of either plaster, composition, embossed paper or stamped tin or steel. This plaster ceiling is a mix of 16th-century Renaissance and 17th-century Baroque.

2 Few Edwardian houses had an electricity supply, so gas lights, oil lamps and candles remained in widespread use. In reception rooms, chandeliers were augmented by wall sconces and table and standard lamps, while in corridors and bedrooms small pendant lights with cut-glass shades were preferred.

3 While sliding sash windows were installed in many houses, this wooden-framed window bay, with its leaded casement windows and tinted glass, is typical of terraced and larger Edwardian houses. (Gunmetal or bronze frames provided maintenance-free alternatives.) The built-in seat reveals the enduring influence of the Arts and Crafts movement.

4 Oak, walnut or, as here, pine wainscotting was often installed in Edwardian houses. However, papered or stencilled friezes, papered fields and painted Anaglypta or Lincrusta dados – divided by linear wooden mouldings – were also popular, with patterns and motifs mostly derived from Georgian, Adam or Regency prototypes.

5 Renaissance-, Georgian-, Arts and Crafts- and Art Nouveau-style fireplaces were all fashionable during the Edwardian era. Many surrounds were wood, either stained and polished or painted – gloss white and matt green being popular colours. However, cast-iron, slate, brick and fully tiled surrounds were also much in evidence, as were briquette and plain or patterned tile slips. Framed by matching wainscotting, this pine surround is inspired by English Renaissance models, and features a dog grate suitable for burning large logs.

6 Oriental-style rugs were laid in many Edwardian reception rooms, and were bordered with either butt-jointed boards or herringbone-pattern parquet. However, quarry tiles, mosaics, linoleum and even marble were favoured in hallways and kitchens.

ART NOUVEAU

From *c*.1890 to *c*.1910, Art Nouveau – a distinctive style of architectural detail and decoration – became fashionable in Europe and, to a lesser degree, Britain and the United States. In Scotland, Germany and Austria this style was characterized by the use of austere, elongated rectilinear forms; in France and Belgium by flowing curvilinear elements and in England; and the United States by a combination of the two (as in the copper fire surround embellished with stylized plant-form motifs shown left). Other keynote elements of Art Nouveau included the abandonment of the tripartite division of walls and the use of "greenery-yallery" colours, such as lilac, violet, sage green, olive and mustard.

THE DETAILS

Following the outlines of the predominant styles of architecture and decoration from the late Middle Ages to the end of the First World War (*see* pp.8–33), the focus shifts to specific architectural fixtures and fittings – in other words, the basic components of each of the historical styles. You will therefore find sections devoted to various exterior details (including external doors, fanlights, porches, verandas, shutters, railings and gates); internal doors; windows; stairs; floors; ceilings; walls; fireplaces and lighting. In each of these sections, representative examples of these different elements are illustrated either in their original or restored form, or as modern reproductions, or both.

You will also find two sections dedicated specifically to bathrooms and to kitchens. These two areas are treated in a slightly different way to others in the book, as they were really only incorporated into most houses from the 19th century onward. Consequently, unlike other rooms, they have not been subject to the full range of period styles of decoration and ornament. Moreover, given the major advances made in bathroom and kitchen technology during the course of the 20th century, it was inappropriate to illustrate many pre-19th-century appliances that are now either inefficient and impractical (such as prototype water closets), or are simply unreliable and dangerous (notably some of the early enclosed cooking ranges).

Of course, such restrictions are not applicable to the other principal rooms of a house, where the primary considerations are aesthetic, and the onus is on an attention to authentic detail. However, successful results are also dependent upon keeping an eye on the bigger picture – on marrying the micro to the macro, matching the right doorknob to the right door, wall, floor and ceiling treatment. For this reason the majority of individual fixture and fittings, and different decorative treatments, are displayed and described within the context of their period settings, rather than in isolation.

FRONT DOORS

The style and fashion of door design evolved from practical requirements – access, materials, strength and weather. In Tudor doors, nail studs, sealing strips and decorative chamfered mouldings protected the frames. Baroque doors were often glazed, inscribed and ornamented, and framed by ornate columns and hoods. The Georgian door's facade – its principal decorative feature – followed the classical form and detail of the pattern books. Doors had six field panels, were made from oak – later from fir or pine – and were often painted black. Regency doors had reeded mouldings, and geometric panelling or studs in the Graeco-Roman style, and were set within a brick or stucco arch or shallow porch with pilasters or console brackets. Victorian door style could be Gothic, Greek, French or Italianate Revival. The Edwardian door's simplified style was influenced by the Arts and Crafts movement.

1 This typical 15th-century English Tudor door is made of broad oak planks, which have been strengthened with extended iron hinges and nails driven into the interior ledges or battens. Oak pegs were used as an alternative to iron nails. Here, quatrefoils decorate the spandrels within the simple carved frame, whose shallow arched (four-centred) heading is characteristic of the period.

2 Gaps between vertical planks were often protected by strips of oak, and cross-boarded on the interior for strength. Doors had either strap hinges secured by a pintle (hook) let into the door jamb, or were hung on a pivot with a plate nailed into the jamb. The window and the later addition of over-door lights maximized the available daylight.

3 Copied from a period example, this door is a fine reproduction only distinguishable from the original by its pale colour, as yet unpatinated by age. As in door 2 door, the vertical lapped planks have covered laths to exclude draughts, and the interior is cross-boarded. This version, however, has disguised integrated door locks.

4 Most door designs during the 18th century were taken from pattern books. This c.1725 entrance has Doric columns flanking a deep-set panelled door. The door was reduced in height during the mid-17th century to accommodate the period rectangular fanlight – a common alteration that did not disrupt the architectural equilibrium.

5 American architects of the late 18th and early 19th centuries favoured the use of columns – particularly Ionic – to support their porches, porticoes and balustrades. Here, elegantly tapered reproduction columns are incorporated into a restored facade which brings together English Regency, Gothic and American Classical Revival influences.

6 Dating from the mid-18th century, this handsome door has raised panels and reeded mouldings, and is set between classical fluted pilasters. In accordance with contemporary style, it may have been finished in white lead paint, but in this case is painted black, also a popular colour of the time. Unlike many doors, this one has retained its original proportions without the addition of a fanlight.

4

5

6

7

8

9

7 This grand mid-18th-century entrance is of aedicular (literally "little house") design and displays the fashion for neo-classical elements. (Aedicules reappeared during the Victorian Neo-classical Revival.) The columns are embellished with classical motifs and support a pedimented hood, giving protection from the elements and adding architectural elegance to the typical four panels. The door has been shortened to include a fanlight.

8 From the mid-18th century, chinoiserie decoration in metal was used as an architectural device. Here, it embellishes a late-Regency porch beneath a pagoda-shaped leaded hood. The design's lightness is complemented by the white paint and the elegance of its panels.

9 This late-19th-century four-panelled door in Philadelphia, Pennsylvania, is simply decorated and detailed. Made of hardwood, the door is plain; the surround is unembellished; and the fanlight has only the house number for decoration – all typical features. Other designs of this period were more flamboyant, with Gothic, Renaissance, neo-classical and Italianate influences.

1 The double-doors to Cliveden, in Philadelphia, Pennsylvania, dating to c.1763, have an aedicular arrangement of Doric half-columns and bracketed pediment. They exemplify the period's style and fashion for focusing on the Georgian facade's doorway as the main architectural embellishment. In America, however, this example is uncharacteristic, as the surround is carved from stone rather than wood.

2 Architectural symmetry and harmony were all-important throughout the 18th century. This c.1793 doorway in Fitzroy Square, London, is typical of late-Georgian urban development. A solidly constructed six-panelled door, it is made from oak, painted black and set within a dignified classical surround. This type of door would have been employed throughout the entire square.

3 Of similar style and date to door 2, this entrance is in Bedford Square, London. Wooden door- frames were banned by the London Building Act of 1774 to reduce the effects of fire. Stone and Coade stone (artificial stone invented in the late 18th century), which were used as replacements, allowing greater architectural versatility.

4 Although many doorway designs were taken directly from pattern books, designers such as the architect Sir John Soane still created ingenious innovations. Here, he rethought the contemporary Regency doorway for a London house c.1812 by adapting Greek or Roman studding in symmetrical rectangles instead of panels. Double-doors permitted generous proportions without jeopardizing the overall scale. The arrangement of the lantern and the fanlight illuminate both the interior and exterior.

5 This Regency doorway (c.1815) is located in King's Cross, London. Typical doors of this period had lozenge or circular heavy panels, and an arch containing a fanlight. Painted black or bronze-green, the doors were fitted with a knocker and handle.

6 This reproduction of a typical Edwardian suburban front door (c.1912) was copied from a contemporary London builders' merchant who mass-produced popular patterns of the period. The glazed panels maximize light filtered into the hallway, which is shadowed by the porched entrance. Extra light is afforded by side lights and by the plain rectangular 20th-century over-door glazing.

7 This late-19th-century doorway is a combination of different influences: early Georgian classicism in its architectural surround and fanlight frame; the aesthetic craftsmanship of the Arts and Crafts movement of the door itself; and a hint of Queen Anne Revival in the upper glazing bars, brought up to date with coloured glass.

8 Characteristic of a late-Victorian middle-class suburban dwelling, this doorway has a Gothic hood supported on composite columns, rectangular panels of coloured glass and a pair of decorative door panels. Incorporating the house number in the fanlight is typical of this period.

9 This modest but stylish door is a reproduction of an Arts and Crafts door of the type favoured by the influential architect C.F.A. Voysey, who much admired the vernacular form and abbreviated decoration. Plain glazed lights and flat vertical lower panels exemplify this style.

10 A pair of simple Victorian doors in a row of terraced houses is united and embellished by a purely ornamental machine-tooled hood. Typically this would be matched by barge-boards beneath the gables. The Victorians used a variety of paint colours, but external doors were mainly painted green, or they were wood-grained.

7   8   9

ARTS AND CRAFTS DOORS

The Arts and Crafts movement shunned mass industrial production and promoted the artisan craftsman. Proponents sought to create an aesthetic environment that was based on historical and vernacular precedents, using fine craftsmanship and high-quality materials. The door on the left characterizes this ideology. It shows the interior of the front door of the Red House, in Bexleyheath, near London, designed by Philip Webb in 1859 for William Morris, a founder of the Arts and Crafts movement. It is obviously medieval in influence in its use of planks and battens for the door, and iron hinges and latch in place of a knob or handle. However, the door is beautifully crafted and also highly contemporary in the way that it employs the chevron decoration and stained-glass inserts.

10

FANLIGHTS

Fanlights allowed natural light into hallways and passages. Those of the 1720s were often rectangular, and were created by cannibalizing the upper register of a tall door's panels. Early styles had semicircular dimensions, and were made of wood in modest houses and of wrought metal in grander dwellings. As doorframes became plainer, fanlights became more fanciful. Mid-18th-century examples featured an inner tracery arch divided into segments using a thin iron frame with cast-lead details. In 1774, Francis Underwood patented a composite glazing bar made by soldering a lead moulding to a strip of metal – this became standard methodology. The 1760s and 1770s were the great age of fanlights. Influenced by the Adam brothers, fanlights had delicate radiating iron tracery overlaid with cast-lead ornamentation of fans, scallops and lacy motifs. The early 19th century saw simplified geometric circles and curves, teardrop and bat's wing, loops and spider's web to match more adventurous door design. Cast iron allowed for mass production and the introduction of gas lighting meant lanterns could be incorporated. From 1832, sheet glass negated the need for segmentation and glass was often inserted into the door's body and surround. Many Victorian fanlights were simple rectangles with geometric glazing bars or coloured glass inserts.

1 The entrance door to the Morris-Jumel Mansion, in New York, is embellished with an elliptical fanlight and side lights that previously were much plainer in style. They are part of the extensive alterations that were made to the original c.1765 building during the early 19th century, and were influenced by the owner's travels to Europe. The coloured glass inserts are a variation of the classic tracery that is more usually seen during this period. This style of door, with its substantial side lights, is typically American in design.

2 This elliptical fanlight is contained within the top storey of the c.1800 Gaillard-Bennett House, in Charleston, South Carolina. The elegant semi-circle and the unfussy glazing pattern are a perfect foil for the dentilled pediment above. Such an arrangement illustrates how well this device could be incorporated as an architectural feature in its own right, and not merely as a light source over a door.

3 Here, a classic fanlight of the mid-18th century is identified by its semi-circular shape and simple "fan" design. This form is well-suited to the geometry of the door-frame, whose key stones echo the shape of the tracery. The generous shape of the fanlight maximizes the filtration of available light more effectively than later fanlights of elliptical design.

4 Fanlights became more delicate and complex in design as the 18th century progressed and cast-iron manufacturing techniques became more sophisticated. Robert Adam's designs of intricate tracery epitomize the zenith of this fashion between 1770 and 1790.

5 The classic fanlight form, such as this example from c.1793, has an inner semi-circle and "fan" spokes that radiate from the centre base. This is typical of the designs in A Book of Designs, written by Joseph Bottomley, the influential fanlight-maker, and published in 1793.

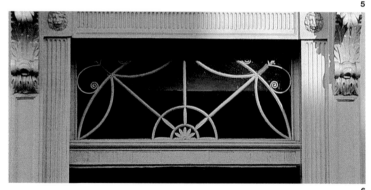

6 Early Georgian doors were often reduced in height in order to accommodate a fanlight, which would therefore have been rectangular in shape. Here, the glazing is in simpler form than fanlights 4 and 5, and the bars are slightly thicker.

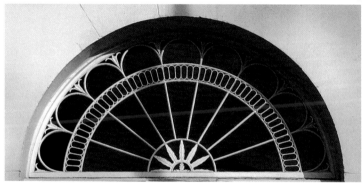

7 This simple fanlight is in the Morris-Jumel Mansion, in New York. The c.1765 door itself escaped the extensive 19th-century alterations elsewhere in the building. The fanlight exhibits sturdy wood glazing bars, precursors of later wrought- and cast-iron tracery.

8 The interior of the entrance to the Morris-Jumel Mansion illustrates the contrast in style after the owner's European travels influenced the alterations. Coloured-glass insets add a purely decorative dimension to the large fanlight and generous side lights.

9 This characteristically American doorway has a black-painted, classically panelled door that is framed by side lights and has a broad-arched fanlight. The delicate spider's-web glazing in the fanlight was very popular on both sides of the Atlantic.

HOODS AND PORCHES

Tudor doorheads often had hoodmoulds and projecting cornices or drip mouldings, but in the 16th century more robust porches became popular. Mid-17th-century hoods and porches were intrinsic to the doorway's design, adding canopies decorated with shells, acanthus leaves, fruit, flowers and cherubs to an otherwise flat-fronted house. From 1720, doorways often had a plain, flat shelf supported by carved brackets. The over-door of the Palladian house was superseded by the neo-classical surround, although, in America, porches were fashionable and were often added to the facades of older houses. The Regency period saw a porch revival, using delicate filigree ironwork, while in America balconies and verandas were favoured. The Victorian porch conveyed social standing – a projecting porch denoted a higher status than a recessed one. The Arts and Crafts movement adapted past styles such as Queen Anne shell and double-ogee canopy shapes. The Edwardian period also featured informal timbered porches and mass-produced cast-iron porches with glazed roofs.

1 Tudor houses often had a jettied upper floor which gave some protection to the entrance below. Here, a beam has been added to the length of the overhang, shaped to sluice off the rain and protect the fabric of the lower storey. At this time, many streets were so narrow that there was no room for a more substantial frontage.

2 Uniquely American in character, this elaborate c.1758 entrance features pilasters and a segmented arch with extravagant pineapple carving, reminiscent of a Chippendale-style high chest. Hoods were popular in town and country houses alike as they provided a stylish accent without the expense of porch construction.

3 A typical Edwardian practice was to borrow a Queen Anne motif of a shell design on carved brackets, adding iron and glass details. The glazed door – again echoing Queen Anne style – and original green paint are very much of this period.

4 Large town houses of the last quarter of the 18th century were often fronted by a classical porch, which was typical of those favoured by the architect John Nash for his grand London squares and terraces. Severe and noble, and without any unnecessary ornamentation, such a porch gives the entrance stature and interest.

5 This Victorian middle-class house is fronted by a Gothic Revival porch, whose pointed roof apex over double inner arches is raised on steps leading to wood-grained double-doors. The porch was a good way to dress a facade to exhibit social standing.

6 Heavily influenced by the Renaissance architecture of rural northern Italy, this c.1860 American house has the addition of an open, balustraded porch balancing the bracketed deep eaves. American Victorians were very enthusiastic borrowers of international and historical styles.

7 This is an Edwardian interpretation of a Queen Anne canopy on brackets with an integral glazed porch. Its dimensions echo that of an 18th-century door with a fanlight and side lights. The squared glazing bars, white woodwork and chequered paving are typical of this period.

8 Imaginative American architecture created this c.1889 mansion in Port Townsend, in Washington State. Although designed in Craftsman style, the porch is influenced by a mixture of French château style and Colonial detail in its raised, pedimented porch with a fanlight.

9 Characteristic of the American fashion for mixing simple and ornate elements, the main entrance of the c.1888 Hale House, Los Angeles, has an ornate pediment, turned supports and broad steps leading to relatively plain double-doors.

10 David Whitcomb built this magnificent edifice on the Hudson River in New York in 1983. The temple-front portico, plain triangular pediment and unfluted columns are all classical features.

5

7

9

6

8

10

43

BALCONIES AND VERANDAS

The balconet, the mid-18th-century precursor to the balcony, had diagonal railings, with rosettes, anthemia, crossed spears and Gothic tracery. By 1770, balconies were more fashionable – running the width of three drawing-room windows on the *piano nobile*, and generally painted green. Some late-18th- and early 19th-century cast-iron balconies were partly glazed and roofed in copper or zinc, and often in the typical Regency pagoda style. These developed into elaborate double-storey verandas, often with *chinoiserie* or Greek key motifs, or rectangular balconies in simple geometric trellis and floral designs. By 1820, cast iron had superseded wrought iron, and verandas were manufactured in pieces and sold by catalogue. Balconettes in wrought-iron "bellied" form were favoured after 1830. In America, neo-classical, Chinese and Greek key designs in ironwork were used in the late-18th-century Federal period, while European craftsmen popularized old continental and neo-classical styles. Cast-iron carvings were used in the two-storey verandas of the 1850s, while turn-of-the-century balconies and verandas had decorative woodwork.

3 The abolition of the Window Tax in England in 1851 encouraged a more generous use of glass. Consequently, the bay window became almost a required feature for the modest Victorian house, allowing good light and viewing. It also provided a broad balcony on the first floor, which was often echoed, as here, with a balustraded parapet to provide symmetry as well as a safety route in case of fire.

1 This elegant wrought-iron balcony (c.1810) fronts the width of the first storey, or piano nobile, of a stucco-faced residence. Balconies of this period were usually fashioned in geometric or key shapes, with running floral top and bottom rails. This style of narrow rectangular balcony was more decorative than practical.

4 This interior recessed balcony of an early 19th-century American mansion overlooks a double-storey hallway embellished with neo-classical pillars and cornice. Interior double-doors open onto a semi-circular balcony, guarded with a dignified railing of geometric design, with a delicate filigree "apron" centrepiece.

2 By the early Victorian period, manufacturing cast iron had become a highly skilled operation, and foundry catalogues began to sell ready-to-assemble panels for verandas, balconies and conservatories. During this period, windows became larger and balconies sturdier, as seen in this example on a London town house.

5 Drayton Hall in South Carolina, c.1738–42, is America's finest Palladian mansion. Its noble proportions are graced by a two-storey pedimented portico. This classic feature, often seen in the grandest American architecture, displays minimal decoration in its balcony railing below a dentilated pediment with lozenge-shaped relief.

6 *The c.1800 Gaillard-Bennett House, in Charleston, South Carolina, underwent alterations in 1819 and 1850, at which time the portico and balconies were added. American architects were very enthusiastic about giving their buildings an updated look, although it took time for English fashions to become popular. Classical Revivalists rejected the neo-classical idiom of the Adam brothers, and instead embraced a uniquely American robustness that relied more on structure than on applied decoration. This portico is a good example. Its Doric columns on the first tier and Corinthian columns with cast-iron capitals on the second are topped by an imposing dentilated pediment and fanlights.*

7 *The Inn at Antietam, in Sharpsburg, Maryland, was built before the start of the Revolutionary War in 1775 and, although some of the architectural elements are similar to the later Gaillard-Bennett House, it has a more accessible, domestic aspect. This homeliness is characterized by the combination of weather-boarding, shutters, bargeboard detail and typical wrap-around veranda. In later years, these verandas and porches became highly decorative features.*

6

7

8

9

10

8 *The veranda gave great scope for inventive architecture, either as an integral part of the original design, or as an addition to an older property to update the look, provide an outdoor "room" or simply to create a place to shelter from the elements. Here a round-ended loggia fits neatly into an angle of this 1880s' New York house.*

9 *Hale House, in Los Angeles, California, is late 19th century in style, and mixes both simple and complex architectural devices in a harmonious manner. The turned wooden columns that support the elaborate painted entrance porch are continued around the house, providing a shady veranda.*

10 *American houses have adopted every style of veranda and balcony to suit their architectural and domestic requirements. These ranged from the wonderful ironwork confections of Spanish and French inspiration in New Orleans, to the chinoiserie and classic Greek motifs gracing the facades of Boston mansions, to the highly decorative woodwork of the Victorian crafts-men, to this simplest of glazed porches, provid-ing space and shelter.*

45

SHUTTERS

Exterior shutters protect the interior of houses from the elements – whether it is winter snow or summer heat. They also allow the control of light and the passage of air; provide security, privacy and decoration; and can dramatically change a window's proportions, and indeed the character, of a building's face. Shutters seem more suited to these uses and to the architecture of the continent and of the hotter states of America than they do to Britain, as they blend well with different styles of window and building materials. Also, Britain does not have such extremes of temperature, nor the intensity of light, nor (usually) the need to protect glass against hurricanes. In Britain, shutters were nearly always added to the inside of buildings, not to the exterior. The Building Act of 1709 in Britain dictated that windows should be set back from the facade of a building by one brick's width and, as a result, windows from this date were very often furnished with interior shutters folding into the reveals. Early American Colonial shutters were sometimes louvred with simple cutouts as a decorative detail. As a rule, internal shutters were used in brick houses, but external panelled and louvred shutters were common on wooden buildings in the early 18th century. In the second half of the 19th century, louvred and Venetian shutters continued to be standard, although canvas awnings were sometimes used as a substitute. In Britain during the Edwardian period, continental travel on a large scale brought back a taste for wooden louvred shutters, called jalousies, and these worked quite happily on the villa-style houses so popular at the time.

1 *The simplest type of unpainted plank shutters on a farmhouse window creates a charming picture bordered by a white surround within a pink limewashed "frame". The shutters keep the interior cool in the summer heat, and are then opened in the evening to let in the cool air.*

2 *Cliveden, built in c.1763, in Philadelphia, Pennsylvania, is associated with grand Colonial-style houses, but, surprisingly, these shutters front a window in the service area of the house, unseen by the public. Such battened shutters, hung on iron strap hinges, were typical of modest houses, too.*

3 *Despite their rustic simplicity, shutters on the windows are typical of many French country houses of standing, and afford great character to the building. This batten-and-hinge style also provides good security with its heavy locking bars.*

4 *This sturdy, rough stone dwelling has a practical arrangement of solid, serviceable shutters, which close out the extremes of weather, and de rigueur lace curtains behind a flytrap window screen.*

46

5 This sash window is located on the raised entrance level at Cliveden, in Philadelphia, Pennsylvania. The design is borrowed from the English Queen Anne style, with that period's characteristic twelve-over-twelve pane window pattern. The panelled shutters take their design from classic early 18th-century door proportions, and their dimensions are a suitable complement to the key-stone arch and the lipped window-sill. Interior slatted blinds control the filtering of light into the room.

6 Louvred shutters have never gone out of fashion. In addition to their decorative appeal, they allow air into rooms and, at the same time, provide shade to keep out the heat. They can also be given an individual flavour, as here, with personalized embellishment. This example, painted in cool gray, which is suited to the unpretentious country style of the property, has a sentimental horseshoe for good luck and a letter box inserted into the structure.

5

6

7 Dick Dumas painted this brilliantly executed trompe l'oeil pair of shutters to embellish and give a sense of fun to this stone house. Painted shutters can also give a house a period feel, or disguise an unappealing wall.

8 Sometimes mountain houses have the tiniest windows – they are more like portholes rather than windows – on the north side of the building, and they will be well protected by basic, functional shutters such as these.

9 This c.1890 American house in Middletown, Maryland, appears to have been influenced by Dutch architecture, with its steep gables, red-brick structure and very narrow-louvred shutters.

7

8

9

47

DOOR FURNITURE

Medieval door furniture consisted of an iron pull or drop handle. Wrought-iron and brass box locks were a luxury in the early 16th century, but iron latches lasted well into the 20th. The Baroque period saw decorative hinges in L-shape, butterfly and cock's-head form, and the rich displayed their wealth with decorative brass locks. Knockers, originally simply styled, became more ornate by 1700. Georgian door furniture was often black-painted cast iron – not brass. Knobs were usually at waist level, centred in the middle door rail. As door design was modernized in the early 19th century, pull handles in the form of rosettes or solid turned balls became popular. Knocker shapes were numerous – from neo-classical heads to lion masks. By 1890, electric bells in brass and porcelain replaced knockers and bell pulls.

1 Only a ring handle was needed on medieval and Tudor doors, which were barred from the inside at night. Early wrought iron had a twisted ring, but here the backplate is more ornate than usual.

2 Stylistically, this simple clutch handle could belong to the 15th century onward. Brass, however, was a luxury until the Industrial Revolution, and only available to the rich.

1

2

3 The functional purpose of a front-door knocker may have remained the same over the centuries, but the material, style and placement give clues to the correct date. This reproduction knocker would be fitting for a late-19th-century door.

4 This knocker is a reproduction of a style dating to the 15th century. It is made from simple forged iron with an authentic-looking hammered ring, and is suited to a rustic oak door.

5 Here is an updated version of the knocker shown in 4, but this time it is reproduced in brass. Although not genuine period material, this knocker would be appropriate if the rest of the door furniture was also brass.

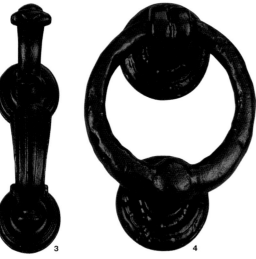

3 **4**

5

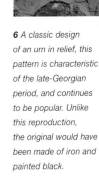

6

6 A classic design of an urn in relief, this pattern is characteristic of the late-Georgian period, and continues to be popular. Unlike this reproduction, the original would have been made of iron and painted black.

7 This charming lion-and-wreath iron knocker is in the grand classical style, and is well-suited to the weathered door that it graces.

8 The Georgian period saw the arrival of many kinds of knocker design. Apart from the somewhat sad-faced lion, there were fish, classical heads and vases. This reproduction has an unusual bronzed finish.

9 This ornate "knocker" is in fact a modern door bell. Made of solid brass, it is based on a turn-of-the-century design at a time when the Victorians were fond of "novelties".

7

8

9

10 *A variety of letter box styles has been utilized since 1840. This reproduction's minimalist lines make it perfect for a modern door.*

11 *The earliest Victorian letter boxes were small and slim. This elegant shape, with curved, chased edges, would suit a late-19th-century four-panelled door.*

12 *Of an unusual style, and with a sinuous outline, this reproduction letter box may have been derived from the Art Nouveau fashion of the late 19th century.*

13 *This sophisticated reproduction letter box, with its integrated knocker handle, is an early 20th-century design. It is finished in polished metal.*

14 *A sleek design in unadorned brass would look well as a letter box where the date of the doorway is in doubt. This example would suit doors after the 1900s.*

15 *Here, a reproduction mid-Victorian letter box is combined with its own knocker. The earliest examples were inset vertically, and so were separate to the knocker.*

16 *This black-iron letter box is in Arts and Crafts style, its fixing plates echoing medieval hinges.*

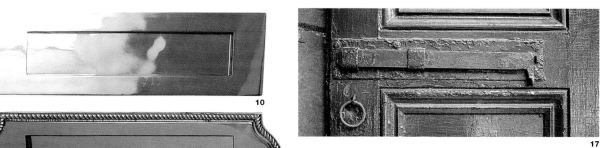

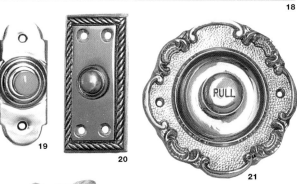

17 *Before exterior locks, security was provided by barring the door from the inside, as here, on this American 19th-century house.*

18 *Unusually, this lock has been fashioned from wood, but it is of a timeless rustic construction.*

19–21 *By 1890, electric bell pushes had generally superseded manual bell pulls. These reproductions show some typical examples in brass.*

22 *This is a twin to the gargoyle knocker/bell ring illustrated in 9. The bronze finish lends it an element of antiquity.*

23 *An early Victorian house bell would have been placed in the service passage to alert the staff to the arrival of a guest. Originally wire-and-pulley operated, today's reproduction has battery or mains power.*

49

RAILINGS AND GATES

The character and prestige of a house are greatly affected by its exterior boundaries. Aesthetically, much can be won or lost by the choice of barrier between private and public property. Moreover, walls, fences and hedges all reflect the standing and impact of the building – and homeowners – within. Ironwork fencing was introduced to Britain in the late 17th century, and its versatility has kept it in constant use ever since. It looks well combined with stone and brick; it can be painted or gilded; and it lends itself to myriad designs. The most enduring styles had plain railings with, for example, spear-head or fleur-de-lis finials, which became the uniting face of the Georgian urban development. In the American Colonial period, iron gates and fences were most often a feature of public buildings, but their grandeur appealed to the owners of pretentious domestic dwellings. Cheaper cast iron, sold by catalogue, made stylish fencing readily available to all by the Victorian period. Wooden fencing maintained its popularity in America. In Britain, apart from continuous rustic usage, it made a fashionable reappearance during the Arts and Crafts period of the second half of the 19th century, and as a companion to the Edwardian decorative trelliswork and Tudor Revival buildings.

1 The open front of this classic country-style property has a pleasing visual definition. This is achieved through the whitewashed weatherboard, gray panelled shutters, steeply pitched stone roof, a low picket fence, and the driveway with its timeless post-and-chain borders.

2 The picket fence is particularly associated with the American Eastern seaboard, where an abundance of readily available continental timber made wooden construction a natural choice for houses and gates. This kind of fencing is as appropriate and charming today as it is in an historical setting.

3 A late-Victorian house, built c.1897, in Middletown, Maryland, is influenced by Gothic Revival style in its church-like spire turret and dormer windows. The street-side garden fence illustrates another shape of picket – flat-cut with spear-top Gothic spindles. The straight line is interrupted by the arch of the gateway. The picket fence is a purely decorative device to delineate the boundaries of a property.

4 In Italianate fashion, this Edwardian villa has been embellished with a balustraded stairway entrance that matches and balances the first-floor balcony. The Edwardians were influenced by their travels to the continent, especially the romanticism of Italian architecture and gardens. This reproduction balustrade is made of reconstituted stone and is a realistic light-buff colour.

5 This stone balustrade was designed and carved for a show stand at the Chelsea Flower Show of 1997. Such a classic design will never go out of fashion, and even a short length – which is sometimes to be found in reclamation yards – will make a fine architectural statement in a garden.

6 *Suitably classic and timeless, arrow-headed, wrought-iron railings front an early 19th-century London house. The uncluttered treatment of the paved frontage enhances the classical symmetry.*

7 *The same type of railings as 6 has been used in a different setting at the entrance to a newly built Dutch Colonial- style mansion. Here, however, the spindles are finer, and are finished with delicate gilded finials.*

8 *The plainest iron fencing is suitable to use as a neutral barrier between the house and the road. Durfee House, which was built c.1880, in Los Angeles, California, is a bright confection of painted weatherboard, and is known as a "pink lady". Its fancy fretwork decoration needs no further ornamental distraction.*

9 *The scale of the entrance gate is important, especially when it partners such an imposing-looking building. This c.1877 house, built in early 19th-century style, has tall narrow windows on the piano nobile that accentuate its height, which is reflected in the tall sweep and decorative detail of the wrought-iron gate.*

6

7

8

9

GILDED IRON

Most wrought- and cast-iron gates and railings have been simply painted, mainly in black or green. However, as with this scrolling plant-form finial (on a neo-classical, Greek-key pattern gate), some of the most prestigious examples have also featured gold-leaf detailing. This was a popular decorative convention during the 17th and 18th centuries, and was often replicated using less expensive gold-metallic paint during the 19th century.

ORNAMENTATION

Exterior ornamentation embraces many forms, from the addition of a naïve carved wooden detail on a doorframe to the ornate statuary of High Victorian architecture – all of which in some way refines a building's aesthetic impact. Baroque style saw a plethora of voluptuous carved-stone decoration, particularly above main doorways. The more studied classicism of the Georgian period confined exterior ornament to such elements as porch brackets, *pateras* and carved pediment insets. The style for embellishment in the second half of the 18th century was greatly influenced by Robert Adam's sinuous, elegant swags, ribbons and arabesques. Later, Coade stone (an artificial, castable material) permitted cheap high-relief decoration. Strongly accented moulding, reeded and incised patterns, and blind niches are the essence of sophisticated Regency architectural detailing. The broad use of decorative elegant metalwork heralded a Victorian passion for ornamentation in Britain and America.

1 The Victorians were conscious of creating a good first impression, and an elaborate entrance was therefore desirable. Holly Village, in Highgate, London, was built in 1865 by Henry Darbishire, who conceived a pastiche of an English village green, surrounded by medieval cottages. This gateway characterizes his passion for Gothic detail, with its church-like archways and flêches (spires), its decorative lattice fascias, small oriel window and pious-looking statuary. Sadly, the ravages of pollution have obscured much of the subtle detail, and this has resulted in a far gloomier impression than was originally intended.

2 This detail is from a c.1880 Queen Anne Revival-style mansion block in Cadogan Square, London. The ornamental brickwork shows Flemish, Gothic, Renaissance and Chinese influences, with the exuberant decoration combining terracotta, red brick and Portland stone. The Victorians loved to mix historical architectural styles and diverse materials, using both traditional and modern manufacturing methods. The Rococo-patterned frieze divides the two levels of leaded windows, and carved stone figures hold up a pagoda-shaped copper canopy.

3 Griswold House, home to the Newport Art Museum on Rhode Island, is a splendid example of American Tudor Revival during the Victorian period, adapted to the eccentricities of the architect. This pastiche of a Stick-style building is based on the traditional English half-timbered house. Its picturesque effect is achieved with timbers that are in fact only applied decoration, and a structure that is composed of ornamental wooden cladding, rather than plaster and decorative pargetting.

4 An example of exterior embellishment favoured by the Victorians, this impressive entrance facade makes use of crafted Portland stonework for the spandrels, pilasters and statuesque finials.

5 A detail of Hale House, Los Angeles, c.1880, shows a delicate filigree ironwork veranda cresting on the roof, with a newel-post division that matches those on the ornate porch. From the 1870s, iron roof crestings often appeared around the square roof line of Second Empire houses.

6 A rare stone edifice in its time, Cliveden, c.1763, in Philadelphia, illustrates the classical idiom in the pedimented roof, where a grand urn tops the chimney.

7 Inventive architectural ornamentation is shown on this roof edge, which has been designed as a cornice, with deeply overhung eaves supported by twinned console brackets.

8 Bargeboards, as here, provide a decorative seal between tiles and wall on the gable end of a roof. Used since Tudor times, bargeboards became more decorative and widespread when machine-cutting made complex designs cheap to produce.

4

5

6

7

8

9

10

11

12

13

9 Medallions, plaques and cartouches have been used from the Baroque period to embellish doorways and walls. This reproduction of a late-Georgian terracotta-and-plasterwork piece typically portrays a woman in classical dress. Other examples have a shield of crossed arrows.

10 This modern version of a Georgian carriage lamp with its shaped storm cowl serves today's requirement for exterior lighting and security. It is made of solid cast brass and has bevelled plate glass.

11 Medieval or Arts and Crafts houses would have used this type of wall lantern, which has very simple lines. This, example, however, is an electrified reproduction.

12 Copied from a traditional Georgian wall-light design, this modern lamp is made of weathered bronze, but black-aluminium and verdigris finishes are also available.

13 An alternative style to 12 is this squared wall light, which would have been seen throughout the English Georgian period. American lamps were more usually made of wrought iron.

53

INTERNAL DOORS

From a constructional point of view, two basic types of internal door have been in widespread use since the Middle Ages: battened-plank and panelled. The former (*see* pp.56–7) were prevalent in most houses up until the 17th century, and thereafter were mostly confined to those dwellings (predominantly, but not exclusively, rural) built in traditional vernacular styles – such as many late-19th- and early 20th-century Arts and Crafts and Colonial Revival houses. Conversely, panelled doors (*see* pp.58–61) were relatively rare from the Middle Ages through to the early 17th century – the high standards of craftsmanship required to hand-cut their mortised-and-tenoned frameworks rendering them more expensive and the preserve of the wealthiest households. Nevertheless, by the early 18th century they had supplanted battened-plank doors in most houses. This was in part due to a reduction in the skill, time and cost of their manufacture, following the introduction of semi-automated cutting techniques (these were often fully automated by the Victorian era). However, it was also fuelled by the fact that most panelled doors required less solid wood than their plank counterparts – an increasingly economical option as timber resources (particularly hardwoods) began to diminish, especially in Britain, as early as the late 17th century.

The vast majority of doors since the medieval period have been made entirely from wood: either hardwood or softwood. As nowadays, hardwoods were invariably the more prestigious and most expensive. This was largely due to the attractive figurings displayed on their surface when they were cut at various angles or from different parts of the tree, and enhanced by staining, waxing and varnishing – the preferred finishes for hardwood doors. The most popular hardwoods have included oak and elm (for battened-plank doors), and mahogany, rosewood, oak, walnut and, notably in America, cherry and maple (for panelled doors). Softwoods are blander in appearance than most hardwoods, but being faster-growing and more abundant, they have provided a cheaper raw material –

especially for panelled doors since the early 18th century. The most commonly used have been the various species of pine and fir; to conceal their blandness, these were traditionally flat-painted or wood-grained in imitation of a hardwood – in both cases, often *en suite* with the other joinery in the room or house.

In addition to the display of figuring and grain, or the particular colour of flat paint, the factors that have determined the overall appearance of a door are the structure and style of the surrounding framework (*see* pp.62–3), the type of wooden, metal or ceramic door furniture employed (*see* pp.64–5) and, most significantly, the configuration of the basic structural components. For example, during the Middle Ages and early Renaissance, many battened-plank doors were constructed from vertical planks of varying width. Thereafter, however, the planks gradually became more uniform and narrower. Similarly, while panelled doors have always been divided into as little as two and as many as twelve panels, specific historical periods or styles have become strongly, albeit not exclusively, associated with particular numbers – for example, between two and five for Baroque, six for Georgian and four for Victorian.

Equally subject to changing fashions in architecture and ornament have been the shape and decoration of the panels. Thus, carved linenfold patterns were in vogue during the early Renaissance and in the 19th-century Gothic and Renaissance Revivals; cartouche-shaped panels were often employed in Baroque, and Baroque and Renaissance Revival houses; and rectangular panels – sometimes fielded in the 18th, 19th and early 20th centuries, and usually defined by thin, rectilinear mouldings – were prevalent in Classical Revival and neo-classical interiors. Other decorative conventions of note have included the use of engraved glass panels in many Victorian houses, and the application – particularly in neo-classical, Aesthetic and Art Nouveau houses – of painted motifs and imagery, the majority of which were based on plant forms.

BATTENED-PLANK DOORS

Internal battened-plank doors were in widespread use in all types of houses up until the 17th century. Thereafter, they were gradually supplanted by panelled doors (*see* pp.58–61), although they continued to be used in houses built in the vernacular tradition, and enjoyed a revival in the Arts and Crafts houses of the late 19th and early 20th centuries. The simplest examples were made up of two or more vertical, butt-jointed or tongue-and-groove, wooden planks nailed to two or more horizontal wooden battens on their reverse side – the number of cross-battens usually increased in relation to the weight of the planks. Variations have included the insertion of diagonal braces between the battens; "double-boarding", in which a set of horizontal planks, rather than spaced battens, is fastened to the reverse of the vertical planks; the use of wooden mouldings to create decorative panelling on the surface of the planks; and nailhead ornament (*see* right). Traditionally, battened-plank doors are hung on surface-mounted hinges (*see* p.64). Favoured woods have included oak and elm, and softwoods such as pine – the latter often painted, rather than stained, waxed or varnished.

1 *Frog Pool Farm, in Avon, England, which dates to the 15th century, has retained many of its original doors. The substantial three-plank, battened oak door on the right has a wrought-iron latch, and is hung on a pair of large strap hinges. The five-plank oak door on the left is lighter, and is hung on a pair of wrought-iron pivots and plates. Both are typical of the period.*

2 *Hung in a converted olive mill, in Andalucia, Spain, this heavy plank door is a type often used in European vernacular architecture from the Middle Ages to the 20th century. The planks on the show side, displaying ornamental nailheads, are secured on the reverse by a set of planks laid at right angles to them. This configuration is known as "double-boarding".*

3 *Apart from exposed nailheads, decorative embellishments on early plank doors were non-existent or very minimal. On this reproduction oak example, they are restricted to simple mouldings along the edges of the planks.*

4 *Prior to the 17th century, doors were often constructed from planks of varying widths (up to 26in/66cm). Here, in an English cob house, they are made of elm.*

56

5 Chamfered battens are often found on American Colonial plank doors. In this restored period house, the three-plank, cross-battened door is made of softwood, and is painted en suite with the wall panelling in a rust-red milk paint.

6 This arch-top, English Jacobean door is of a type only employed in very grand houses. The main body of the door is constructed from butt-jointed vertical planks. However, unlike most plank doors, these are secured within a frame, and are embellished with a series of linked, geometric-shaped panels made up of applied wooden battens. The fan-moulded arch top is a particularly prestigious addition.

7 As on door 5, this milk-painted plank door in an 18th-century American Amish log house has chamfered cross-battens. For extra security, its iron latch is supplemented with a sliding wooden bolt.

8 To prevent warping, the cross-battens on lightweight plank doors were often augmented with a pair of diagonal braces mitred at the ends to sit flush with the cross-battens. This modern reproduction is hung in an English farmhouse kitchen.

5

6

7

8

NAILHEAD ORNAMENT

Since the Middle Ages, a fashionable decorative convention employed on battened-plank doors has been to leave the heads of the wrought-iron nails (which secure the planks to the battens) exposed, rather than sinking them under the surface of the wood. Usually, the pattern formed by the nailheads exactly corresponds to the number and position of the battens on the reverse – in other words, a series of horizontal, parallel lines. These were also sometimes interspersed with vertical rows of nailheads running up the inner and outer edges of the doors – as on this pair of limewashed Moroccan cupboard doors. However, on some plank doors, purely ornamental nailheads were employed, in addition to those that also served a constructional purpose. The former were usually configured as simple motifs or emblems. Notable examples include shields and stylized floral forms (such as fleurs-de-lis), mainly derived from the heraldic vocabulary of ornament.

PANELLED DOORS

Although panelled doors were sometimes employed in grander houses prior to the 17th century, they gradually replaced battened-plank doors (*see* pp. 56–7) as the standard internal door that was used in most houses. The basic construction – in which the panels are secured in a wooden framework of (vertical) stiles and (horizontal) rails, mortised-and-tenoned together – has never altered. However, there have been numerous stylistic variations. For example, the number of panels has ranged from two to ten, or more – with four, five and six panels being the most prevalent. The embellishment of the panels has also varied: they can be flat and sit below the frame, or be raised ("fielded") in the centre to lie flush with it; be defined around their perimeter with decorative mouldings; and be plain, or decorated with carving, or additional applied mouldings, or painted motifs and imagery. Although glass panels have been used, most panelled doors have been made entirely of wood – the finest from finely figured, waxed or varnished hardwoods, such as oak, mahogany or rosewood, but more commonly from cheaper, painted or wood-grained softwoods, such as fir or pine.

2 Highly characteristic of early 18th-century reception rooms, this pair of full-height, three-panelled double-doors echoes the configuration of the wall panelling. The doors are made of deal, and are painted in one of the grayish green-brown colours – collectively known as "drabs" – that were very fashionable in early and mid-Georgian houses. Also typical is the plain brass rim lock, which would have been made of iron in poorer houses, and probably engraved or chased with motifs in wealthier ones.

1 From the early 16th to the mid-17th centuries, linenfold carving was a fashionable method of embellishing the panels of reception-room doors in wealthy households. (It enjoyed a notable revival in the second half of the 19th century.) Inspired by the folds in the fabric wall hangings used in medieval and Renaissance interiors, the carving was often extended to adjacent wall panelling, as on this reproduction oak-panelled door and full-height wainscotting. As here, the linenfold patterns in the top panel of the door and wain-scotting could be offset with other carved motifs and imagery, usually of organic origin.

3 While battened-plank doors retained their popularity in some rural areas, the six-panelled door, with the panels configured as here, became the standard choice in town and city houses, although two- and three-panelled versions (see 2) were also employed. The panels on this door are flat, and defined by simple mitred linear mouldings; fielded panels became more common during the second half of the 18th century (see doors 4 and 6). A popular alternative to this flat-painted finish – applied over fir or pine – was wood-graining, notably simulations of expensive hardwoods such as mahogany or rosewood.

4 Bearing a painted faux-limed finish, this grand reproduction Georgian door has the same panelling configuration as door 3. In this case, however, the panels are raised and fielded, and are defined by more ornate linear mouldings, carved as bands of stylized foliate motifs. Its prestigious surround is similarly ornamented with carved acanthus leaves, scrolling foliage, rosettes and, in the tympanum of its broken pediment, a shell motif. All of this decorative imagery is derived from the classical Graeco-Roman vocabulary of ornament, and is typical of grander neo-classical interiors on both sides of the Atlantic during the second half of the 18th century.

5 Framed by a surround capped with a row of neo-classical rosettes set under a dentil moulding, this pair of wall-cupboard doors is in Home House, London, which was designed c.1775 by Robert and James Adam. The lower section of each door has a raised and fielded panel; the larger upper section is fitted with a latticework metal grill, backed with pleated fabric. More expensive than glazing, latticework panels were also often fitted without the fabric to bookcase doors in the late 18th century.

4

5

6

7

8

6 Decorated with a red milk paint, this large, six-panelled door is in an Amish farmer's log house that was built in the mid-18th century, and moved by its current owners from Lancaster County to Chester County, in Pennsylvania.The door's panels are raised and fielded; its latch is made of wrought iron.

7 This four-panelled, painted softwood door is hung in a restored, late-18th-century Connecticut farmhouse. The panels are set flush with the frame, and their sides defined by simple mouldings. The damaged lower panels have been reinforced with an extra bottom rail. The wrought-iron thumb-latch is of a type in widespread use in the late 18th and 19th centuries.

8 This pair of white and gilt doors is in a New York apartment, and was designed by the owner, Bernd Goeckler. The panels are made of applied mouldings, and the applied motifs are derived from the neo-classical vocabulary of ornament. The winged figures in the lower panels, like the winged Pegasuses on the frieze above, are strongly associated with Empire style – the source of inspiration for the overall decorative scheme of the apartment.

1 *Ionic columns frame this substantial pair of eight-panelled sliding doors at the Old Merchant's House, which was built in New York, in 1832, in the Greek Revival style (see pp.22–3). Sliding doors were often hung in American Greek Revival townhouses, usually to divide the principal reception rooms. These are made from, flame-cut mahogany, and are known as "pocket doors" because they slide into compartments recessed into the walls.*

2 *This four-panelled door is of a type commonly found in modest Victorian houses built during the second half of the 19th century. The stiles and rails that make up its framework are no more than 1in (2.5cm) thick, and thus substantially thinner and lighter than the 3in (7.5cm) frame-work of the sliding panel doors in 1. As a consequence, its door's sound-proof qualities are far less impressive. Moreover, while sliding doors were constructed from expensive, solid mahogany, this door is made of much cheaper deal (fir or pine), and has been wood-grained to simulate the colour and attractive figuring of mahogany. Its door handle is a black-china knob – again, a cheaper alternative to brass.*

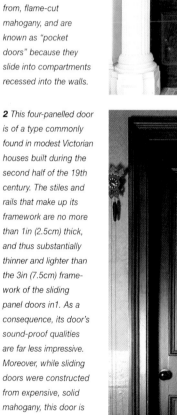

3 *Framed by a pair of swagged portières (door curtains), these Victorian double doors have upper panels of "frosted" etched glass. Used to introduce more light into a room, while preserving a privacy, such panels became very popular in the late 19th century. The sophistication of the decorative motifs usually reflected the status of the household – these are particularly ornate, and are based on the stylized, interlaced foliage patterns known as arabesques, which originated in Islamic art.*

4 *Clear-glass door panels provided a less expensive alternative to "frosted" etched glass panels, as in the doors in 3. To provide insulation and, when necessary, to shut out what the Victorians sometimes referred to as "borrowed" light, a fabric portière was usually draped from a rod or wire fixed to the top of the door. This painted and glazed, seven-panelled door is made of softwood, and is in a mid-19th-century French château. Its lower wooden panel is characteristically picked out in a paler shade of the gray-blue colour applied to the frame and glazing bars. The chequer-pattern portière is original, and made from a cotton Carreaux du Perigord fabric.*

5 These stained and polished mahogany double-doors are in a substantial French Renaissance Revival mansion built on Rhode Island, in the late 19th century. Each door has five panels: plain rectilinear at the top and bottom, and three cartouche panels in between. Cartouches were widely used in Renaissance ornament, and can have concave, convex or flat centres – either decorated with motifs or, as here, plain. (The fingerplates and lever handles are brass – the former stamped with a Renaissance-style tracery pattern.)

6 These double-doors are made of oak, and hung in an American "Tudor-style" mansion, built in Forest Hills, New York, in the late 19th century. Six panels are carved with a stylized, linenfold pattern, relieved with diamond motifs. The other two are carved with portraits of English royalty.

7 Leaded, stained-glass door panels were very fashionable in the late 19th and early 20th centuries, particularly in Arts and Crafts houses. These elaborate panels, set in an oak door and surround, incorporate arcading and a central roundel, and display colourful images of flora and fauna.

5

6

7

PAINTED PINE

From the late Renaissance to the end of the Edwardian era, most doors made from pine – such as this late-18th-century English kitchen door – were painted or wood-grained. This was because the figuring and grain of pine were usually thought too bland for the semi-translucent, stained and polished finishes favoured for the more decorative hardwoods, such as oak and mahogany. However, during the late 20th century, it became fashionable to strip off the paint, and replace it with a clear wax or varnish. Decoration has always been subject to the vagaries of fashion, but such treatments do almost inevitably compromise period authenticity.

DOOR SURROUNDS

Most internal door surrounds are made of either hardwoods or softwoods – the latter usually painted. However, stone has also been used, mainly in grander houses, prior to the 18th and during the late 19th and early 20th centuries, as has plaster – the latter generally restricted to entablatures or pediments in neo-classical and Classical Revival houses. The form and decoration of surrounds have been largely determined by changing fashions in architecture and ornament. For example, flat-headed surrounds have been consistently employed since the Middle Ages, while pointed-arch Gothic surrounds (either four-centred or ogee) were also popular in medieval, "Gothick" and Gothic Revival houses, and curved Roman-arch surrounds were often installed in Renaissance, Baroque and Roman Revival Federal homes. Similarly, the jambs (the sides) of the surrounds have been chamfered, especially if they are stone; moulded to various profiles, mostly derived from classical architecture; and carved or painted (and sometimes gilded) with motifs from the Gothic, classical or oriental vocabularies of ornament. In terms of visual impact and prestige, the most impressive surrounds – confined to the finest houses – have been topped with classical pediments (broken and unbroken), or with classical entablatures supported on consoles, columns or pilasters, and encompassing friezes bearing carved, moulded, painted or gilded imagery.

1 Stone door surrounds were in widespread use during the Middle Ages and early Renaissance. This example, framing a plank door, is at Frog Pool Farm, in Avon, which dates to the 15th century. It has chamfered jambs and a four-centred arch.

2 These reproduction, late-15th and early 16th-century door surrounds have four-centred arch inserts spanning the tops of their jambs. Like many internal door surrounds of this period, they are made of oak.

3 In 1912, the Edwardian library at Temple Newsam, in Leeds, was converted into a replica early Georgian library. Like the other architectural mouldings in the room, those of the door surround are elaborately carved, and highlighted with gilding. Notable elements include the scrolled, acanthus-leaf consoles, and a frieze of scrolling foliage flanking an urn.

4 This painted, built-in cupboard is in Mount Pleasant, Philadelphia, Pennsylvania, and dates to 1761–2. Its arched door surround breaks into an acanthus-carved key stone – the latter invariably used to support, within the broken pediment, a classical bust, urn or, as here, a vase.

5 *This late-Georgian panelled door and surround are in Home House, London, which was designed c.1775 by Robert and James Adam. The painted wooden architrave that frames the door opening is in the form of simple, rectilinear mouldings. Characteristically, the entablature above is more elaborately ornamented, with strings of husks swagged-and-tailed from ribbons, and a plaque depicting nymphs at play.*

6 *Located in Richard Jenrette's early 19th-century American Empire-style house on the Hudson River, in New York State, this door surround displays the essential symmetry and proportion of neo-classical architectural fixtures and fittings. Mounted on marble blocks, and joined by corner blocks bearing gilded floral motifs, the rectilinear architrave mouldings have the look of a classical temple-front opening.*

7 *The double-doors between the parlour and dining room of the Belle of the Bends Inn, in Vicksburg, Mississippi, are hung in a painted wooden, elliptical-arched surround – the latter typical of grander American Victorian houses designed in the Italianate style.*

8 *During the second half of the 19th century, it was fashionable in houses designed and decorated under the aegis of the Aesthetic and Arts and Crafts movements (see p.31) to ebonize (stain and black lacquer) woodwork. This ebonized panelled door and surround are in Leighton House, built in the 1860s in London. The carved plant-form motifs on the surround are typical Aesthetic details.*

9 *This late-Victorian five-panelled door and surround are made of pine and wood-grained with a faux-walnut finish. The basic surround is made up of a bulbous, pilaster-like, rectilinear moulding, which is stop-chamfered on either side of the bottom of the door. The arched pediment on top of the surround is inset with an elaborately carved shell motif which provides, in turn, the backdrop to an aegricane (a ram's skull).*

63

DOOR FURNITURE

The basic categories of internal door furniture are hinges; locks and latches; knobs and handles; fingerplates; and keyhole escutcheons (*see* right). Prior to the 17th century, all hinges were surface-mounted, and fashioned as either long straps (simply tapered, or terminated in decorative shapes, such as arrowheads, hearts or stylized flowers), or as smaller H, L, cock's-head or butterfly forms. These were superseded on panelled doors by less decorative, "concealed" iron, brass or steel hinges, which were cut into the side of the door. Until the early 19th century, doors were secured with wooden or iron latches or, in grander houses, expensive, surface-mounted box locks made of wood, iron or brass – the latter largely confined to the late-17th and 18th centuries, and often engraved with decorative motifs. While latches continued to be used in some vernacular houses, box locks were gradually replaced on panelled doors by cut-in mortise locks, which were usually faced with decorative fingerplates housing the lever handles or door knobs. Favoured materials for the plates, handles and knobs included wood, iron, brass, china and, in affluent households, even silver or gold. As with box locks, the plates and knobs often bore geometric patterns or decorative imagery.

1 *The large strap hinge is made of wrought iron, and is of a type used to hang battened-plank doors since the Middle Ages. The strap is fixed to the face of the door, and pivots on a plate screwed or nailed to the doorframe. Some strap hinges pivoted on a pintle (hook) sunk into the frame. The wrought-iron, H-shaped hinge above it came into wide-spread use during the 17th century. Popular variations of this hinge included the butterfly and S-shaped cock's-head hinges.*

2 *This wrought-iron thumb-latch is on a late-American Colonial framed-plank door. These latches were used from the Middle Ages to the early 20th century. It is locked from the inside with a wooden wedge. The iron hook above secures the opened door to a wall or post.*

3 *This combination thumb-latch and door handle is also late-American Colonial, and fitted to a door in Hunter House, on Rhode Island. While the profile of the thumb-shaped lever, which operates the latch on the reverse of the door, has remained largely unaltered over the centuries, the handle and fingerplate have been subject to many variations of shape and decorative detail.*

4 *Rim locks were luxury items prior to the 18th century, but came into common use after that. The example at the top is made of wood, and fitted to the front door of the Red House, built in 1859 near London, for William Morris, the leading exponent of* the Arts and Crafts movement. The middle lock, which is on a panelled American Colonial door, is made of brass, but painted black to simulate cast iron. The example at the bottom is polished brass, and dates to the late 18th century.

5 *Both of these door pulls are made of brass. The top one is modelled in the Gothic Revival style; the shape of the bottom one is primarily based on classical forms. Pulls such as these are traditionally used on both room and cupboard doors.*

6 These three door-knobs are made of, in descending order, polished brass, transfer-printed white china and white china. Round doorknobs first became fashionable in the 17th century, and were especially popular in the late 18th and 19th centuries. Prior to the

Victorian era, they were usually made of brass, but also gilt or silver in grander houses, and could be either plain or engraved (see 7). China knobs – porcelain or glazed earthenware, and mostly white, black or, as here, patterned – were much in favour during the Victorian era.

7 In the finest houses, (particularly on their reception-room doors), brass, gilt and silver escutcheon plates and doorknobs were often embellished with motifs and patterns in relief – mostly either chased, engraved or repoussé. This American reproduction knob and plate display a highly intricate Renaissance Revival pattern of stylized foliage motifs.

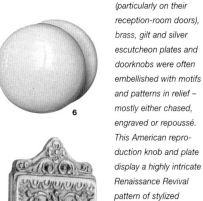

8 Brass lever handles first became widely fashionable in the Georgian interiors of the early 18th century, although thereafter never proved quite as popular as round or oval doorknobs. As these three polished brass examples illustrate, differences of style centre on the profile of the handle, and on the

shape and decoration of the fingerplate. In contrast to the plain, rectangular example on the right, the one in the centre, like the one on the left, is arched at either end. The perimeter of the latter is ornamented with bead moulding – a popular definitional device derived from classical architecture.

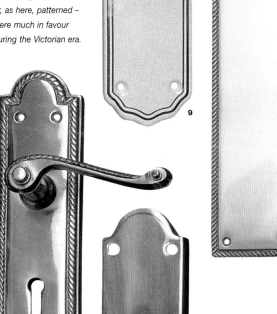

9 Separate fingerplates were fashionable from the late 18th century onward. The Victorian blue-china plate has ogee-arch-style ends and black banding around its perimeter. The perimeters of both the Georgian brass plates are defined with rope moulding.

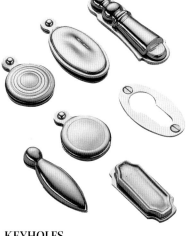

KEYHOLES

Small metal escutcheons, designed to protect the door surface around the rim of a keyhole, became widespread during the early 19th century. Used with the newly developed mortise locks which, unlike surface-mounted rim locks, were cut into the door, they were mostly made of brass, although gold, silver and china were also employed. Produced in a wide variety of shapes – including round, oval, cartouche and teardrop – many were fitted with pivoting covers, which were intended to protect the keyhole from accumulations of dust.

10 The knob and key-hole escutcheon of this late-19th-century brass door furniture display raised relief patterns, and the fingerplates show pierced fretwork vases and foliage.

WINDOWS

The orchestration of window architecture affects not only the aesthetic aspect and technical structure of the exterior, but also the interior proportions and the way light affects them. Mullioned and transomed windows – those with upright posts and horizontal bars – were common by the late 16th century, as was diagonal leaded glazing. The monastic trefoiled and four-centred arched style of the early Tudor window (see left) were superseded from the 17th century by square heads and panes. Later, casement windows were fitted within these with a variety of glazing patterns. Mullions and transoms were reduced in number and size as window proportions became taller and narrower. The first uncorded sash windows of the mid-17th century had a fixed top half and sliding bottom half, but by 1700, sashes were counterweighted, allowing larger areas of glass to be moved vertically.

After 1709, windows were set back four inches (10 centimetres) from the wall face, and thereafter the reveals were often plastered and painted white. However, vernacular buildings retained casement windows and leaded panes for much longer. The Baroque period saw great sophistication in window design, and windows included such features as decorative scrollwork or rustication, key stones, pedimentation, and curved window heads.

Pattern books affected the evolution of Georgian buildings and ensured structural integrity. The Venetian window is characteristic, with its arched section between two narrower side windows, adapted to suit classical fashion. Exterior embellishment included classical window pediments supported by console brackets or pilasters, cut brickwork, and stonework lintels. In America, these devices were heavier and more elaborate. Dormer windows were also popular, especially in America, where they carried the fenestration pattern into the deep-hipped roof line. Glazing variations included ornamental lattice or stained glass, and the arrangement of six-over-six panes. In Britain, the old, thick, hardwood glazing bars became more refined in softwood, and were always protected by white lead paint.

After 1774, frames were rebated within the wall face to meet the British fire-safety regulations, and Coade stone or rusticated surrounds on the ground floor restored visual weight to hidden frames. Below the attenuated window line of the *piano nobile* the string course formed a unifying running sill and, by the 1780s, French doors gave onto balconies. Round-headed, Gothic, Venetian (sometimes with spider's-web tracery or squared with a pedimented heading) and, by mid-century, bay windows, were popular. By 1780, some windows were painted a darker colour, usually gray, particularly with white stucco facades, but by 1800 brown paint was also fashionable.

The classical, mannered style of the 1800s loosened as the 19th century progressed. The Regency period is typified by tall, narrow French windows and delicate ironwork balconies and verandas. Windows had narrow margin lights, sometimes paned with coloured glass, arched windows enlivened with Gothic tracery and sophisticated bow windows. American style c.1800–50 is typified by attenuated mouldings, Greek Revival surrounds, semicircular and oval windows on the upper storeys, and Queen Anne or Empire-style dormers enhancing the roof line.

Glass was cheaper after 1850, and sash windows became plainer and had more glass, counterbalanced by decorative brickwork, stucco, and terracotta decoration. Gothic, Queen Anne, Italianate styles, and stained and leaded glass had a following in Britain and America. Late-19th-century windows favoured small, square panes in the upper sash and plain glass below, or vernacular casements with leaded glass. Coloured glass was extensively used in both countries.

Edwardian facades had more window space than Victorian, and bow and bay were popular. Multiple "Queen Anne" glazing divisions were often used in the top section only, and stained glass screened secondary windows. American turn-of-the-century style was more flamboyant, with Colonial Revival six-over-six paned tall windows, Italian Renaissance-style aedicules or pedimented heads, French classical arched or carved surrounds, and Spanish Revival ornamental iron grilles.

CASEMENT WINDOWS

Glass was so precious in the mid-15th century that casement windows were considered separate pieces of furniture and not part of the house structure. They were commonly fitted into existing mullion openings of notable houses from the mid-15th century, but they were not used in country dwellings until the second half of the 18th century. Stone houses had iron casements and timber houses had wooden ones. In urban areas these initially opened inward to avoid the elements buffeting the fragile glass and the proximity of passing traffic. Casements again became fashionable in Arts and Crafts and Edwardian Tudor Revival houses, when they were inserted into the prepared brick or stone openings or wooden subframe, and embellished with decorative coloured-glass transfers or stained-glass panes.

1 *This is a mid-16th-century eight-light window with typical four-centred headings. Casements were often inserted into older mullion and transom windows, but the size of the panes indicates that the glazing is 17th century.*

2 *This early 20th-century stone-dressed Tudor-style window also has four-centred arches and a stone mullion and transom, but it is glazed with plate glass, as the Edwardians preferred to have as much natural light as possible.*

3 *In this 18-century château, the verticality of these narrow casement windows is accentuated by being divided into four separate panes. The panes are simply glazed and the frame is painted softwood.*

4 *Very small windows were generally found in rustic dwellings because glass was unavailable until well into the 18th century. Shutters, waxed paper, oilcloth or skins were used instead to keep out the elements.*

5 *French windows, beloved in England from the 1780s, are seen here in their place of origin – a c.1765 Normandy château, which shows the exquisite attenuated lines of the window and architrave.*

6 *Bay windows had several periods of being in vogue, from medieval times to the mid-18th century, and then from the Regency to the Edwardian periods. In this example, the metal casement windows and the large area of glass indicate the latter period.*

7 *A distinctive Gothic Revival example of the mid-19th century, this window has the typically fashionable ogee-shaped top and fragments of 16th- and 17th-century stained glass set in the heading.*

8 *Such a dominating element as this glorious Victorian stained-glass window should always influence the interior style. Here, the bathroom fittings are well-suited.*

9 *There were numerous movements during the 19th century inspired by rural lifestyles. This lodge at Blue Mountain Lake, in New York State, has beautifully crafted wooden leading to hold the glass quarries.*

10 *In this Tudorbethan house, the casement windows have leaded lights that are arranged in a rectangular pattern, which is appropriate to the period and the vernacular tradition.*

6

7

8

9

10

69

SASH WINDOWS

By the end of the 17th century, better glass-making techniques allowed larger quantities of glass to be used and, as a consequence, a completely new window composition was required. Probably introduced to Britain from France or Holland in about 1640, the first sash windows were kept open by means of pegs that were inserted into notches in the bottom frame's grooves, but from 1700 weighted sashes radically changed the face of architecture. The British fire-safety regulations stipulated that the wooden frames be recessed from the wall face, and this gave a lighter architectural profile while at the same time accommodating the weighted sash mechanism within the window jamb. These developments resulted in the ability to raise greater areas of glass and create a more elegant frame with increasingly narrow glazing bars. Endless permutations of glazing formations followed until, by the mid-18th century, the twelve-pane sash became standard in the majority of buildings. The next two-and-a-half centuries saw designers exploring the aesthetic possibilities of the sash window in all its endless variety, as evidenced here.

1 These beautifully proportioned mid-18th-century sash windows are in a Connecticut farmhouse, where they are complemented by simple but generous curtains. The number of panes, the size of glazing bars, and the placement of the pair of windows are indicative of the period.

2 Perhaps more than any other element, the tripartite Venetian window, adapted to suit the fashionable classical idiom, most clearly identifies the early Georgian period. The window was employed to draw focus to the facade's centre. From the 1730s, the design was freely interpreted both in Britain and in America.

3 Here, an imaginatively designed American "bay" window, dating from the second half of the 18th century, not only provides a window seat, but also lets in as much natural light as possible.

4 The six-over-six panes and louvred shutters of the c.1800 Gaillard-Bennett House, in Charleston, South Carolina, put it ahead of fashion. The green and cream paints are historically accurate.

5 In the windows of this c.1720 house in Spitalfields, London, there is the usual arrangement of panes and double shutters. The panelled room is painted a deep, dusty red which, with the other dull, muted colours, is in keeping with the period.

6 Well-balanced window proportions and a corner position favour this elaborate American Empire-style interior treatment and luxurious fringed pelmet.

7 This mid-19th-century Shaker house reveals the uncluttered symmetry, the soothing colours and the unadorned furnishings that epitomize the Shaker ideology. The window is similarly plain and unembellished, and devoid of curtains or other types of covering.

8 The Victorians favoured the double-storey bay with two narrow windows set on either side of the larger one. However, they draped the interior heavily, thereby keeping out the natural light.

5

6

7

8

9

10

9 This mid-Victorian double-storey bay arrangement, which is very much of its period, has a mixture of types of brick banding across the upper storey, stucco piers, and a broad lower sill for holding a window box.

10 Here, a reproduction oriel window is used in an early 20th-century house of idiosyncratic design. It has a panelled base and blind covers and a lead half-bell canopy, and permits a broad sweep of the fine views of the surrounding area.

WINDOW SURROUNDS

There were numerous treatments that influenced the look of a window's exterior and interior environment. Historically, this consideration was of great importance as it affected many aspects of design. For example, great thought was given to the pediment detailing that was considered best-suited to the building's classical references – correct geometry was intrinsic to an 18th-century architect's rule book. Certainly, the choices were determined by the availability of materials, the skill and imagination of the craftsmen, and the vernacular architecture of the locality (it should be remembered that the fashion of the city was not the national standard). On another level, the designer's aesthetic decorative quest could be satisfied when attention was given to the minute detail within the broader plan. Thus the type of questions that would have been addressed were as follows: Should marble or stone be used for a heading key stone? Which would be more pleasing and appropriate for a surround – quartered columns or pilasters? And should a mahogany cornice or fabric pelmet be employed for the window's embellishment? The mid-18th-century designers, Robert and James Adam, excelled at marrying their dignified classical-exterior ensemble with interior decoration of exquisite refinement and, of course, the windows were of utmost importance, being the gateway between the two.

2

1

3

1 The interior view of the window surrounds at Wenlocke Abbey in England reveals a monastically austere atmosphere that has not been dissipated by modern overdressing. The trefoil surrounds have a tiny casement window, sturdy oak shutters strengthened with metal cross-bracing, and heavy carved stone window headings. The deep window reveals have room enough for integral carved-stone side sills, which may have been used as book supports, thereby making the best use of space and the available natural light.

2 In the c.1775 Home House, in London, Robert Adam used neo-classical style to provide the complete architectural vocabulary to richly decorate this room. The treatment of the window surround integrates the grand "hardness" of the architecture with the "soft" opulence of the green, gold and black ornamentation.

3 The faux stone walls, the marble baseboard, and the classical artefacts and window surround re-create the American Empire style of Edgewater, in New York, c.1854.

4 The Nathaniel Russell House in Charleston, South Carolina, dates to 1808, and this window arrangement embodies several typical elements of the period. The long sash window is placed in a shallow arched recess capped by a key stone that is paired with the lintel design. The delicate balcony and a line of stone stringing provide a strong visual link between the windows, unifying the overall architectural geometry.

5 Reproduction mahogany brass-mounted cornices, with corded pennant valances of striped crimson moiré silk, give these floor-to-ceiling windows a balanced proportion and a period feel. Their corner position prohibits the use of curtains, which would, in any case, hide the architectural symmetry of the window surround.

6 This example illustrates a Victorian Gothic theme within a genuine medieval building. The window initiated the collection of numerous modern and antique pieces that do credit to the house's origins.

PELMETS
Pelmets have been in and out of fashion since they first appeared in the 16th century in France. Pelmets and window cornices played a part in defining the proportions of a window, and in giving decorative emphasis to the blank area of a room between the window and the ceiling. Careful choice of the fabric, colour, style and embellishment will help to enhance the period feel of the room.

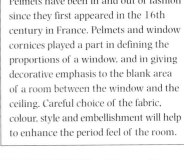

7 Grange, a late-19th-century house in Philadelphia, Pennsylvania, has a charmingly ornate exterior. The carved Gothic tracery of the window pediment draws the eye toward a tiny circular window and "gingerbread" bargeboard beneath the eaves.

8 This American Italianate bay window in a house in Los Angeles is also late 19th century, and shows great complexity and craftsmanship in its quest to make a flamboyant statement.

73

SHUTTERS

Before glass was in widespread use, window openings were often covered in wood, waxed paper, oilcloth or skins, and then sometimes in a primitive wooden shutter. Shutters were often needed both inside and out to eliminate light and draughts, protect privacy and repel burglars. From 1620 they were fitted in pairs, each side having two hinged leaves. Aesthetically, shutters could be used to play with the effect of light, and to protect precious furnishing materials from fading. Grand houses with sliding sash windows generally had shutters. Each pair was divided into two or three tiers, and closed vertically to fold away in the window embrasure which was either at right angles to the window or, increasingly in the Georgian era, splayed back in order to maximize light. Their panelling matched that of other woodwork, but, toward the end of the 17th century, shutters began to be decorated *en suite* with the room, or painted in a darker colour. Victorian softwood shutters, like those of the Georgian period, were always painted, while Arts and Crafts shutters and other areas of woodwork were mainly left unpainted.

2

3

5

1 *Even a very basic shutter adds to the theatricality of this medieval interior. A similar shutter could quite easily be made from old floorboards or part of a door.*

2 *The windows' structure and the surrounding architecture indicate that curtains were never envisaged in this Empire-style New York apartment. The window opening is elegantly served by slender panelled shutters.*

3 *The architecture of the wall face is continued with these 18th-century shutters. The window rests comfortably on top of the dado, its outline continued to the floor, and the whole ensemble is united by period-gray paint.*

4 *The finely louvred shutters in the early 19th-century Nathaniel Russell House, in Charleston, South Carolina, are multi-hinged and arranged in several tiers in order to manage the flow of air, heat, humidity and light.*

5 *On the garden door of John Keats's house, in Hampstead, London, which was built c.1820, the shutters are set in shallow, splayed boxes, and the door retains its coloured and acid-etched glass.*

1

4

WINDOW FURNITURE

Seventeenth-century casement windows had several parts to their opening mechanism: the hinge, the wrought-iron handle for opening and closing, and the stay for holding the window open. In a domestic interior, decorative furniture allowed a noticeable element of status to the house and its occupants. Made by the local blacksmith, the window furniture was beautifully crafted and came in a great variety of designs, including cock's-head and zoomorphic shapes. Some examples were highly sophisticated: they could twist, have a spring mechanism, or function as a simple latch. Brass was very expensive, and therefore was the most desirable for the wealthy. Early sash windows, which were without counterweights, were very heavy and had wooden lifts until 1760, but weighted sashes, with more glass, required tougher brass or cast iron. As brass became cheaper, and decorations generally more ornate, the window furniture became more elaborate as well.

3 *Apart from looking serviceable, there is a certain aesthetic about the tangible chunkiness of this rustic window fastener, which is made of brass (but has been painted over).*

4 *The first patent for a sash fastener – a barrel-type with a spring and screws – was registered in 1776 in Britain. This type (above right) and the variation (below right) – both reproduction-brass examples – are strong and authentic-looking.*

5 *The addition of a sash lift, which evenly distributes the upward draw, helps to protect the counterweight mechanism and paintwork. These reproduction Georgian examples are both made of brass.*

1 *Good reproduction casement fittings should offer an historically correct type of fastener. For example, the wrought-iron fasteners and mortise plates (far left) are accurate for medieval and revival windows, while the brass catches and plates (left) are more appropriate for the mid-1850s.*

2 *The top window stay is forged iron and is of a type used since the Renaissance, particularly in Jacobean Revival, Arts and Crafts, and vernacular houses. Brass superseded iron from the 18th century. The second stay is Georgian, and was used until the 20th century; the third is late-18th- to early 19th-century neo-classical; and the fourth is early 20th century.*

CURTAIN POLES

The fashion for hanging a curtain or curtains from a pole over a window or interior door has appeared in some form throughout the last five hundred years. The most frequently revived style is the Gothic, and today there is a great assortment of pole finials available reflecting that period's motifs. The one illustrated is a fleur-de-lis style made from cast resin. Today, curtain poles and finials are manufactured in a number of period styles and materials, including wood, brass, steel and painted metal.

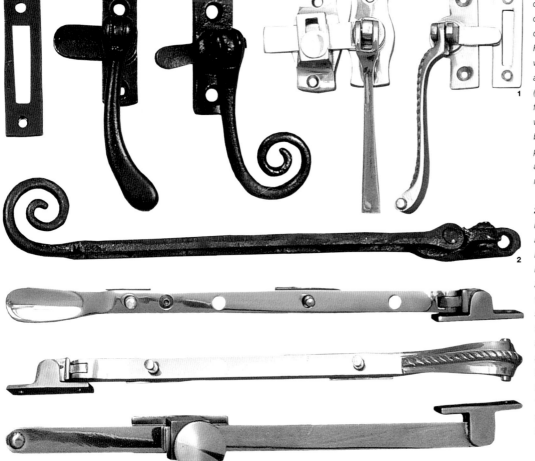

STAIRS

In terms of their constructional role, the basic components of a staircase have remained largely unaltered since the Middle Ages. Individual steps consist of an upper, horizontal surface known as a tread, the front edge (or nosing) of which rests on (and slightly overlaps) a vertical section, called a riser. On most staircases, the sides of a run or flight of steps are keyed into supporting diagonal members, known as strings, although on spiral staircases the narrow ends of the steps are keyed into a central newel post (*see* spiral stairs, right). The structure that runs up one, or both, side(s) of a flight of steps is known as a balustrade. This is made up of balusters, newel posts and a handrail. Balusters are vertical posts that support the handrail and serve as a barrier to the open sides of the steps. (If the bases of the balusters are keyed into the strings, the staircase is referred to as closed-string; if they are keyed directly into the steps, and the latter are not enclosed by the string, the staircase is open-string.) The balusters are flanked at each end of a flight of steps by a vertical newel post. Newels, which often bear decorative finials and, sometimes on floors above ground level, pendants, are much larger than balusters. They support the ends of the strings and the handrail(s), and are keyed into the floor or the landing – the latter being either a platform between flights of steps, or the floor at the top of the stairs.

The materials used to make these components include stone, metal (especially wrought and cast iron, but also steel) and, most commonly, wood. Apart from basic structural requirements – notably, the need to bear given loads under compression or tension – their form and decoration (carved or moulded) has been determined by prevailing fashions. For example, vase- or columnar-shaped balusters are mostly found on staircases where the architecture of the house is influenced by Graeco-Roman classicism, while newel posts capped with chamfered pinnacles are confined to Gothic or Gothic Revival staircases (*see* pp.8–33 for the predominant historical styles of architecture and ornament).

Over and above variations in the shape and decoration of their component parts, staircases are divided into a number of basic categories or types. Straight flights, as the name implies, provide a direct, diagonal link between floors. Dog-legs provide the connection via two straight flights, which run parallel in opposite directions to one another, have no space (or "well") between their outer strings and are joined, between floors, by an intermediate landing. A variation on the dog-leg is the open-well, which has a wider landing and a space between the outer strings of the flights. Turning stairs link floors with a single flight of steps, but instead of the flight being straight, it is angled or turned at one or more points along its rise or descent. The angle of turn varies, but quarter-turns, half-turns and three-quarter turns are most common. Spiral or newel staircases connect two or more floors and consist of angled steps wound around a large central newel post. A variation of the spiral is the framed newel, in which the inner edges of the steps are keyed into a timber-framed tower, rather than a solid, central newel, and the outer edges into the surrounding brick or stone walls of the stairwell. The final basic category consists of cantilevered (or "flying") stairs, in which only the outer edges of a flight of steps are keyed into and cantilevered from a straight or curved side wall – the inner edges having no visible means of support.

Other, less commonly employed types of staircase worthy of note include bifurcated, in which a single flight divides at a landing into two flights to the floor above, and a double-return, where a single flight joins a floor above, but divides and returns to the original floor in two flights. Both of these tend to be used as grand staircases in large houses. Also used, mainly prior to the 19th century, as the principal staircase in smaller houses, and secondary stairs in grander ones, were box-winders. Turning between floors, they were concealed within a narrow stairwell which, especially in American Colonial houses, was often sited next to a chimney flue, and accessed by a door in the fireplace wall.

STAIRCASE STYLES

Many types of staircase have been employed during the various historical periods from the Middle Ages to the end of the First World War. However, because most staircases (especially the main ones, rather than the secondary staircases that were primarily installed for the servants) have been conceived of as a domestic showpiece, reflecting the status of the house and the homeowner, the style of their construction and ornamentation has almost invariably followed prevailing fashions in architecture and ornament. For example, Gothic shapes and motifs dominate medieval staircases, and are combined with classical equivalents on Renaissance stairs. Similarly, classical forms and imagery dominate Baroque and neo-classical staircases – exaggerated and heavily sculpted in the former and more refined, symmetrical and historically accurate in the latter. Victorian stairs can be characterized by the numerous reproductions and pastiches of almost all of the preceding period styles (*see* pp.8–33) revived under the banner of "eclecticism".

1 *Made of oak, this reproduction, framed-newel, closed-string staircase is of a type originally found in grander houses of the early to mid-16th century. It has carved and pierced flat balus-ters, their curvaceous shape inspired by strapwork. They were especially favoured in English Jacobean houses, although turned columnar shapes were also popular. The square-section newel posts, topped with urn-shape finials, are quite plain for the period – more decorative examples were carved with motifs and imagery.*

2 *Dated to 1738–42, and installed at Drayton Hall, Charleston, South Carolina, this was probably the most elaborate staircase in the American Colonies of this period. Made of mahogany, open-string, and with three turned balusters to each tread, it has two double-dog-leg flights, and is based on English Palladian models.*

3 *Built 1764–7 at Cliveden, in Philadelphia, Pennsylvania, this open-string, American Colonial staircase is a very refined classical composition. Its turned balusters are elegantly attenuated, and the sawn tread ends display wavescroll profiles.*

4 As in 3, this 18th-century, American Colonial, open-string staircase is made of softwood, and painted in a typical Colonial colour. The fielded side panelling, and the plain, square-section newel posts and balusters – two of the latter to each tread – are characteristic of rural Colonial houses.

5 This painted "Gothick" staircase at Strawberry Hill, Twickenham, England, dates to c.1754. Closed-string, and with a balustrade of carved tracery, and unusual caged, carved birds and animals on the newels, its form is based on 17th-century models.

4

6 Cantilevered from the wall, this white-painted, open-string staircase is a reproduction of a mid- to late-18th-century model. Its stained and polished mahogany handrails terminated in fashionable spiral forms on and around the classical, columnar-shaped newel posts. Fitted runners became increasingly common toward the end of the century.

7 The central stair-hall is typical of classically inspired, American Colonial architecture of the mid-18th century. This example, at Hunter House, on Rhode Island (built c.1758), follows the characteristic pattern of a long hall, divided by a bracketed arch, and with an open-string staircase to the rear. A typical feature is the absence of a runner on the treads.

6

7

8 When the prestigious French decorator, Frédéric Méchiche, "transformed" his Parisian apartment, giving it the appearance of a late-18th-century neo-classical, French Directoire-style town house, he installed a restored, original Louis XVI staircase. Closed-string and cantilevered, it has white-painted strings and risers, bare wooden treads and an elegantly simple cast-iron balustrade – the latter painted black to be en suite with the striped upholstery.

5

8

79

1 Cantilevered into the wall of a stairwell, this curved staircase is an American reproduction of an early 19th-century model. Made of stained and polished wood (with metal balusters), it is a good example of the flying staircases which became popular in many grander neo-classical houses during the late 18th and early 19th centuries. As with other examples, the main handrail, which is supported on balusters secured to the tread ends, rather than the tops of the treads, is supplemented with a secondary rail fixed to the wall of the stairwell. Also typical of the period is the central stair runner, which displays a pattern derived from the oriental vocabulary of ornament.

2 & 3 Both of these cantilevered, winding staircases date to the first half of the 19th century, and are of a type much favoured in larger American houses of the Federal period (see pp.18–19). The example on the left rises from the ground floor to attic level at the Bartow-Pell Mansion, in New York, and dates to c.1842. Its tapering balusters are turned and reeded and, like the treads and handrail, are made of stained and polished mahogany. The equally fine example on the right is in Patrick Duncan House, in Charleston, South Carolina, and dates to 1816. While it also features a mahogany handrail and treads, its thin balusters display the simpler and more delicate profile popular in early 19th-century neo-classical interiors on both sides of the Atlantic.

4 This reproduction early 19th-century English staircase is also curved, cantilevered and open-string, and, like staircase 3, has a balustrade of refined neo-classical simplicity. In contrast to staircase 1, its runner spans the full width of the treads, and is patterned with repeat floral motifs taken from the European, rather than the oriental, vocabulary of ornament.

5 *Constructed c.1880, this majestic staircase rises from the centre of a large stair-hall in an 18th-century, English Georgian country house (with later and major Victorian modifications and additions). Quite often referred to as bifurcated – because its initial flight rises to a half-landing and then divides into two dog-leg flights – it is made from stained and polished mahogany. The deep, shallow-rising treads, the closed-string balustrade, with robustly turned balusters and the large urn, obelisk and ball finials on the newel posts, are typical mid-Victorian features, as are the arched niches in the side panelling (which serve as bookshelves and a small storage closet).*

6 *In contrast to example 5, this classic dog-leg staircase is far more utilitarian in both its form and decoration. Early American Victorian, and sited in the hallway of a house in Galena, Illinois, it is open-string and has a simple, but elegant, balustrade, with a tapered newel post and balusters turned from walnut. The painted risers and walnut treads are left bare, although in American houses of this period they could also be covered with a carpet or floorcloth runner.*

CAST-IRON SPIRAL STAIRS

Spiral staircases – also known as newel, turngrece, vice, turnpike, winding or cockle stairs – consist of a series of steps wound around a central pier or column (a newel). They have been used since the Middle Ages, but prior to the 19th century had to be enclosed, for supportive reasons, within a tower or a stairwell, so that the broad end of the steps could be keyed into a circumference wall – the narrow ends being keyed into the newel. However, by making the newel from interlocking sections of heavy cast iron (rather than stone or wood), and by integrating a cast-iron step with each section, the Victorians were able to mass-produce free-standing spiral staircases. This example has been installed between two floors of a converted malt house, near Bath, in England.

7 *Designed for the Red House (built 1859), in Bexleyheath, near London, England, by the architect Philip Webb (working with the house's owner, William Morris), this framed newel staircase is based on late-16th- and early 17th-century models. Like many staircases in Arts and Crafts houses, it is made of oak. Also typically Arts and Crafts are the solid balustrade, consisting of vertical, butt-jointed planks, and the faceted, medieval Gothic-style pinnacles on the newel posts.*

STAIRCASE COMPONENTS

Before the widespread adoption during the 19th century of semi-automated cutting, carving and routing machines, and of techniques for casting iron, staircase components were fashioned – mostly from stone, wood and iron – by hand. This skilled, labour-intensive and relatively expensive process meant that sophisticated decorative embellishments of items such as tread ends, balusters, newel posts, finials and handrails were confined to wealthier households. There were a few exceptions to this. For example, in some quite humble houses, wooden newel posts might be elaborately turned and carved. Generally, however, it was only after the Victorians developed the techniques for mass-producing staircase components that costs were reduced and ordinary householders began to gain access to the wide and diverse range of ornamentation applied since the Middle Ages. Nevertheless, what this development did not change was the premium placed on skilled craftsmanship and ingenuity of design, and the enduring status and cost of raw materials such as intricately veined marbles and finely figured hardwoods, over more abundant, cheaper and less prestigious alternatives, such as softwood firs and pines.

1 The balustrade of this reproduction Jacobean, framed-newel staircase has been given the appearance of Gothic arcading by linking the tops of the chamfered balusters with pierced and carved, double-arch inserts. The square-section newel post – popular during the 16th and early 17th centuries – is topped with an urn-shaped finial, but ball, obelisk and pyramidal shapes, of varying complexity, were also fashionable during this period.

2 The turned sections of the balusters on this early 18th-century, open-string English staircase display the spiral-twist pattern that was much in vogue at this time. Also typical is the use of two balusters per tread; by the mid-18th century, this was often increased to three per tread. The undulating profile and the carved details of the tread ends – like the expensive spiral-twist turnings, and thick mahogany handrail – are indicative of a fairly wealthy household. The columnar newel post reveals the strong influence of classical architectural forms in the modelling of many 18th-century staircase components.

3 The complexity of handrail and stair-end mouldings reflected both the status of the house and the position of the staircase. The finely carved and pierced scrolling plant-form motifs on this grand, mid-18th-century American Colonial mahogany staircase are particularly elaborate.

4 The newel post and balustrade on this mid-Victorian staircase are made of cast iron. Their detailed and lavish ornamentation consists of forms and motifs primarily derived from the classical vocabulary of ornament, and includes rows of rosettes, rows of husks, bead moulding and scrolling foliate forms.

5 Fretwork decoration on this imposing mid-Victorian panelled balustrade is in the form of quatrefoils and, above and below, stylized floral motifs, derived from the Gothic vocabulary of ornament. The diagonal string beneath the intricately carved handrail displays a row of carved rosettes.

6 This superbly carved balustrade is in a François Premier-style house in New York (built 1899). Its dolphins and urn-shaped balusters, like the acanthus-leaf carving on the newel post, were inspired by Renaissance prototypes.

7 Substantial newel posts, exuberantly carved with floral, fruit and foliate forms, and invariably topped with elaborate finials, are highly characteristic of Baroque staircases. This particularly splendid example is at Moulton Hall, in Yorkshire, England, and dates to c.1654–60.

8 Mounted on a carved, cube-shaped plinth, this American newel post is turned as a pair of vases, and carved with acanthus-leaf motifs. Made of stained and polished oak, it dates to the 1830s, and was almost certainly inspired by a 17th-century newel carved from stone.

9 Dated to the 1880s, this impressive, square-sectioned newel post is moulded and carved from mahogany. Square, columnar-shaped newels were particularly fashionable during the late-Victorian era.

10 Turned and faceted wooden newel posts, modelled on medieval Gothic prototypes, were often employed in Victorian Arts and Crafts houses. This example has a faceted pinnacle, which is very typical of the style. However, some newels in the grandest of late-19th-century Arts and Crafts houses were capped with electric lights.

83

1 Designed by architect George Aitchison in 1879–81, the principal staircase at Leighton House, London, England, has stone treads and risers, which are keyed into a wood-panelled brick wall. Largely due to the costs of quarrying, transporting and carving the raw material, stone steps were invariably much more expensive than wooden equivalents, and thus tended to be reserved for grander houses. The oriental runner on the stairs is 19th century, but displays a re-creation of a "Tree of Life" pattern often found on rugs and carpets during the 17th century.

2 Like the balustrade, the treads of this open-string, cantilevered staircase in Richard Jenrette's American Empire-style house on the Hudson River, in New York State, are made of mahogany. Supported on painted softwood strings and risers, the centres of the treads are, as in many other imposing American Federal- and Empire-style houses, covered with a monochrome (dark green), woven-pile runner. This is secured to the risers with ornate, polished-brass stair rods, which feature wavescrolls – a favourite neo-classical motif of the late 18th and early 19th centuries.

1

3 The knotted-pile central runner covering the treads and risers of this reproduction, late-19th-century wooden staircase is secured with plain, lacquered- brass stair rods. These slot into small clips screwed into the treads and the risers, and can be easily removed for cleaning. In order to protect the runner from excessive wear and tear, L-shaped brass strips have been screwed over the nosings of the treads. Although these metal strips were often applied over runners on grander staircases from the late-Victorian age onward, they were rarely used prior to this.

3

4 Marble has retained its status since classical Greek and Roman times as one of the most prestigious building materials. Consequently, marble staircases have been almost exclusively confined to the grandest houses. This example, at The Elms, in Newport, Rhode Island, dates to 1895, and has steps and strings of contrasting-coloured and figured marbles. The interlaced, stylized foliate forms of the wrought-iron balustrade are typical of American Beaux Arts mansions styled on classical French houses.

4

5 Like the balustrades and newel posts, the majority of treads and risers on late-19th- and early 20th-century Arts and Crafts stairs were made of wood. The best examples were polished hardwood (especially oak, as here), although in smaller houses, softwoods such as fir and pine were used, and were often painted. As with most other Arts and Crafts joinery, the aesthetic appeal of these steps resides in the quality of their construction, and the natural colour, figuring and grain of the oak, which was enhanced by polishing, rather than by any applied decorative detail.

5

84

6 *The staircase, like the rest of the woodwork, furnishings and decorations in this late-20th-century American house, is modelled on 18th-century prototypes found in the plank houses of Chester County, Pennsylvania. The simple, but well-executed craftsmanship of the bare wooden treads, strings and risers is echoed in the form and decoration of the chamfered newel post and moulded handrail. These are painted with authentic Williamsburg green-blue milk paint to match the tongue-and-groove side panelling and the window.*

7 *During the second half of the 18th and the early 19th centuries, it was very fashionable to terminate handrails in a spiral – either a tight coil, as here, or a loose curve. The centre of this reproduction mahogany handrail is inlaid with small cuts of mahogany that display contrasting figuring to that of the main body of the rail.*

8 *This cantilevered, winding stone staircase, in an early 19th-century American Empire house, has painted, wrought-iron balusters with a matching handrail. Their simple profiles indicate that this is a secondary staircase – on the main staircase they would be more elaborate.*

9 *Wooden handrails have been made with a wide range of profiles, especially since the advent of automated cutting, carving and routing machines in the 19th century. Most are copies, or adaptations, of mouldings used in classical Graeco-Roman architecture. Notable examples include torus, astragal, echinus, ovolo, scotia and, as here, bolection mouldings.*

10 *This wall-mounted wooden handrail is part of a restored American staircase dated to 1889. Wall-mounted rails were rare prior to the late 19th century, and up until then were mostly confined to the circumference walls of towers or stairwells surrounding spiral ("vice") stairs that wound around a central newel post. Thereafter, they were increasingly used as an additional safety feature, to supplement the main handrail on a balustrade.*

11 *The main staircase at Olana, built in New York in the 1870s, has a brass-pole handrail mounted on its wooden balustrade, and a matching brass finial on the newel post. While wrought- and cast-iron rails were in widespread use during the 19th century, brass ones were rarer, and mainly used in Aesthetic and Arts and Crafts houses.*

FLOORS

Since the Middle Ages, the choice of flooring materials has been determined by a combination of geographic location, constructional restrictions and degrees of affluence. For example, prior to the 18th century, inexpensive floors made of baked, dampened and beaten earth (*see* pp.92–3) were often employed in ground-level rooms by homeowners who couldn't afford, or didn't have access to, more durable and expensive tiles or stone. When tiles (*see* pp.94–5) were laid, more costly, glazed, polychrome-patterned versions, as opposed to cheaper, unglazed monochrome types, were generally the preserve of wealthier households. Similarly, given the high cost of quarrying and then transporting heavy stone over long distances by boat or cart, superior stone flag floors – and particularly exotic, inlaid marble floors – were only employed in ordinary houses in close proximity to local quarries, a restriction eventually eased in the 19th century by the development of extensive and efficient transport systems (primarily the railways, but also better roads).

Timber floors have been subject to similar constraints. The absence of properly ventilated spaces under the majority of houses built before the 18th century meant that any timber floors laid in ground-level rooms were particularly subject to damp and rot. Consequently, up to this period, they were confined in most houses to upper storeys; thereafter, following the introduction of improved sub-floor ventilation and damp-proofing, they vied with stone and tiles at ground level as a worthwhile flooring option. As with stone, the type of timber used was largely determined by availability and cost: durable hardwoods such as oak and elm were abundant prior to the late 17th century, and therefore in common use. However, as supplies dwindled, they were increasingly reserved for better houses, and generally supplanted by plentiful and cheaper softwoods such as pine and fir. In terms of how the timbers were used for flooring, standard floorboards, whether hardwood or softwood (*see* pp.88–9), have been most prevalent, and intricate marquetry and parquetry hardwood block floors (*see* pp.90–1) the more exclusive.

While the styles of decoration applied to floors – particularly the patterns or motifs – have always closely reflected prevailing fashions in architecture and ornament at different historical periods (*see* pp.8–33), the form they have taken was largely fuelled, as before, by availability and cost. For example, stencilled or hand-painted motifs and patterns – especially popular in the United States from the late 17th to the end of the 19th centuries – were often applied to softwood floorboards either as an inexpensive simulation of costly or unavailable hardwood marquetry or parquetry floors, or of even more expensive stone or inlaid-marble floors.

Much the same principle has applied to different types of floor covering. For example, plain woven matting (*see* pp.96–7) was in widespread use up to the late 17th century, primarily because during this period patterned woven carpets were either unavailable or unaffordable to all but the wealthiest householders. Even though flat-weave and woven-pile carpets, of oriental or European manufacture, were increasingly employed in larger houses during the course of the 18th and early 19th centuries, they still remained well beyond the means of most people. Consequently, oil-stiffened canvas floorcloths, stencilled or hand-painted in imitation of fashionable carpet patterns (*see* pp.96–7), were often used in ordinary houses – again, especially in the United States – as cheaper substitutes. Similarly, although the introduction of techniques of automated mass production during the second half of the 19th century helped to increase the supply and reduce the cost of woven carpets, less expensive alternatives were still required. The invention of linoleum (*see* pp.96–7) in *c*.1860 largely fulfilled the demand. Made of solidified linseed oil, resin and gum, heat-bonded to a canvas or jute groundcloth, linoleum was not only relatively cheap and very durable, but it was also made available in a tremendous range of finishes, including simulations of carpet patterns, woven matting, finely figured hardwood boards, marquetry and parquetry, as well as diverse tiled, stone-flag and inlaid-marble floors.

FLOORBOARDS

Before the late 17th century, most floorboards were of irregular width – up to 35 centimetres (14 inches) – and cut from hardwood, notably oak or elm. Hardwood boards, of oak, teak, mahogany, maple and cherry, enjoyed a revival during the Victorian and Edwardian eras. However, from the early 18th century, they were supplanted in most houses by softwood pine or fir boards, which became increasingly uniform in width, and gradually narrower – down to 10 centimetres (4 inches) by the early 19th century. Most hardwood boards have been clear-waxed or varnished, while softwood boards have been either untreated (especially in America), or stained, flat-painted, stencilled, *faux marbred* or wood-grained in imitation of hardwoods.

1 These butt-jointed and dark-stained pine floorboards are in an 18th-century London town house kitchen.

2 Oak or pine boards, unstained, unvarnished, and of random widths, are characteristic of American Colonial houses. These butt-jointed boards are in the keeping room of an 18th-century Rhode Island house. Home of Stephen P. Mack.

3 From the late 17th century onward, fir and pine boards (often imported from the Baltic) gradually replaced oak and elm boards in most English houses. As with these stained and varnished boards in a Georgian drawing room, they also became narrower and of a more regular width.

4 During the 19th century, pine and fir boards become narrower than in the 18th century, and now measured 18–23cm (7–9in). These varnished floorboards are in Lady Hertford's Regency-style bedroom at Temple Newsam, in Leeds, England.

5 Between 1780 and 1840, tongue-and-groove boards were commonly used in grander American Federal houses. Until the late 18th century, white pine was favoured in the New England states; thereafter, there was a gradual switch to yellow pine, which had long been used in the states along the Eastern seaboard and in the South. These yellow pine boards are in the Gaillard-Bennett House, built c.1800 in Charleston, South Carolina.

6 These plain pine boards, of regular width and irregular length, are typical of modest English Victorian houses.

7 While fir and pine boards gradually superseded oak boards in most English houses from the late 17th century onward, the latter remained popular in timber-framed houses that continued to be built in the vernacular tradition. These modern tongue-and-groove oak boards were installed in a restored cottage in Dorset.

8 Also made of oak, these wide-plank modern boards are cut to display the distinctive heart grain of the wood. Like many reproduction boards, they are finished with a clear matt sealant.

5

6

7

8

9

9 Primarily employed for their insecticidal properties, liming pastes and waxes were often applied to boards in Scandinavia, and, to a lesser extent, in British and American rural houses up until the mid-19th century. These limed boards are in the Hansmoen Farmhouse in Norway.

10 In many American Federal houses, pine boards in some rooms were often flat-painted and stencilled, rather than being covered with rugs or floorcloths. Diamond patterns made up of, as here, recurring leaf (or floral) motifs, were particularly popular

11 This more austere grid pattern is in an 18th-century English country house, and is hand-painted in an ox-blood red over pink-painted, butt-jointed wooden boards.

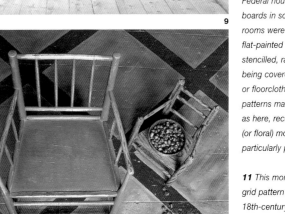

10

11

89

MARQUETRY AND PARQUETRY

Originating in Persia (now Iran), the technique of marquetry involves inlaying a base wood with contrasting-coloured pieces of different woods, or materials such as ivory, bone and various metals, to create decorative patterns. First adopted in Italy during the 14th century, it had become widespread in France by the 17th century, and thereafter was taken up throughout the rest of Europe and in America. As cutting the pieces was time-consuming and required a high level of skill (even after the introduction of automated cutting techniques in the 19th century), marquetry floors were very expensive, and therefore have invariably been confined to the grandest houses. They are primarily associated with late-Baroque, Regency, Victorian and American Beaux Arts houses, with favoured designs ranging from arabesques, to naturalistic floral patterns of Western origin, to geometric, organic and pictorial imagery derived from the classical vocabulary of ornament. The technique of parquetry emerged in France during the 17th century, and involves arranging blocks of hardwood of different, or the same, species and colours of wood, to form geometric patterns. Cheaper than marquetry, parquetry flooring was used in Baroque, Regency, Victorian, Art Nouveau, Edwardian and Beaux Arts houses, either as a complete flooring, or, from the Victorian era onward, as a border for a centrally placed carpet. Latticework patterns have been enduringly fashionable, as have cube, lozenge, diamond, star, octagon and Greek key repeats, sometimes shaded to create *trompe l'oeil*, three-dimensional effects.

1 & 2 Parquetry floors, consisting of hardwood blocks laid in geometric patterns, were first employed in grander houses in France during the 17th century, and soon became popular in Britain, and later in the United States. Both of these 18th-century French floors are laid to a standard design, in which a large diamond-patterned grid, formed by long rectangular blocks, is infilled with repeated latticework patterns made up of smaller rectangular and square blocks.

3 Herringbone-pattern parquet floors such as this became particularly popular for the kitchens, hallways and living rooms of suburban houses in the late 19th and early 20th centuries. The best-quality versions were made up of (2.5cm-) 1in-thick oak or teak blocks, and laid on a cement base covered with bitumen. A cheaper alternative consisted of thinner blocks, ready-assembled in panels fixed to a cloth backing, and designed to be laid directly onto existing boards.

4 This close-up of some oak parquet reveals how the illusion of woven, three-dimensional latticework is created by alternating longer and shorter, butt-jointed rectangular blocks.

90

5 & 6 Some parquet floors feature wooden blocks of almost uniform pattern and colour, and therefore rely for visual effect purely on the configuration of the blocks when they are laid down. However, many parquet floors also exploit the variations of figuring and grain of different woods, or in different cuts of the same wood, as in the American octagonal-pattern oak parquet in 5. Others utilize inherent colour contrasts which, as in the English rectilinear-pattern oak parquet in 6, can also be artificially enhanced by selectively staining some of the blocks.

7, 8 & 9 Marquetry floors first appeared in the West during the Renaissance, and feature patterns and motifs created by inlaying contrasting-coloured woods (or materials such as ivory or bone) into a more uniformly coloured base wood. Floor 7 displays a neo-classical border of S-scrolls and anthemia composed of ash, mahogany, bubinga and walnut. Neo-classical floor 8 has a rope and banding border, made of red oak, maple and mahogany. The early 20th-century floral motif border in floor 9 is created with mahogany, maple and American cherry.

5

6

7

8

9

10

10 Numerous and diverse geometrical and figurative patterns have been employed in marquetry floors. These range from figures and scenes from classical mythology, through stylized or naturalistic floral and foliate motifs, to "faceted" diamonds and stars. This classic interlaced, eight-pointed star motif is made of walnut, mahogany, red oak and cherry.

91

EARTH, BRICK AND STONE

The simplest type of ground-level flooring in general use from the Middle Ages until the end of the 17th century was beaten earth. These floors, sometimes enlivened with scratched designs or covered with straw, continued to be used in Georgian country cottages and the basements of poorer Georgian town houses, but thereafter were rarely employed. Throughout this period, floors made of bricks, laid on edge, were considered a better and more durable alternative to beaten earth; they were still laid in the cellars and service areas of many houses, on both sides of the Atlantic, well into the 19th century. Better still, and costlier, were stone floors. Most were laid as sandstone or limestone flags, although granite and slate – the latter usually cut to smaller, tile-size proportions – were also employed. Up until the 18th century, these stone floors were used in many ground-level rooms, but subsequently they were generally restricted to entrance halls, covered porches and kitchens. The most prestigious and expensive, however, were stone floors made of marble. Employed in grander houses from the Renaissance onward, they could be laid either like other stone floors, in simple geometric patterns, or in more complex inlaid designs inspired by classical Roman prototypes, in which the contrasts of colour and figuring inherent in different types of marble were exploited to enhance the basic symmetry of geometric patterns, and to enrich them with *trompe l'oeil*, three-dimensional, parquetry-like effects.

2 *Brick floors were in common use at ground-floor level up until the 18th century, particularly in rural areas, and provided a cheaper alternative to stone flags. This brick floor is in an English farmhouse.*

3 *Stone tiles are mostly laid in traditional brick-work patterns, as with this 18th-century English floor. In addition to the mortar lines, patterns are often created by alternating different-coloured stone tiles.*

4 *Although rare by the late 18th century, ground and below-ground level floors made of stamped earth were often used in ordinary houses prior to that, and were a less expensive option than brick or stone.*

1 *Large flagstones have been used for ground-level flooring since the Middle Ages, although the high costs of transporting stone over long distances meant that, with the exception of the most prestigious buildings, its use was restricted to areas where there was an abundant supply of the material. This flagstone floor is in the kitchen of a large house in London, but it is made up of stone pavers imported from Tuscany, in Italy, which also provides the source of inspiration for the neo-classical decoration.*

5 *Flagstone floors remained popular in hallways and kitchens well into the 20th century, even though they were superseded by suspended wooden floors in most ground-level rooms from the 18th century onward. In some houses, flagstones were laid onto a beaten earth or cement base, while in others, as here, they were laid onto boards supported on a grid of strong joists. The limestone pavers in this English Victorian hallway are laid in a traditional diamond pattern used since the Middle Ages.*

6 & 7 During the 17th and early 18th centuries, there was a fashion for embellishing sandstone and limestone paved floors with colourful marble inlays to create often highly elaborate geometrical patterns. However, in the late 18th and early 19th centuries, simpler and plainer flooring patterns also came into vogue. Both of these grand, late-18th-century English entrance halls have been paved with large, French limestone flags.

8 Contrasts of colour and figuring between different types of marble (and within individual marbles) have often been exploited by architects and designers to relieve the rigidity of of many traditional rectilinear flooring patterns. This marble flooring is in the cloakroom of an early 19th-century house.

6

9

9 Chequer-patterned stone or marble floors, consisting of regularly spaced squares of alternating colours, were popular in classical Roman architecture, and have subsequently been associated with medieval, early Renaissance and Victorian houses. This black and white marble floor is in the hallway of a restored English Renaissance house. Red or green alternated with black or white as popular options.

7

10

10 The neo-classical geometric pattern of this hall floor is composed of contrasting-coloured granite and marble inlays. Granites, like porphyries, are quarried from igneous rocks and, unlike many marbles, which are quarried from metamorphic rock, display an intricate, but broadly uniform, pattern across their surface.

8

11

11 Because marble can be prohibitively costly, it has often been simulated in paint over either a wooden or plain stone ground. This black and white faux marbre floor is in the hallway of a Federal-style New York apartment. The pattern is neo-classical, and features a central fan motif encompassed by banding and four corner roundels – the latter displaying stars (one of the symbols of American independence).

93

TILES

Floor tiles have often been employed since the Middle Ages, mainly at ground-level, as an alternative to stone floors (*see* pp.92–3). Made from fired clays, the simplest – particularly, but not exclusively, favoured in rural areas – are unglazed quarry tiles, produced in natural clay colours ranging from off white to various shades of brown and red. Where other monochrome colours – notably, black, greens and yellows – have been required, these are created by adding mineral dyes to a thin tin or lead glaze fired onto the surface of the tile. Made in basic geometric shapes, such as squares, rectangles, triangles, hexagons and octagons, monochrome tiles have either been laid to intricate mosaic designs (*see* right) or, more often, in simple or complex, overall geometric patterns. More elaborate tiled floors, especially favoured during the Middle Ages and the Victorian era, have been created by combining monochrome tiles with patterned encaustic tiles bearing inlaid and colourful motifs and imagery – the choice of the latter always reflecting the prevailing styles of architecture and ornament, but mostly medieval, classical or oriental in origin.

1 *Smooth-surfaced and highly durable, encaustic tiles made of inlaid earthenware were often laid in the entrance halls and passageways of British and American Victorian houses. In a typical arrangement, the encaustic tiles in this English Victorian entrance hall feature a border that follows and defines the contours of the main architectural fixtures and fittings, namely the doors and the staircase. The recurring motif, in both the border and centre of the floor, is a simple diamond or lozenge shape, set in a small square. Diamonds, either used as individual motifs or as diaper patterns, were very popular during the Victorian era.*

2 *Although far more intricate than 1, the pattern of this late-Victorian encaustic-tiled hallway is also highly symmetrical, and made up of basic square and triangular geometric shapes. However, in terms of imagery, it differs from floor 1 in the use of a number of floral-patterned tiles, sited at intervals along the border and at the centre of the octagonal star patterns. Floral motifs were rarely used in the late 18th and early 19th centuries, but they came back into vogue from c.1860 onward under the aegis of the Aesthetic movement and the fashionable influence of oriental styles of ornament.*

3 *Hall Place was built in the mid-19th century by associates of the influential British architect Sir Gilbert Scott. Like many other Victorian Gothic Revival houses, the hallway features a plain and patterned tiled floor in which the patterned tiles display heraldic and medieval-inspired Islamic motifs. Prominent among these are the stylized floral and foliate motifs, and the lions – the latter symbolizing, since ancient Egyptian times, strength, courage, pride, fortitude, goodness, majesty, watchfulness and victory.*

4 This spacious entrance hall is in a Victorian Gothic Revival mansion built in 1855 in Galena, Illinois, USA. The simple, but striking, geometric pattern of the tiled flooring comprises alternating diagonal rows of monochromatic burnt-orange and buttercup-yellow octagonal tiles that are linked on the diagonals by smaller, rectangular, powder-blue spacer tiles.

7 Small, black diamond-shaped tiles mark the intersections of the larger, octagonal-shaped, "white-vein" marble tiles in a late-19th-century English bathroom. The overall pattern of the tiles (like the basin in the alcove) is French in origin, and known as carreaux d'octagnes. It was very popular in both Europe and the United States throughout the 18th and 19th centuries.

5 The Calhoun Mansion was built in the 1870s in Charleston, South Carolina. The encaustic tiles in its entrance hall are laid in a geometric pattern, and display motifs inspired by classical Romanesque prototypes. These include bands of white and blue guilloche, enriched with small rosettes, naturalistic floral forms, and, at the centre, anthemia and gently scrolling foliage.

8 Terracotta tiles have been used as a flooring material for centuries, especially in the rural areas of Europe. Made by firing a mixture of clay and sand, and usually unglazed, they range from a pale-orange hue to a deep reddish-brown, depending on the colour of the local clay. Mostly square, they are traditionally laid, as here, in a simple, rectilinear grid pattern.

6 The classic black and white chequer pattern at the centre of this Victorian hallway is bordered with a black-on-white chevron pattern. V-shaped chevrons were an ancient symbol of both water and lightning. Usually strung together to form a zigzag pattern, they were often used in Romanesque, Gothic and Renaissance architecture and their 19th-century revivals.

MOSAIC TILES

Classical Roman and Islamic Middle Eastern mosaic floors, in which geometric, floral, foliate or pictorial patterns are created from up to thousands of small, plain tiles in contrasting colours, provided much of the inspiration for the elaborate mosaic flooring laid (often at ground level) in grander houses from the Renaissance onward. Mainly employed in entrance halls, passageways and bathrooms, mosaic floors were particularly popular in early 19th-century Regency and mid- to late-Victorian houses. This early 19th-century example is modelled on a classical Roman design.

FLOOR COVERINGS

Woven rush matting was the almost universal floor covering prior to the late 17th century, and lighter equivalents made of sisal, coir or jute were often favoured in late-Colonial, Federal and Arts and Crafts interiors. Floorcloths made of oil-stiffened canvas, and stencilled or hand-painted with patterns, were used during the 18th and 19th centuries, notably in America, as a cheap substitute for carpets. Inexpensive, home-made, rag, shirred and hooked rugs were also popular at this time, especially in rural American homes. Expensive Oriental carpets were only used to cover tables prior to the mid-17th century. Thereafter, together with Western-made, flat-weave and woven-pile carpets, they were increasingly used in on floors in grander houses, and, following the mid-19th-century development of automated production, in ordinary houses as well. Linoleum, made of solidified linseed oil, resin and gum bonded to a canvas or jute backing, was developed in 1860. Durable and relatively inexpensive, it was mostly employed in hallways, kitchens and bathrooms.

1 & 2 Woven rush or straw matting was often employed as a floor covering in grander houses from the Middle Ages to the early 17th century. It could either be laid on a damp plaster screed (so that it fused to the floor when the plaster dried), or, as in the Elizabethan manor house in 1 and Jacobean manor house in 2, loose laid in strips on stone flags or wooden boards, then stitched together and nailed or stuck down.

3 & 4 *Made of canvas or other stout cloths, and stiffened with linseed oil, floorcloths first appeared in the 17th century, and provided a cheaper alternative to flat-weave or woven-pile rugs and carpets. Employed on both sides of the Atlantic, but especially in the United States, well into the 20th century, they have invariably been decorated with either stencilled or hand-painted patterns. The floorcloths shown here are English, and date to c.1892. Floorcloth 3 is stencilled to simulate a geometric-pattern tiled floor, while 4 is inspired by an oriental mosaic design. Other popular patterns include various faux marbres and fake marquetry and parquetry flooring.*

5 Home-made rag, shirred and hooked rugs were often laid on top of either rush or sisal floor coverings, or bare wooden floorboards, in rural houses during the 18th and 19th centuries, and were particularly popular in American houses. In this bathroom, the larger of the two rugs is a Victorian rag rug, and the smaller is a 20th-century French hooked rug of ethnic design.

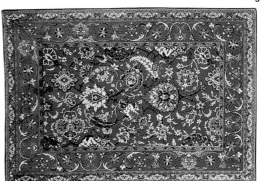

6 Until the late 17th century, oriental rugs such as this were too rare and expensive to be laid on floors, and were mostly used as table coverings. Thereafter they were employed on floors, and also provided inspiration for cheaper, Western-made copies – known as "turkeywork".

7 Although European
pile carpets became
increasingly fashionable
for the reception rooms
of grander houses in
the late 18th and early
19th centuries, oriental
rugs were also used.
This Persian rug is in a
Regency drawing room.

8 An Empire-style
drawing room in the
Calhoun Mansion, in
Charleston, South
Carolina, has a knotted-
pile carpet patterned
with small, stylized floral
motifs, and a guilloche
border enriched with
naturalistic floral sprigs.

7

8

9

10

11

12

13

14

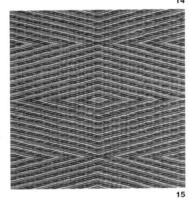

15

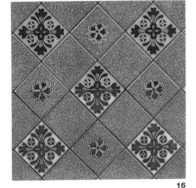

16

9 A British Victorian
carpet, custom-made
to fit the contours of
a room, and patterned
with naturalistic floral
and foliate motifs of
Eastern origin.

10 A 19th-century
European copy of a
Turkestan carpet, with
a symmetrical pattern
typical of the region,
and made up of
geometric motifs
based on stylized
foliate forms.

11 Anthemia and
paters with floral motifs
are incorporated in a
neo-classical geometric
pattern in this early
19th-century American
woven-pile carpet.

12 A detail of a late-
19th-century faux
marbre American
linoleum, with an
alternating curlicue
and star border.

13, 14 & 15 English
linoleums, all dated to
c.1892: 13 is based
on a naturalistic floral
carpet pattern; 14 is
an "inlaid" linoleum
(in which the colours
penetrate to the full
depth of the material)
imitating encaustic tiling;
15 is patterned to look
like woven matting.

16 Similar to, but less
durable than, linoleum,
this English cork carpet
is modelled on plain
and stylized floral-
patterned ceramic tiles.

97

CEILINGS

Prior to the mid-17th century, ground-floor ceilings in the majority of houses were made up of the structural timbers (beams and joists) of the floor above, together with either the exposed undersides of the floorboards or, in better houses, lath-and-plaster infills between the joists. In single-storey dwellings, and in the upper-storey rooms of other houses, ceilings consisted of the structural timbers of the roof and the underside of the roof covering – the latter made of woven matting, wooden boards or lath-and-plaster infills. In the reception rooms of grander houses, the beams and joists were often arranged to divide the ceiling into a grid of symmetrical compartments (or coffers). Decoration of the beams and joists – reflecting the status of the room, the household, or both – ranged from simple chamfering, to carved motifs (notably of birds, animals, flowers and foliage), to the application of carved ribs or straps in compartments, and carved pendants where the timbers intersected. Sometimes, painted decoration was also used: the simplest, white lime-wash, was applied to lath-and-plaster infills (and occasionally to the timbers, primarily to protect against insect infestation), while the most flamboyant had polychrome stencilled or hand-painted medieval, heraldic or Renaissance motifs and imagery.

Exposed timber ceilings continued to be used well into the 20th century, notably in vernacular timber-framed, and Arts and Crafts and Renaissance Revival, houses (*see* pp.100–2). However, from the 16th century onward in many grander houses, and from the mid-17th century in most other houses, they were generally supplanted by suspended ceilings. These ceilings fall into three basic categories: wooden-boarded, tin-panelled and plaster. Wooden-boarded ceilings, made up of painted, butt-jointed or tongue-and-groove planks, nailed to the undersides of the joists, were employed in some American Colonial, Federal and Victorian houses, and embossed tin-panelled ceilings, also nailed or screwed to the joists, were installed in some (mostly American) 19th- and early 20th-century houses (*see* p.102). However, in most houses, suspended plaster ceilings were used.

In its most basic form, the plaster ceiling consists of a smoothed coat of plaster bonded into a network of wooden laths that are nailed to the undersides of the joists, and trimmed around the perimeter, at the junction with walls, with a decorative cornice moulding (*see* pp.102–3). From the 18th century to the present day, plain plaster ceilings – usually flat-painted and often embellished with a central ceiling rose (*see* p.103) – were used throughout most houses, and in the secondary rooms of larger homes, but more ornate versions have also been favoured, especially in the reception rooms of grander houses. For example, some Renaissance and Baroque ceilings were covered with plaster mouldings – such as bosses, pendants, ribs, roses, and rectilinear and foliate strapwork – which, during the course of the 17th century (and under the prevailing influence of classicism in architecture and ornament), became increasingly systematic in the manner in which they compartmented (or coffered) the ceiling. These heavily ornamented plaster ceilings continued to be employed in many grander reception rooms on both sides of the Atlantic up until the early 20th century, with the mouldings sometimes highlighted (notably in Victorian houses) with polychrome painting and gilding against flat-painted monochrome grounds.

Fashionable additions, or alternatives, to plaster mouldings on elaborate ceilings included polychrome hand-painted (and gilded) imagery and patterned papers. The former are particularly associated with early Georgian, Rococo and neo-classical interiors. For example, many of the compartmented ceilings designed or influenced by Robert Adam during the late 18th century feature painted figures and scenes from classical mythology in plaques, cartouches or roundels, set in a combination of flat-painted and plaster-relief mouldings. During the 19th century, sets of printed polychrome papers, bearing pictorial imagery and *trompe l'oeil* simulations of plaster mouldings, were used to create much the same effect and, following the development of machine-printing, provided a cheaper option.

CEILING TYPES

Particular types of ceiling are strongly associated with specific historical periods or styles of architecture and decoration. Ceilings in which most or all of the structural timbers – such as beams, joists and braces – of the floor or roof above are exposed were commonplace in the Middle Ages, and continued to be used in most houses until the mid-17th century. Thereafter, they were largely confined to vernacular, timber-framed dwellings – particularly the Arts and Crafts houses of the late 19th and early 20th centuries – as well as some 19th-century Gothic and Renaissance Revival houses. Suspended ceilings made of jointed wooden boards or panels were used in many late-Colonial and some Federal and late-Victorian American homes. However, having first appeared in the grandest Renaissance and Baroque houses, suspended plaster gradually superseded all of the above in the majority of houses from the 1650s onward. The simplest – monochrome-painted flat plaster – has been widely used since then in most secondary rooms. However, in reception rooms and some main bedrooms, especially in larger houses, more ornate treatments dividing the ceiling into compartments have been favoured. Most of these have been created with plaster mouldings – systematic and grid-like on late-Baroque, early Georgian, neo-classical, Victorian and Edwardian ceilings, and more organic or fluid on Renaissance and Revival ceilings. Alternatives include polychromatic painting and stencilling, notably in neo-classical houses, and the application of printed papers – the latter much favoured during the Victorian age.

1 The dining room at Frog Pool Farm, in Avon, England, dates to the early 16th century. Its grid-like coffered ceiling consists of heavily moulded oak beams, infilled with painted lath-and-plaster panels. On many earlier coffered ceilings the undersides of the floorboards above would have been exposed, rather than concealed under plaster panels. More ornate ceilings had carved motifs on the beams, and moulded bosses or pendants at the intersections.

2 The oak coffering of this 16th-century English manor-house ceiling is denser than that of 1. The joists of the floor above, supported on the cross-beams, are left exposed, with only the undersides of the floorboards covered by plaster panelling.

3 A series of arched oak braces and horizontal oak purlins supports the painted lath-and-plaster vaulted ceiling in this Elizabethan dining room. Such ceilings enjoyed a revival during the early 20th century.

4 *Coffered wooden ceilings were sometimes used in the 18th century. This example is in a pine-panelled English library that dates to the reign of George I (1727–60). The grid-like pattern and the profiles of the moulded beams recall late-medieval coffered ceilings, and are indicative of mid-18th-century revival of interest in medieval "Gothick" architecture. However, the modillion cornice used to define the ceiling's perimeter – and derived from the Corinthian, Composite and Ionic Orders – also illustrates the prevailing influence of classicism during the period.*

5 *In the 16th and early 17th centuries, plaster ceilings in the reception rooms of grander houses were frequently embellished with a maze of ornament. During the second half of the 17th century, the ornament, although still profuse, was applied within a grid-like system of compartments, which usually radiated out from the centre of the ceiling to the corners. However, by the late 17th century, as on this English Baroque dining-room ceiling, the grid was often omitted, leaving only the ovals or circles of ornament surrounding a large, usually plain, expanse of painted flat plaster.*

4

5

6

7

8

6 *This compartmented, polished-hardwood ceiling is in an American Victorian mansion in Newport, Rhode Island. The combination of arched ribs around the perimeter of the ceiling and the diamond and quartered-octagonal panelling in the centre was much in vogue during the second half of the 19th century.*

7 & 8 *Both of these plaster ceilings display the structure and type of ornamentation that was the height of fashion in neo-classical houses of the late 18th and early 19th centuries. Ceiling 7 is Roman-inspired, and divided into a regular grid of diamond- and octagonal-shaped coffers, embellished with rosettes. Ceiling 8 has a plain field bordered with recessed coffering, containing pateras. Both ceilings are "supported" by purely decorative, rather than structural, classical columns.*

101

1 *This plaster ceiling is in a small drawing room at Drayton Hall, built c.1740, near Charleston, South Carolina. The liveliness and refinement of the plasterwork, in which gently scrolled foliate motifs are compartmented by classical mouldings, are highly characteristic of the best mid-18th-century Palladian-style American houses.*

2 *Neo-classical ceilings designed by Robert Adam were segmented and embellished with either plaster mouldings, painted decoration, as here, or both. This centrepiece of a ceiling at Newby Hall, built in the early 1770s in Yorkshire, England, features a central roundel painted with scenes from classical mythology. Notable among other popular neo-classical motifs are rings of guilloche and wavescrolls, as well as candelabra forms incorporating anthemia and husks.*

3 *This detail of an English Victorian ceiling reveals the edge of the papered field, bordered with an ornate plaster moulding displaying rosettes and gently scrolling foliage. Foliate-pattern papered fields, in realistic colours such as browns and greens, were a popular choice in Victorian interiors.*

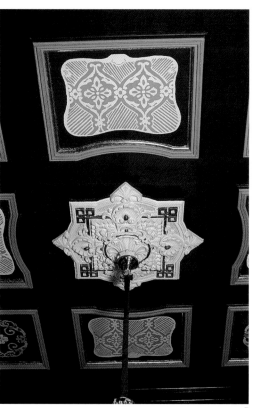

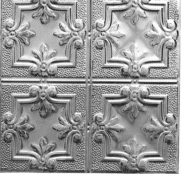

4 *Proportion and symmetry underpin the decoration of this Adam ceiling at Home House, built c.1775 in London. As was often the case with neo-classical ceilings, the ground colour and most of the motifs were painted onto the plaster, while the figurative plaques and roundels were painted onto paper, which was then glued in place.*

5 *Small and colourful compartments of decoration, which combined stencilling with painted and gilded plaster mouldings, were fashionable in American Victorian mansions.*

TIN AND STEEL CEILINGS

During the 19th century, stamped-tin ceilings were often used instead of more traditional plaster or wooden ceilings in American houses. Produced in a range of historical styles, assembled from separate panels, and often painted *in situ*, they were fireproof and supposedly "non-absorbent and free from bacteria". In the early 20th century, they were generally supplanted by pressed-steel versions, which also proved popular in some English Edwardian houses.

CEILING ROSES

A focal point of the majority of plastered ceilings since the beginning of the 18th century, especially during the Victorian period, ceiling roses have been fashioned in all the predominant architectural styles. Originally, they were made of plaster, but nowadays resin is also used. Their circumference and degree of ornamentation have traditionally been related to, respectively, the size of the ceiling and the status of the room for which they are intended.

1 This plaster ceiling rose is in the dining room of an American Empire-style house in New York State. Its rings of foliate motifs are typical neo-classical forms of ornament.

2 The ceiling rose in the drawing room of the same house is a rosette and a ring of caulicoli. Set in a recessed coffer, it is encircled by a plain moulding, and framed with four corner fans and key-pattern mouldings.

3 Fruit and, as here, vegetable motifs have often been employed on ceiling roses, usually to symbolize fertility, wealth or abundance.

4 Of a type found in 18th-century "Gothick" and 19th-century Gothic Revival houses, this ceiling rose draws on medieval Gothic forms and motifs. Notable elements include cinqfoils and lozenges containing naturalistic flowers and foliage, and a brattished (crested) perimeter embellished with alternating ball flowers and fleurs-de-lis.

5 On this segmented Robert Adam ceiling, dated to the 1770s, the central rose is a fluted, circular fan, topped with a rosette and a ring of foliate forms. Set in a recessed, octagonal compartment, the rose is encompassed by a circular, scoop moulding, and by strings of husks swagged from ribbons. The white, blue and cream colour scheme is a modern restoration of the original decoration.

6, 7 & 8 As with these reproduction Victorian examples, most ceiling roses made from the early 18th to the early 20th centuries have been decorated with stylized or naturalistic floral and foliate motifs.

103

CORNICES

Because of their purpose and prominent position – to disguise and ornament the junction between ceilings and walls – cornices have played a significant role in establishing the architectural and decorative style of interiors. They were rarely employed with the timber-framed ceilings in widespread use prior to the 17th century, and in many houses built in the vernacular tradition thereafter, because the perimeters of these were usually defined by wooden beams (supporting cross-beams or floor joists), or by full-height wainscotting. However, they have invariably been used with plaster and wood-panelled ceilings. Mostly made of plaster or wood, but also of stone, papier-mâché and, nowadays, resin, the extent of their moulded or carved ornamentation usually reflects the type of room for which they are intended – generally, more elaborate in reception rooms and principal bedrooms, and plainer in other rooms. The simplest ones consist of concave- or convex-profile mouldings – such as ogee, ovolo, torus, scotia, bolection and *cyma reversa* and *recta* – and are mostly derived from the Classical Orders. More elaborate examples combine these with key and scoop patterns, dentils and modillions; repeat motifs such as egg-and-dart, bead-and-reel and ribbon-and-rosette; or devices such as vases, urns, cartouches, plaques, and human and animal forms. However, the most enduringly fashionable imagery has been stylized or naturalistic representations of plant forms.

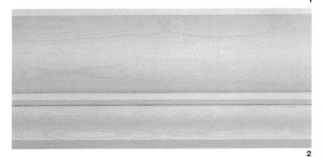

4 *The cornice and its accompanying frieze are part of an elaborate curved ceiling designed by Robert Adam in 1772. The cornice contains a continuous band of guilloche, set above a strip of bead moulding. The frieze is dominated by pateras and aegricanes, linked by swagged strings of husks, and is painted in Pompeiian colours.*

5 & 6 *The foliate motif that dominates these reproduction cornices is the acanthus leaf. The most widely used foliage ornament from the Graeco-Roman era to the end of the Victorian period, it is based on the leaves of the Mediterranean species Acanthus spinosus. Generally, acanthus-leaf mouldings inspired by Greek prototypes are sparser than their heavier, droopier and more elaborate Roman-inspired equivalents.*

1 *Carved from oak, this American Victorian cornice features alternating rose and stylized English Tudor flower motifs, set above a rope moulding.*

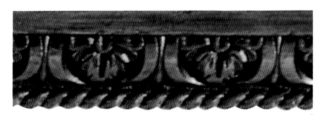

2 *This double-bolection cornice moulding is of a type that was in wide-spread use during the 18th and 19th centuries. Made of pine, it would have almost invariably been painted to match the ceiling, or other joinery in the room.*

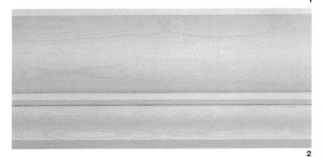

3 *Neo-classical imagery here includes plaques of foliage and trophies-of-arms, wreath heads and egg-and-dart moulding.*

7 *Waterleaf or stiff-leaf is the motif that is used in this neo-classical plaster cornice. Feather-shaped in appearance, this foliate motif was often employed by the architect Andrea Palladio to enrich mouldings on Ionic, Corinthian and Composite Orders, and also by Robert Adam as an alternative to acanthus leaves on columns, friezes and, as here, cornices.*

8 The modillions on this classical cornice are inspired by the consoles that support the cornice in the Corinthian and Composite Orders.

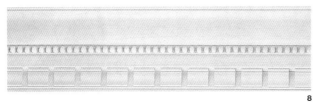
8

9 Also derived from the Corinthian, Composite and Ionic Orders, dentil mouldings have often been applied to cornices in classical interiors, notably in the 18th century.

9

10 This neo-classical modillion cornice is early 19th century. The modillions are fluted, alternated with recessed rosettes, and set above egg-and-dart moulding.

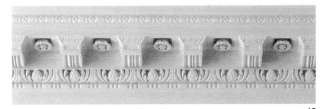
10

11 This painted-plaster cornice-frieze is in the oval Music Room of Nathaniel Russell House, built 1808 in Charleston, South Carolina. It incorporates strings of husks, guilloche, scoop mouldings, and lozenges and cartouches filled with floral ornament.

11

12 The pomegranate was a popular motif in oriental and Graeco-Roman ornament, and was also fashionable, especially in plasterwork and woodcarving, during the Renaissance and the 18th- and 19th-century classical revivals. A symbol of fertility, it is depicted surrounded by leaves in the formalized vegetal pattern that dominates this American Greek Revival cornice.

12

13

13 This plaster cornice is in a mid-19th-century Gothic Revival house in New York. The upper section is an ogee moulding; the lower a series of trefoil arches, alternating with smaller, flower-like quatrefoils. Trefoil and cinqfoil arches were often used on Gothic Revival cornices, sometimes embellished with spike-like pendants.

14

14 Apart from acanthus, the most popular leaf motifs for cornices have been vine, laurel, lotus, ivy, oak, palm and, here with its fruits, lime.

15

15 Prominent features in this American Victorian cornice are a Greek key-pattern moulding along the bottom, a series of modillions around the centre, and rosettes along the top.

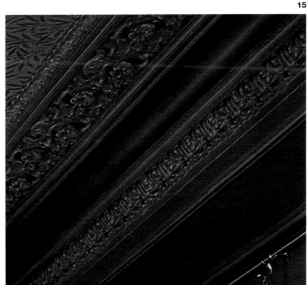
16

16 This cornice-frieze is in a Victorian drawing room. Its centre is made up of a deep, concave scotia moulding and, above that, scrolling foliage interspersed with rosettes. Flanking these are parallel bands of stylized leaf ornament. To highlight all the prominent motifs, the green paint has been rubbed back on raised areas to expose a muted gold ground colour – a decorative finish similar in appearance to aged or distressed gilding.

CORBELS

Used in classical and Gothic architecture, corbels are projecting stone or wooden blocks or brackets that are attached to a wall and used to support beams, arches and cornices. S-shaped corbels, such as this reproduction Renaissance example, are called consoles. Like many, it is carved with scrolling forms and foliate motifs, here derived from the classical vocabulary of ornament. A series of small, block-like consoles regularly spaced along cornice's length, and usually more decorative than functional, are known as modillions (see cornices 8 and 10).

WALLS

Internal walls fall into one of two broad stylistic categories: those in which the basic structural components are either wholly or partly exposed, and those in which they are clad with various materials. The first category is comprised of stone, brick and half-timbered walls. The latter consist of a grid-like network of vertical posts and studs, horizontal cross-rails and, in some cases, curved or arched braces. The spaces between these exposed, structural wooden components are traditionally infilled with either limewashed lath-and-plaster panels, or bricks laid in various decorative patterns (notably chevron or herringbone). Such walls were in widespread use in timber-framed medieval and Renaissance houses, and continued to be employed in some vernacular timber-framed houses thereafter – mainly in rural areas of England, but also in early American Colonial homes, and in some Arts and Crafts houses of the late 19th and early 20th centuries. Exposed stone walls were also much in evidence during the Middle Ages and the Renaissance, but generally were confined to residential castles and palaces. Subsequent use was mainly restricted to the entrance halls, passageways and stairwells of neo-classical, and Gothic- and Classical Revival houses of the 18th, 19th and early 20th centuries, although, in many cases, *faux* stone (including marble) effects painted onto flat plaster were employed instead of real stone. Apart from in basements, internal walls with exposed structural brickwork have been much rarer than half-timbered and stone walls. However, exceptions include inglenooks in British and American houses built prior to the early 18th century, and inglenooks and some projecting chimney breasts in Arts and Crafts houses.

Walls in which the structural components are covered have been far more prevalent than their exposed equivalents. One fundamental reason for this has been because they help to minimize the loss of heat from the interior of the house. For example, from the 18th century onward, most walls in American timber-framed houses were clad with boards or panelling to insulate against the harshness of the winter climate. However, architectural and decorative considerations have also influenced the choice. The impact of classicism on European, and later American, architecture from the Renaissance onward saw walls increasingly divided, horizontally, into three sections. These were a frieze at the top (*see* pp.112–13), a field in the centre (*see* pp.114–15) and a dado at the bottom (*see* pp. 116–17), with the relative proportions of each of these derived from the architrave, column and base of Classical Greek and Roman Orders. This tripartite division was much easier to create if the structural elements were covered, and various materials and decorative techniques have been employed to this end.

Polished hardwood, or painted softwood, panelling applied to the full height of the wall has often been used (*see* pp.108–11), and the distinction between frieze, field and dado created with applied mouldings or carved detail. Alternatively, frieze-height panelling has been combined with a flat or moulded plaster frieze, or dado-height panelling has been surmounted by a painted or papered plaster field – with the latter usually separated from the plaster frieze by a picture rail or similarly positioned lengths of wooden or plaster moulding.

Where wooden panelling has not been employed, flat plaster has been applied over the entire surface of the wall, and the tripartite division marked by rectilinear skirting boards, and dado and picture rails – the last two usually of wood or plaster, but sometimes stencilled, hand-painted *trompe l'oeil* simulations, or thin strips of patterned wallpaper. These horizontal divisions have then been further defined by infills of either applied plaster mouldings (usually painted or gilded), hand-painted motifs, fabrics stretched over battens and wallpapers, or ceramic tiles – with the latter mostly applied to dados from the 19th century onward. In all cases, the motifs and patterns that were employed – whether carved, moulded, stencilled, hand-painted or printed – have invariably reflected prevailing fashions in decoration and ornament (*see* pp.8–33).

PANELLING

In grander medieval and Renaissance houses, oak panelling was often applied to brick, stone and timber-framed walls – either to full-height or frieze or dado level on the brick or stone type, and always to full-height on the timber frame. Polished oak or walnut panelling, as well as pine or fir panelling painted in imitation of finely figured hardwoods, marbles or even tortoiseshell, was also prevalent in larger Baroque houses, and was regarded as furniture that could be dismantled and taken to a new house when the owner moved. Having remained in vogue in early Georgian and American Colonial homes – mainly in the form of flat-painted, sometimes gilded, and wood-grained or *faux marbred* softwood – it generally fell out of fashion (apart from on some Federal fireplace walls), until it enjoyed a resurgence of use beginning in the 1830s. Full- or frieze-height panelling was then often employed in hallways, studies and dining rooms. Victorian panelling was dark-stained and polished hardwood; Arts and Crafts was polished hardwood or flat-painted softwood; while Art Nouveau panelling was of painted or lacquered softwood. In the late 19th and early 20th centuries, Tudorbethan- and Georgian-style panelling was also used throughout Edwardian homes, as was Renaissance-, Baroque- and Colonial-style panelling in larger American Beaux Arts houses. Much of this panelling, as with its forerunners, bore elaborately carved decoration (*see* right).

1 & 2 From the late 15th to the early 17th centuries, oak wall panelling was often used in grander houses. Fashionable carved decoration included linenfold patterns, and, later in the period, arabesques, strapwork, foliage forms, busts and roundels. The linenfold panelling in 1 is in an Elizabethan manor house, and in 2 in a Jacobean manor house. The latter, topped with a foliate frieze, provides a backdrop to panelled cupboard doors decorated with shield-like cartouches with portraits of knights, clerics and patrons of the arts.

3 The influence of classical Renaissance architecture is evident in this fine quality, carved wall panelling at Parham House, an Elizabethan manor house in Sussex, England. Made of oak, and limed, the ornately carved panelling flanks an arched doorway, and features fan-arched niches, fluted pilasters and an entablature bearing corbels and scrolling foliate forms. (The tapestry hanging in the doorway is typical of the period.)

4 *Like many other Jacobean houses, the oak wall panelling here is more elaborate on the fireplace wall than on the other walls of the room. While the latter have an unadorned, grid-like configuration, the former incorporates the fire surround, shelving and a central panel with a double, blind arch and a pair of pilasters.*

5 *As in 4, this fireplace at Drayton Hall, built c.1740 in Charleston, South Carolina, is conceived as an extension of the wall panelling (and vice versa). The whole ensemble is Palladian in style, and, as in many Colonial houses, has been painted. Notable features include the low chair rail, and a triglyph and metope frieze just below the egg-and-dart moulding of the cornice.*

6 *Also painted, this wall panelling features fielded panels. The rigid symmetry of their rectilinear configuration, together with the absence of ornament, is highly characteristic of 18th-century American Federal interiors.*

7 *Made of pine, the panelling and doors in this Adam-style room are embellished with corner pateras and rope and transverse scoop mouldings. The painted frieze is Pompeiian style.*

8 *The rectangular wall panels, like the chair rail and the tops of the skirting boards in this neo-classical room, are made up of simple, classical rectilinear mouldings, and picked out in white against a lilac ground. Additional definition is given to the panels by using a darker tone of lilac (also used on the frieze) than on the rest of the field.*

9 *Fluted pilasters and rectangular and oval panels define the walls of the neo-classical style Music Room in Lillian Williams's 18th-century French château. Made up of wooden mouldings, they are decorated in a yellow-and-gold colour scheme that was particularly fashionable in late-18th-century European reception rooms.*

1 In some 19th-century timber-framed American houses, the walls were panelled with horizontal tongue-and-groove planks. In this restored cottage near Houston, Texas, the planks have been stripped of layers paint to reveal the original stencilled frieze. Stencilled decorations such as this – especially foliate patterns – were very popular in the United States, and are mostly attributed to itinerant artists and craftsmen of German and Scandinavian origin.

2 When wall panelling was employed in British Victorian houses it was usually confined to halls, studies and dining rooms. The panelling here is at Cragside, built in 1870 in Northumbria. It is made of oak, has a castellated cresting, incorporates sunflower and animal carvings in the upper panels and is topped with a floral-patterned wallpaper.

3 In this American Victorian house, the dado level in the oak wall panelling is defined at intervals by fretwork, in this case a simple latticework pattern with rosettes on the overlaps. Latticework – a type of diaper pattern – had been very popular in 18th-century "Gothick" houses, and enjoyed a notable revival during the Victorian age.

4 Full-height, or, as here, three-quarter height wall panelling, was often used in the hallways of late-19th- and early 20th-century Arts and Crafts houses. Oak, stained and polished, was the preferred hardwood. However, softwoods, usually painted ivory white, sage green or olive green, were also employed. This oak panelling incorporates a large pair of bi-fold double-doors leading to a reception room. Because the simple rectilinear panels on the walls and the doors are the same, the latter are "concealed" within the former when closed – a popular architectural convention in Arts and Crafts houses.

5 While flat-painted or wood-grained pine was used for wall panelling in the majority of American homes during the second half of the 19th century, more expensive, stained and polished native American hardwoods were usually employed in grander houses. This elaborate, full-height mahogany panelling dates to the 1880s. The larger panels at dado level are carved with a linenfold pattern. The panels in the field above feature mahogany veneers inlaid to form geometric patterns, which incorporate recurring star motifs.

6 This superbly panelled library is in an American Queen Anne-style house. It features fan niches, fretwork-style panels and interlaced glazing bars – all highlighted with gilding to contrast with the painted green ground.

7 Designed 1902–3 in Art Nouveau style by C.R. Mackintosh, the hallway at The Hill House, in Helensburgh, Scotland, is lined with black-stained pine panelling. The vertical straps are enlivened at the frieze height with small, pink-painted, fluted panels. The latter flank stencilled motifs (of stylized organic forms) applied to the white-painted plaster panels framed by the straps.

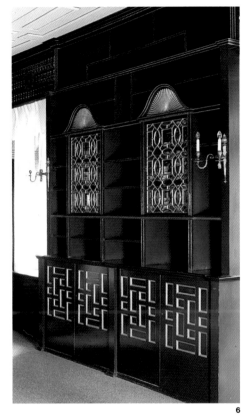

8 This mahogany-lined inglenook at the Gamble House, in Pasadena, California, dates to 1908–9, and is inspired by 16th-century European inglenooks. However, the horizontal emphasis and the relatively plain surfaces of the panelling clearly identify this as a 20th-century composition.

9 Built in the vernacular tradition of the Southern states, this 20th-century house in Florida has pine-boarded walls. It is distinguished from its predecessors by a plain, white-painted finish, without, as in 1, stencilled decoration.

8

CARVED DECORATION

While decorative geometric shapes applied to wall panelling have mainly been created with wooden mouldings, figurative embellishments have either been painted or carved in relief. Carved decoration has been employed from the Middle Ages to the early 20th century, most extensively and elaborately in medieval Gothic, Renaissance, Baroque, Gothic Revival (as in the panel above), American Beaux Arts and Edwardian Tudorbethan houses. However, the finest and most flamboyant carving was produced in English Baroque houses by Grinling Gibbons during the late 17th century. His incredibly naturalistic carved animal, marine and plant-form imagery was much copied but it has never been surpassed.

7   9

FRIEZES

Derived from the Classical Orders (*see* p.107), friezes have mainly been defined at the tops of walls in houses where classicism or neo-classicism has influenced the overall style of architecture and ornament (*see* pp.8–33). For the same reason, the patterns and motifs used to decorate the frieze have primarily been classical Greek or Roman in origin, although Gothic and oriental imagery have also been employed – the former in the early Renaissance, and during the late 18th, 19th and early 20th centuries. Favoured materials and forms of decoration have included carving – where wooden panelling was employed (*see* pp.108–111); painted plaster mouldings – sometimes gilded, often combined with hand-painted imagery and especially favoured in neo-classical interiors; stencilling – notably in Colonial, Arts and Crafts and Art Nouveau houses; and hand- or machine-printed strips of wallpaper – the latter increasingly common from the Victorian era onward.

1 *This early 1770s neo-classical painted plaster frieze is at Newby Hall, Yorkshire, England. It has bands of interlaced foliage and rosettes against a Wedgwood-blue ground, and scrolling flowers and foliage, interspersed with Greek urns and winged chimeras, on a Pompeiian red ground.*

2 *The painted and gilded frieze in this domed niche is at Home House, designed by Robert Adam c.1775. It has a row of anthemia above strings of husks – the latter flanked by urns and swagged around a row of pateras.*

3 *This French Empire-style frieze is at the Morris-Jumel Mansion in New York. Made of paper, it displays neo-classical urns, lyres and flower and foliate motifs.*

4 *Also at Home House, this Adam frieze features a thin band of pateras, linked by strings of husks and anthemia, and alternating plaques and roundels showing figures and scenes from classical mythology.*

5 *This paper frieze is in a reception room in the Eastlake-style Durfee House, built c.1880 in Los Angeles, California. The upper section is patterned with scrolling foliage and flowers, and the lower section with a two-tone chequer pattern sandwiched between rope and bead motifs.*

6 *In a recreation of a 19th-century Shaker interior at the American Museum in Bath, England, the painted plaster walls are divided into a field and deep frieze by a wooden peg rail. Simple, utilitarian wooden mouldings such as this are a feature of Shaker houses.*

7 *This reproduction cornice-frieze (which can also be used as a pelmet) is carved from oak, and has a limed finish. It is modelled on an 18th-century plaster-on-wood original first used in an Irish castle.*

8 *Carved from oak, this reproduction Jacobean cornice-frieze displays small rosettes set in a band of guilloche.*

9 *Although inspired by a Victorian original, the combination of rosettes and gently scrolling foliage on this oak cornice-frieze is ultimately derived from 17th-century carving.*

10 *Also inspired by a 17th-century original, this cornice-frieze features acanthus leaves carved in deep relief.*

11 *Similar to, and often used interchangeably with, hop plants and ivy, grapevine imagery has been employed on architectural ornament since ancient Egyptian times. This cornice-frieze is based on an 18th-century original.*

12 *The repeat floral motifs on this frieze moulding are palmettes (formalized palm leaves). A feature of Etruscan ornament, they are a recurring motif in neo-classical and Classical Revival architecture.*

13 & 14 *These two turn-of-the-19th-century picture rail mouldings have repeat floral motifs.*

15 *This torus picture-rail moulding is of a type in common use in the 18th and 19th centuries.*

113

FIELDS

While various types of wooden panelling (*see* pp.108–11) have often covered the fields of walls since the Middle Ages, many other forms of decoration have also been favoured. In medieval, Renaissance and Baroque houses, pictorial tapestries or painted cloths were hung over limewashed flat plaster, or the latter was embellished with hand-painted or stencilled imagery. In early Georgian and Colonial homes, flat-painted plaster was most prevalent, although *faux marbre* and other painted stone effects, silk and woollen fabrics stretched over a network of battens, and, more rarely, hand-printed or flocked wallpapers, were also used in grander houses. All of these treatments continued to be widely employed in late-Georgian, Federal, Empire and Regency homes. However, in reception rooms, much greater use was made of stretched fabrics, especially damasks and brocades, and, increasingly, of patterned wallpapers. The introduction of cheaper, machine-printed papers in the mid-19th century saw patterned-papered fields become commonplace thereafter even in ordinary houses, although alternative finishes were never supplanted. In addition to flat-painted plaster, notable examples included a revival of tapestry hangings in Arts and Crafts and Renaissance Revival houses; colourwashed flat plaster in Art Nouveau-style interiors; and ceramic-tiled fields in most bathrooms, but also in some hallways designed under the aegis of the Aesthetic movement.

1 Walls decorated with painted simulations of stone and marble blocks were employed in many grand Renaissance, Baroque and neo-classical houses. These faux marbre walls are in the study of Richard Jenrette's American Empire-style house on the Hudson River.

2 Flat-painted plaster fields have been employed in many houses since the Middle Ages. The painted field in this fan-arched wall niche is at Home House, London, designed c.1775 by Robert Adam.

3 Apart from in kitchens and bathrooms, tiled fields have rarely appeared in British and American houses. However, largely due to oriental influence, they were fashionable in the entrance halls of some grander houses during the late 19th century. This tiled field is at Leighton House, built in the late 1870s, in Kensington, London.

4 In the 18th and 19th centuries, in the rural areas of Europe and America, stencilling was a cheaper alternative to costly wallpapers. This flower-and-foliage pattern, in the hallway of an English country house, is copied from an 18th-century bedroom at the American Museum in Bath, England.

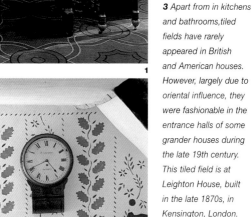

5 & 6 Stencilled and hand-painted decoration overpainting plank fields is highly characteristic of timber-framed American and Northern European rural houses built during the late 17th, 18th and 19th centuries. The "pattern-box" stencilling in 5 was applied in the late 19th century by itinerant German painters on the plank walls of a cottage near Houston, Texas. Its stylized foliate forms are taken from the classical vocabulary of ornament. The hand-painted decoration in 6 was produced c.1796–1820 in a Norwegian country house. It consists of a garland of roses entwined around a simple, rectilinear trompe l'oeil *moulding.*

5

6

7 Hand-painted grisaille (monochrome trompe l'oeil) has been used to decorate plaster fields since the Renaissance. Set in a plaster panel, this bouquet of fruit and flowers is in a bedroom of a mid-Victorian house in London, England.

8, 9 & 10 Due to the cost of hand-printing, wallpapered fields were confined to grander houses prior to the mid-19th century, but following the advent of cheaper machine-printed papers, they came into common use. Paper-panelled field 8 is in an American Federal house. The "Chinese Garden" paper in 9 is in a Georgian room c.1800, and has imagery from Audubon's The Birds of America. The colonnaded paper field in 10 is in the American Empire-style Morris-Jumel Mansion, in New York.

7

8

9

10

DADOS

A wide range of materials and decorative techniques have been used to define dados on walls since the Middle Ages. In houses where full- or three-quarter-height wooden panelling was applied (*see* pp.108–11), the distinction between the dado and the field above was often made within the overall composition of the panelling by applied rectilinear mouldings or bands of carving, which could also be highlighted with contrasting-coloured paints, or by gilding. An alternative treatment for full-height panelling composed of butt-jointed or tongue-and-groove planks was the application of hand-painted or stencilled dado rails – a decorative convention much favoured in 18th- and 19th-century rural American dwellings. In some Renaissance and early Georgian houses, and many late-Georgian, Regency, Federal, Victorian, Arts and Crafts, Art Nouveau, Edwardian and American Beaux Arts homes, wooden panelling was simply extended up only to dado or chair-rail height, and the contrasting plaster field above painted or covered with fabric or wallpaper. Where panelling was not used, definition of the dado has been achieved by the combination of chair and dado rails above and wooden skirting boards below, infilled with painted or papered plaster; by the use of tripartite wallpaper sets (which include separate dado strips); and by ceramic tiles – the latter particularly popular in bathrooms, kitchens and hallways from the mid-19th century onward.

1 In most American Federal houses built c.1780 to 1830, wall panelling was taken to dado level only – the exception being on fireplace walls where, as in the Colonial period, full-height panelling was often used. This painted wooden panelling is in a hallway of the American Empire-style Morris-Jumel Mansion, in New York. The classical mouldings framing the centre panel are typical of the period. However, more ornate beading, guilloche and gouge-work were also used, as were painted neo-classical motifs on the centre panels.

2 Set above a mahogany skirting board, this Victorian dado panel is painted over flat plaster. The bands of flowers and foliage have been stencilled over a painted faux sienna marbre.

3 Dated to c.1822, the dado on the plank walls of this farmhouse is divided from the blue colourwashed field above by a hand-painted floral border and a contrasting red colourwash.

4 & 5 Tiled dados became increasingly common in bathrooms, kitchens, and, to a lesser extent, hallways, during the last third of the 19th century (and thereafter). As here, rectangular tiles in one or two colours were usually laid in traditional brickwork patterns, and topped with bands of patterned and three-dimensional tiles, the latter profiled as classical mouldings.

6

7

6 *The dado in this late-Victorian hallway is covered with Anaglypta. Invented in 1886, made of cotton-fibre pulp and incorporating relief patterns made by hollow moulding, it was always painted, and it provided a lighter and cheaper alternative to Lincrusta.*

7 *Invented in 1877, Lincrusta was made of linseed oil, gum, resins and wood pulp spread over canvas, and had embossed patterns created with engraved metal rollers. This Art Nouveau Lincrusta dado is painted to resemble ceramic panelling.*

8

9

10

11

12

13

14

15

16

8 *A reproduction dado rail with a Tudor-style reeded pattern, carved from oak and based on a 16th-century original.*

9 *A reproduction dado rail with alternating pineapple and dart motifs, based on an 18th-century original.*

10 *A classical dentil-pattern dado rail, carved from whitewood and based on 18th- and early 19th-century originals.*

11 *A Greek key pattern dado rail, with an egg-and-dart border, based on an early 19th-century Greek Revival original.*

12 *A reproduction neo-classical dado rail, with repeat swagged ribbon motifs carved in deep relief.*

13 *A wavescroll pattern dado rail, of a type used in Classical Revival and neo-classical houses since the Renaissance.*

14 *A rope (or cable) moulding dado rail, of a type used in neo-classical, and especially Regency, houses.*

15 *A reproduction classical astragal moulding, in common use during the 17th, 18th and 19th centuries.*

16 *A classical-style egg-and-dart moulding, carved in oak and copied from an 18th-century plaster original.*

17

18

19

20

21

22

23

17 *A reproduction oak skirting board, of a type often used under carved linenfold wall panelling. Available in different depths to suit the proportions of the room.*

18 *A whitewood skirting board topped with a bolection moulding – the latter is directly above a band of classical egg-and-dart motifs.*

19 *A pine skirting board topped with a stained band of naturalistic leaf motifs – the latter set above a classical concave torus moulding.*

20 *A classical skirting board featuring a fielded band set underneath a thin rope (or cable) moulding, and topped with a repeat bead-and-reel moulding.*

21 *The moulding on top of this skirting board is a variant of the concave and convex ogee moulding in widespread use from the 17th to the 19th centuries.*

22 *Also fashionable from the 17th to the 19th centuries, a pine skirting board topped with a classical convex astragal moulding (with a chamfered top edge).*

23 *Another variant of the classical convex torus moulding topping a skirting board. Torus profile mouldings were particularly popular in the late 19th century.*

FIREPLACES

Prior to the late 15th century, an open hearth in the centre or near one end of the main living room of a house – its smoke allowed to meander up through a hole in the roof – was the most common form of fireplace. However, the introduction of wattle-and-daub or wooden canopies above the hearth, designed to channel smoke more efficiently out of the room, increasingly led to the relocation of the fireplace to one of the walls – it being easier to support the canopy there, rather than from a wooden stand or the ceiling. From the early 16th century, the open hearth and canopy was, in turn, largely superseded by the enclosed wall fireplace, consisting of a brick or stone stack (a chimney) with a hollow centre (a flue) designed to conduct smoke up from a hearth (recessed in the base of the stack) and out via a louvre in the roof. Most hearth openings were rectangular and spanned by a stone or wood lintel, but in some grander houses they were shaped as a Gothic four-centred arch. Lintels and arches could be plain, chamfered, or carved and painted or gilded with decorative motifs – the extent of this reflecting the wealth of the household.

Despite its new position and increased ornamentation, the early 16th-century fireplace was, in many respects, treated as just part of a wall. However, it rapidly thereafter became not only a dominant feature in its own right, but also the architectural focus of most rooms – an effect primarily due to the development of the fire surround (or mantelpiece). Initially devised in Italy during the Renaissance, and inspired by the Classical Graeco-Roman Orders of architecture, the surround took the form of a pair of jambs (flanking the hearth) linked (just above the hearth) by an entablature; the jambs could be columns, pilasters, carved figures or simple architectural mouldings, while the entablature was essentially a decorative frieze. The surface of the chimney breast above was also invariably subject to a decorative treatment – in the form of a wooden or stone overmantel, consisting of either a large, projecting smoke hood, an architectural structure mirroring the surround below or, more usually, carved, or painted and gilded, panelling.

This basic model for the fireplace has survived to the present day, although it has inevitably been subject to numerous technical and decorative changes over the intervening centuries. Notable among the former are canting of the sides of the hearth to help project heat into the room; reductions in the size of the hearth and the flue (and also the depth of the chimney breast) to increase the draw of air and improve combustion; the invention of, in turn, dog, hob and register grates designed to burn coal, rather than logs – the latter traditionally burned on firedogs (*see* pp.134–5); and the introduction of enclosed stoves and heaters as alternatives to open fires (*see* p.136). Significant decorative developments include lining the areas between the sides of the jambs and the hearth or grate with marble, slate or ceramic tiles (*see* pp.123 and 133); incorporating a picture panel or, from the late 17th century, a mirror-glass within the overmantel structure (*see* pp.138–9), or dispensing with the overmantel and hanging a picture or mirror directly on the chimney breast; and, during the 19th century, increasing the depth of the mantel-shelf to accommodate clocks, candles and numerous decorative artefacts. Nevertheless, aesthetically, the most pronounced changes have occurred in the style of the fire surround. Made of stone, slate and brick (*see* pp.120–3), marble (*see* pp.124–7), wood (*see* pp.128–31), or cast iron and copper (see pp.132–3), they have always closely reflected changing fashions in architecture and ornament.

During the 20th century, the fireplace suffered a demise in popularity, largely due to the widespread adoption of central-heating systems (*see* p.137). Indeed, in the 1960s and 1970s, many fire surrounds were stripped out and their hearths boarded up, thereby removing the architectural focal point of the room. Fortunately, this trend has now been reversed by numerous homeowners intent on restoring the architectural equilibrium and period authenticity of their properties, and by the many salvage companies and manufacturers now supplying a diverse range of restored original and fine-quality reproduction fireplaces.

STONE AND BRICK

Many of the earliest fire surrounds, dating to the late 15th century, were cut and carved from stone, a material that has proved enduringly fashionable for this purpose ever since. Like marble (*see* pp.124–7), stone has always been expensive to quarry and transport, and therefore usually reserved for more prestigious surrounds, although reconstituted stones, such as the Coade stone developed in the 18th century, have provided cheaper alternatives. Their appeal to architects and craftsmen largely resides in the receptiveness of most types – notably various limestones – to carving and chamfering. Consequently, numerous examples have displayed elaborate decorative embellishments on their jambs, lintels, entablatures and, where deployed, hoods or overmantels. However, many stones are equally prized for their variations of colour and figuring, which range from the largely monochromatic off-white and yellow limestones, and black and gray slates (very popular during the 19th century), to the polychromatic purple, brown, white and red porphyries – the latter often used as decorative inlays set in plainer stones. Variations, and particularly subtle gradations, of colour also explain the visual appeal of bricks. Unsuitable for carving, they have not often been employed (except in later Arts and Crafts houses) to make fire surrounds as such. Yet, because of their load-bearing qualities, and their resistance to high temperatures, they have been regularly used since the Renaissance to construct hearths, chimney breasts and inglenooks. Their aesthetic qualities (which also include different patterns of mortaring) have often been exploited by leaving them exposed, rather than cladding them with materials such as cement, plaster, wooden panelling or ceramic tiles.

2 *Large smoke hoods, as on this neo-Gothic limestone fire surround, were often employed in medieval, Renaissance and Baroque houses. Here, late-medieval decoration includes the coat-of-arms on the hood, stylized floral roundels along the frieze, clerics' heads on the pilasters and a four-centred arched hearth.*

3 *The drawing room in Plas Teg, a Jacobean mansion in North Wales, retains its original 17th-century stone fireplace. Its columnar jambs, four-centred arch and breakfront mantelshelf were carved as separate sections and assembled with mortar on site.*

1 *Hand-carved from limestone, this fire surround is modelled on 15th-century English Tudor style. Essentially classical in form, it also incorporates lingering elements of the medieval Gothic style – in this case a pointed arch over the hearth. The latter features a cast-iron fireback with lion and unicorn motifs, and a cast-iron, swan's-nest firebasket flanked by a pair of black-iron and brass firedogs.*

4 Modelled on an original Queen Anne stone fireplace, this modern reproduction displays the robustness and simplicity of line that characterized many turn-of-the-17th-century fire surrounds – qualities that were consolidated during the later 18th-century Georgian era. Available in Portland, Bath or reconstituted stone, it is shown here with a cast-iron insert.

5 Classical ornament is evident in the pair of turned roundels, and in the reeded pilaster jambs and frieze, of this reproduction, late-Georgian fire surround. Roundels and reeding were very fashionable forms of decoration on early 19th-century Regency fire surrounds. Classical flower and bead motifs are employed on the arch-top, cast-iron insert.

7 This reproduction of a classic Louis XV carved-stone fire surround, with its serpentine-profile frieze and mantelshelf, and scrolling motifs, is very characteristic of late-18th-century French neo-classicism. Intended for use with a free-standing dog grate, surrounds such as this one were exported in considerable numbers to both Britain and the United States.

6 Classical decoration on this late-18th-century English Coade stone fire surround is far more ornate than on 5. The bacchanalian figures on the pilaster jambs, Pomona and Flora, are inspired by murals found c.1738–65 during the excavations of Herculaneum. They are surmounted by myrtle wreaths, bows and quivers, and these flank a frieze embellished with a trailing vine heavily laden with grapes.

8 Carved from a creamy coloured limestone, this reproduction of a mid-19th-century fireplace displays the minimum of applied or carved decoration. As such, the emphasis is clearly on pared-down classical architectural

form, rather than as with many other Victorian fireplaces, on classical ornament. The matching limestone slips and infill frame an extremely plain cast-iron insert – a combination that would sit quite happily in many

20th-century Modernist rooms. However, when installed in a Victorian-style interior, a more appropriate insert would feature simple classical motifs, such as reeding, strings of husks, individual rosettes and rows of acanthus leaves.

121

1 Reproduced from a mid-19th-century model, this fire surround, like the similarly austere example 8 shown on page 121, relies for effect on its classical architectural form and simple linear mouldings, rather than on any applied or carved ornament. However, decoration of sorts is present in the subtle mottling and gradations of colour inherent in the stone itself. Moreover, the colour contrast between the elegant beige surround and the black-leaded, arch-top grate that it frames makes a strong visual impact, and thereby consolidates the fire-place's position as the architectural focal point of a Victorian room.

2 This Arts and Crafts fire surround dates from the late 19th century and is made from Welsh slate. While the surround itself is unornamented, the contrasting-coloured blue-ceramic tile slips display subtle but decorative mottling, and the hood of the one-piece, cast-iron insert features Islamic-inspired fretwork. It is also worth noting that the insert is polished, rather than black-leaded, as was usually the case during the second half of the 19th century.

3 Designed in 1870 by the influential Arts and Crafts architect Richard Norman Shaw, this monumental stone fireplace has carved columnar jambs surmounted by a pair of massive corbels. *The latter are intricately carved with foliate and bird motifs, and support a deep frieze bearing a homely Victorian motto. Unusually, the mantel-shelf is made of finely* figured marble. The tiled *slips are Islamic, and the wrought-iron fire-back bears images of medieval chivalry – a military theme extended to the armorial brass shields on the firedogs.*

4 Located in an 18h-century American Colonial house, this is very much a working fireplace designed for open-hearth cooking. Framed by a simple, painted wooden surround, the jambs, lintel and back of the hearth are constructed from mortared bricks. Also highly characteristic of the period are the pair of wrought-iron firedogs and the swivel-crane – the latter designed to support pots and kettles over the burning logs. Home of Stephen P. Mack.

1

3

2

4

5 In an American Colonial house on Rhode Island, a brick fireplace is framed by a painted wooden surround constructed of simple rectilinear mouldings, which blend into the surrounding raised-and-fielded, painted wall panelling. In grand 18th-century American Colonial houses, it was not unusual for all of the walls of some reception rooms to be similarly panelled. In most houses, however, panelling was confined to the fireplace wall. Home of Stephen P. Mack.

6 Large, brick-built, inglenook fireplaces enjoyed a revival during the second half of the nineteenth century, especially in substantial Arts and Crafts houses. As in many 16th- and 17th-century houses, the larger inglenooks sometimes, as here, incorporated a small bake oven set into the rear wall to one side of the main hearth. However, the primary purpose of the inglenook was to provide bench seating, keyed into the side walls, in close proximity to the fire. Typically, the wooden lintel and mantelshelf above it are used to store and display mugs, jugs, bowls, and other useful household wares, as well as many other decorative artifacts.

7 Designed in 1859 by the influential Arts and Crafts architect Philip Webb, for the Red House, in Bexleyheath, near London, this mortared, red-brick chimney breast incorporates a pointed arch and curved lintel infilled with herringbone-pattern brickwork. The cast-iron grate is bordered with a lattice-work pattern, and flanked by English delft tile slips. It also features an adjustable brass smoke canopy, which augments the iron hood (with rosette motif) directly above the grate.

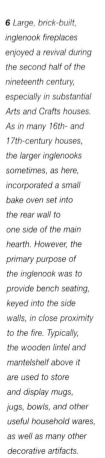

EARLY TILE SLIPS
During the 17th and early 18th centuries, Delft tiles (made in the Netherlands), and English delft tiles, were often used to decorate fireplace slips – the areas between the fire surround and the front of the hearth. Popular in Europe and the American Colonies, they were produced with tin-glazed polychrome or blue-on-white motifs and patterns. The latter (and most fashionable) were inspired by Chinese export blue-and-white porcelain wares. Some simply had corner motifs, such as oak leaves or fleurs-de-lis, but most featured a decoratively bordered central picture of either ships, windmills, landscapes, figures, or moral or religious themes.

123

MARBLE

Marble has been one of the most prestigious building materials since classical Greek and Roman times, and since the late 16th century has been used to make the finest fire surrounds, especially in houses where the design and decoration have been primarily inspired by the classical Graeco-Roman vocabulary of architecture and ornament (*see* pp.10–33). The aesthetic and constructional reasons for this are manifold. First, all types of marble instantly convey an air of solidity, formality and opulence – the latter due to the considerable cost of cutting and polishing marble from dense metamorphic rock, and transporting it from quarries mainly located in Italy, France and Belgium. Second, some varieties, notably the almost pure white statuary marble from Carrara, in Italy, are very receptive to elaborate and finely detailed carving. And third, numerous other types of marble are highly decorative, displaying subtle or bold gradations of colour, mainly in the form of crystalline deposits, such as turquoise, opal and quartz. Typical examples of these variegated marbles, which are either used in their own right, or employed as decorative inlays within paler and more monchromatic marble surrounds, include serpentine, onyx, sienna, breche violet, red levanto and bois jordan.

1 Made from contrasting plain and finely figured marbles, this grand Palladian fireplace dates to c.1720–30. Its composition is characteristically bold, and includes numerous decorative devices derived from the the classical Roman vocabulary of ornament. Notable features include the "earred" egg-and-dart moulding framing the jambs and lintel; S-scroll brackets (bearing gilded pateras) flanking the jambs; a dentil cornice along the top of the stepped frieze, the latter bearing, at its centre, a projecting sculpted mask; and, on top of the mantelshelf, a triangular-shaped pediment.

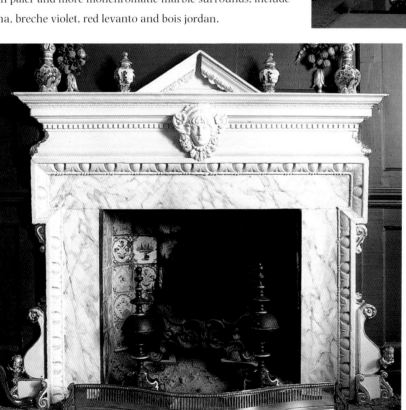

2 The curving sculptural forms of this reproduction, early 18th-century Louis XIV fire surround are essentially 17th-century French Baroque in style, but they also herald the lighter French Rococo style of the 18th century. Characteristic Gallic features include splayed pilaster jambs, and the serpentine-profile mantelshelf and frieze. Both are embellished with simple linear and curved mouldings and, more prominently, scrolling, spiralling and splayed acanthus leaves, as well as "abstract" architectural scrolls. The inner perimeter of the surround is reeded to further define the opening of the hearth.

3 Dated to the reign of George II (1727–60), this fire surround has a "bracketed" mantelshelf. Bracketed surrounds were very fashionable during the first half of the 18th century. Here, each bracket is carved with three long, strap-like, feather-shaped leaves. These foliate motifs are generally referred to as water-leafs, and were often employed in both Palladian and later 18th-century neo-classical architecture. Apart from the carved bust on the frieze, the other notable feature is the use of contrasting plain and fossilized marbles.

4 This is a reproduction of a late-18th-century English neo-classical fire surround. Hand-carved from marble, its frieze and pilaster jambs are fluted. The latter have capitals which are derived from the Ionic Order of architecture, and which surmount stiff-leaf acanthus carving. The frieze is further embellished with a central plaque display-ing an urn and lightly scrolling foliage carved in shallow relief. This, in turn, is flanked by a pair of corner brackets which are carved with ribboned drinking vessels and lend additional support to the mantelshelf.

5 Designed by the Adam brothers c.1776, this white-marble fireplace is located at Home House, in London. Neo-classical ornament includes fluted columnar jambs, a reeded frieze, a frieze plaque with a ribboned urn and mantelshelf brackets with roundels. The surrounding walls are painted faux marbre to match the contrasting-coloured and stridently figured marble slips.

6 Modelled on a French neo-classical fireplace at the Fontainebleau Palace, this reproduction surround is carved from the finest white statuary marble. Its flat pilaster jambs feature carved acanthus leaves surmounted by rosette motifs on the corner blocks of the frieze – the latter is also embellished with splayed branches tied with a ribbon.

7 Dated to the early 1830s, this American Greek Revival fireplace is in a house in New York. It is carved from gray-and-white-veined black marble – one of the most fashionable colours for surrounds in mid-19th-century Greek Revival houses. The columnar jambs are derived from the classical Greek, rather than Roman, Ionic Order

of architecture. Their austere, unadorned forms are echoed in the sparse ornamentation of the rest of the surround. The cast-iron grate, which is framed by a marble insert modelled on the surround itself, is shown with its cast-iron, pierced-fretwork cover – the latter intended for installation during the summer months when the fire was out of use.

125

3 The most prominent architectural feature of this reproduction early Victorian marble fire surround is the pair of scrolled consoles (or corbels) flanking the flat frieze and supporting the mantelshelf, each of which surmounts a demi-oval paterae. The elegant arched insert is trimmed with a string of husks, crested with floral and foliate motifs.

4 Similar to 3, this reproduction marble fire surround is copied from a model that was initially popular during the reign of William IV, but which remained fashionable well into Queen Victoria's reign. It is shown with a black-marble hearth slab. Contrasting black and white marbles were very popular during the first half of the 19th century.

1 Ornamentation of this reproduction Regency marble fire surround is confined to fluting on the flat jambs and frieze, and the roundels on the corner tablets.

2 Inspired by classical temple-front porticoes, this early 19th-century marble surround is topped with a broken pediment. The fluted frieze and flat pilaster jambs are bordered by an egg-and-dart moulding. The frieze plaque displays scrolled foliage, and the corner tablets show rosettes.

5 This fireplace is in the drawing room of a mid-19th-century Greek Revival-style house in Connecticut. It is constructed from lightly veined white marble, although its columnar jambs are in fact painted a contrasting and more stridently figured black-and-gold faux marbre. Typical Greek Revival motifs include carved aegricanes (sacrificial goats' heads) on the corner tablets, and scrolling acanthus and a Greek vase, filled with fruits and flowers, on the frieze plaque.

6 *Made from Belgian black-and-gold marble, this Greek Revival fire surround dates to the 1860s. Its columnar jambs are derived from the rather austere, Classical Greek Ionic Order of architecture. The spiral scrolls which form the capitals of the columns are known as volutes, their shape supposedly derived from the horns of goats or rams. The cast-iron, arch-top register grate is designed to burn coals, but is shown fitted with its summer cover. This is decorated with intricate pierced fretwork, in the form of stylized, interlaced foliage patterns, known as arabesques.*

7 *This plain Victorian marble fire surround dates to c.1892. As with many late-19th-century fireplaces, its glazed ceramic tile slips are monochrome (green), rather than patterned, although they do display subtle mottling across their surfaces. Rather than being individually mortared, tiles such as this were often supplied as ready-made panels that slotted into a cast-iron framework around a register grate. The latter incorporates a smoke canopy, which has a serpentine profile and bears a large, stylized floral motif filled with lightly scrolling foliage.*

8 *This late-19th-century American Beaux Arts fireplace consists of a tabernacle of carved and polished mahogany, enclosing an overmantel and fire surround made of contrasting-coloured and patterned marbles. The entire composition is a hybrid revival of French and Italian Renaissance designs.*

9 *Contrasting-coloured and patterned marbles are employed in this late-19th-century Arts and Crafts fire surround. The blue-and-white ceramic tile slips display motifs and imagery inspired by the Victorian pre-Raphaelite school of painting.*

127

WOODEN

Fire surrounds made of wood have been in widespread use from the late Middle Ages onward, and have been produced in all the major styles displayed in their stone and metal equivalents. Wooden surrounds can be divided into two basic types: hardwood and softwood. Because most hardwoods, such as oak and mahogany, are aesthetically pleasing in their own right, the surrounds made from them have often been stained and waxed or varnished to accentuate the natural figuring and grain of the wood; these woods have also proved particularly suited to carved decoration. On the other hand, softwoods, such as fir and pine, have always been more abundant and cheaper, but relatively bland in appearance. Thus, softwood surrounds have tended to be wood-grained in imitation of hardwoods, or, alternatively, painted to simulate the appearance of other prestigious materials, such as marble; they have also often featured applied, rather than carved, decoration, usually in the form of composition mouldings.

1 The integration of the fire surround with wooden wall panelling was common practice in the reception rooms of 18th-century American Colonial houses. This example is in Hunter House, on Rhode Island, and dates to 1758. Its original overmantel picture panel has survived, as have the imported Dutch Delft tile slips. As in many Colonial houses of this period, the panelled surround is made of softwood (probably fir or pine) and wood-grained in imitation of more expensive mahogany.

2 Flat-painted wooden fire surrounds are also typical of 18th-century American Colonial interiors and, as in this Rhode Island house, were usually painted the same colour as the surrounding woodwork. The simple mouldings that define the jambs, frieze and mantelshelf are also characteristic of the Colonial period. Home of Stephen P. Mack.

3 The ornamentation of the painted wooden fire surround – restricted to the leading edge of the mantelshelf – in another room of the Rhode Island house is even plainer than on the example in 2. The flat-painted, sage-green finish, like the buttermilk-yellow above, is from a Colonial colour palette based on earth and vegetable dyes. Home of Stephen P. Mack.

4 A notable feature of this reproduction of an early 18th-century wooden fire surround is the linear moulding that runs up the sides of the marble slips and then projects outward at 90 degrees, before continuing up the sides and then across the top of the marble lintel. This geometrical configuration, known as "earring", was a popular embellishment of many fire surrounds of the late 17th and early 18th centuries.

128

5 *The painted motifs, such as anthemia, scrolling foliage, husks, masks, urns and mythological figures, on the frieze and jambs of this Adam fire surround, which dates to the 1770s, are derived from the Etruscan vocabulary of ornament. Ancient Etruscan, Greek and Roman ornament was popular in the neo-classical interiors of the late 18th century.*

5

6 *Like example 5, this Adam-style fire surround also dates to the 1770s, and is decorated with painted and gilded neo-classical motifs. Their colour schemes – pale blue, off-white and gold in 6; raw umber, white, off-white and gold in 5 – are typical of late-18th-century neo-classical interiors, as were Pompeiian red, black and white.*

6

7 *Painting softwood fire surrounds, made of inexpensive pine or fir, to simulate expensive and prestigious Italian white statuary marble was a well-established decorative convention during the 18th century. This reproduction of a late-18th-century neo-classical surround has fluted pilaster jambs and a dentil cornice below the mantelshelf. The swags-and-tails and the urn on the frieze are applied composition mouldings.*

7

8 *In contrast to the neo-classical surrounds shown on this page, this detail of a painted wooden fireplace from Strawberry Hill, a house in England, illustrates the "Gothick" style of ornamentation – a revival of late-medieval Gothic forms – that also came into vogue in the second half of the 18th century.*

8

9 *Typical Adam-style motifs – urns, anthemia, husks, caulicoli, ribbons and bead mouldings – ornament this late-18th-century flat-painted wooden fire surround.*

9

1 This reproduction wooden fire surround is copied from an early 19th-century model. The vigour and precision of the hand-carved decoration are evident in the scrolling foliage, swags and a rosette on the frieze; the egg-and-dart moulding around the figured marble infill; and the fluting on the pilaster jambs.

2 Dated to c.1808, this American neo-classical wooden fire surround is carved from softwood and painted a cream colour in imitation of a plain marble. Its reeded consoles support a dentilled mantelshelf, and the frieze plaque displays bacchanalian figures set against a contrasting-coloured, Wedgwood blue ground.

3 This white-painted wooden fire surround is early 19th century, and is in an Empire-style reception room of the Morris-Jumel Mansion, in New York. Ornamentation of the surround is restricted to the rather bulbous classical mouldings on the frieze and on the "earred" jambs. In contrast, the stridently figured, black-and-gray marble slips and lintel that frame the hearth are far more obviously decorative, as is the pair of brass-finialed firedogs on the stone hearth slab.

4 Copied from an early Victorian fire surround, this stained and polished reproduction is carved from mahogany. The decorative details are primarily classical in origin. They include fluting and S-scrolls on the jambs; naturalistic buds, fruits and foliage on the frieze plaque; and rope moulding on the leading edge of the mantelshelf. The cast-iron insert is partly black-leaded and partly burnished. Bordered with palmettes, the insert has vases and scrolling plant forms on the slip panels, and budding shoots surrounding a highly stylized rosette on the smoke hood.

5 Integrating a wooden fire surround into the surrounding wooden wall panelling is an architectural convention which has its origins in some of the grander Jacobean houses of the 15th and 16th centuries. It was subsequently employed in many late-Colonial and Federal American houses during the 17th and 18th centuries. Here it is revived in a late-19th-century interior. The lighter, post-Victorian look is evident in the use of pine, rather than of darker-stained oak or mahogany.

130

6 *This highly elaborate Victorian Gothic Revival fireplace is made of carved, stained and gilt-painted mahogany, although some of the decoration is gilded composition or plaster. The pair of carved inset panels flanking the mantelshelf clock was salvaged from a 17th-century Dutch fireplace. The Gothic and heraldic imagery – coats-of-arms, arcading and tracery – is supplemented with some classical motifs, notably Ionic capitals and rosettes on the columnar jambs.*

7 *The decoration on this plain, reproduction Victorian fire surround, which is made of antique pine, is restricted to reeding on the flat pilaster jambs and the mantelshelf.*

8 *Fire surrounds with integrated overmantels became increasingly popular toward the end of the 19th century. This American example, made of pine and with an inset mirror and* *display shelving, is very characteristic of the type and period. The grate, framed by relief-tiled slips depicting hunting scenes, has its pierced fretwork cover installed for the summer.*

9 *The striking feature of this late-19th-century American Arts and Crafts hardwood fire surround is its pink-marble insert with a Moorish arch. Various stylized floral motifs – inlaid on the frieze, carved on the spandrels of the arch and painted on the tile inserts in the bases of the jambs – provide the decoration. .*

10 *Classical scrolling foliage is combined with the sinuous and elongated organic forms of Art Nouveau in this reproduction, late-19th-century, hand-carved mahogany surround.*

6

9

7

8

10

131

CAST IRON AND COPPER

One of the major developments in fireplace design during the 19th century was the introduction of metal fire surrounds, the most popular and numerous being those mass-produced in cast iron from the mid-century onward. Due to the abundance and cheapness of iron, and the efficiencies of the industrial casting process – which automatically replicated elaborate decorative details that had to be laboriously hand-carved on scarcer and more expensive marbles or hardwoods – cast-iron surrounds proved affordable to the rapidly expanding middle classes of the period. Moreover, as casting techniques improved, and construction and decoration therefore became more sophisticated, these surrounds proved to be an acceptable alternative in many wealthier households to those made of prestigious marble and finely figured hardwoods. Usually made with a built-in cast-iron register grate, and in some cases an integrated overmantel, cast-iron surrounds were produced in all of the historical-revival and innovative styles in vogue from the mid-19th century onward (*see* pp.24–33). Fashionable finishes included white paint (in imitation of statuary marble) and wood-graining. More popular, however, were black-lead and burnishing. The latter, which gave the iron a subtle reflective appearance and thus emphasized the metallic qualities of the fire surround, had an aesthetic appeal fundamentally similar to those surrounds fashioned from hammered and press-moulded copper produced under the aegis of the Arts and Crafts and Art Nouveau movements during the late 19th and early 20th centuries.

1 Modest fire surrounds such as this one were designed to be installed in secondary rooms, especially small bedrooms. Dated to the mid-19th century, it is made of cast iron and painted white to simulate expensive white statuary marble. Decoration – classical in origin – is confined to thin pilasters on the jambs and a small, ribboned wreath on the deep frieze. Like the shallow, overhanging mantelshelf, the plain, beige-coloured tile slips framing the hearth are typical of "lesser" Victorian surrounds.

2 Stylistically, this typical cast-iron, mid-Victorian fireplace, which dates to the late 1850s, is highly eclectic. Architecturally it is classical in form – its flat pilaster jamb topped with a deep mantelshelf and flanking a decorative frieze. Classical influence is further evident in the strings of husks on the jambs and in the scrolling foliage on the frieze. However, Gothic ornament is also used, notably in the pair of quatrefoils (the stylized four-lobed floral forms) on the smoke hood.

3 Made from beaten copper, this distinctive turn-of-the-19th-century fire surround was made by George Walton. Although it is essentially Arts and Crafts style, the sinuous interlacing plant-form motifs on the frieze and jambs reflect the style of the Art Nouveau movement that became popular in the last decade of the 19th century. The free-standing, cast-iron firebasket was designed by C.F.A/ Voysey, and is framed by a slate-lined lintel and matching slips.

4 *With its slender, flat jambs and columnar mantelshelf brackets, and its characteristically elongated organic motifs, this early 20th-century fireplace is quintessentially Art Nouveau. As with many Art Nouveau surrounds, the cast iron is burnished rather than black-leaded, as with example 2.*

6 *Painted off-white in imitation of stone, this Edwardian fireplace combines classical with late-medieval ornament. The former is evident in the fluting and tiny swags on the frieze and the beading on the mantelshelf; the latter in armorial shields on the jambs and a Tudor-style hearth.*

5 *This fireplace was designed by Charles Rennie Mackintosh in 1902–3 for the main bedroom in The Hill House, in Helensburgh, Scotland. It has a burnished cast-iron frieze and jambs, framed by a simple concave moulding, and built-in overmantel shelving. The frieze is decorated with inset coloured-glass mosaics of highly stylized organic motifs.*

VICTORIAN TILES

Having been widely supplanted by marble fascias during the late 18th and early 19th centuries, ceramic tile slips again became popular in the 1840s, and remained very fashionable throughout the Victorian era. Some were hand-painted, such as those made under the aegis of the Aesthetic and Arts and Crafts movements. Most, however, were mass-produced, and often in the form of ready-made panels for slotting into the one-piece, cast-iron inserts of register grates. The vast range of pictorial, floral and other organic patterns and motifs available was inspired by the diverse historical styles in vogue during the period, notably the Gothic, Renaissance, Baroque, Rococo and neo-classical revivals.

7 *One-piece, cast-iron fireplaces and register grates were often fitted with tile slips (see left), but panels made of burnished or black-leaded cast iron, or of brass, were sometimes used instead. These panels depict the Greek goddess Hestia, symbol of fire. Other popular motifs included urns, vases, scrolling foliage and Electra, goddess of hearth and home.*

133

FIREDOGS AND GRATES

Since the Middle Ages, four basic devices – firedogs, and dog, hob and register grates – have been utilized to burn wood or coal in open hearths. Firedogs (or andirons) are pairs of iron bars used to support the ends of logs and raise them above the hearth. Employed almost exclusively until the late 17th century, and for most log fires thereafter, they have been made of both wrought and cast iron, with more decorative examples featuring brass or silver finials, typically in the shape of balusters or globes. Free-standing, wrought-iron dog grates (or firebaskets) appeared in the late 17th century, and were designed to contain and burn coals, although small logs could also be burned. Although they continued to be used in some larger hearths, they were generally superseded in the 1720s by the cast-iron hob grate, which took up the full width of hearths made narrower to promote the greater draw of air required for the efficient combustion of coal. During the second half of the 18th century, hob grates became highly decorative, and displayed a wide range of classical, Rococo and "Gothick" motifs. Their coal baskets were also moved forward, and their sides canted, to minimize heat loss up the chimney and reflect more heat into the room. However, in the 1820s, these were superseded by even more efficient register grates. Cast in one piece, and forming the sides and back of the hearth, they had a damper plate to control the supply of air to the coals, another damper in the chimney, and were usually embellished with built-in tile slips.

2 The hearth of this late-18th-century Adam-style fireplace contains a particularly elegant dog grate. Made of polished steel, it has a built-in, arch-top fireback, and a pierced, serpentine-profile front, supported on columnar legs with urn-shaped finials. It is a type only found in the grandest houses of the period, and displays in its form and classical decorative detail an exceptionally high level of craftsmanship.

3 Set in the hearth of a fine marble fireplace with splayed and fluted, quarter-column jambs, this large Regency register grate is made of cast iron and is equally suitable for burning coals or logs. The absence of decorative detail indicates that the grate was not intended for use in the finest reception rooms.

4 This reproduction Regency dog grate is made of cast iron and is notably sculptural in form. Neo-classical details include the splayed scrolled legs and feet – the former embellished with strings of husks – and small, brass, urn-shaped finials. The reproduction surround is carved from white statuary marble.

1 The hearth of this reproduction 16th-century stone fireplace, with its carved wooden overmantel, has an arch-top, cast-iron fireback, and a wrought-iron grate. The fireback bears an heraldic armorial device – a coronet-crested achievement-of-arms – flanked by naturalistic foliage. The front of the dog grate is in the form of a medieval portcullis. Dog grates, which only came into general use at the end of the 17th century, were better suited to containing and burning coals than firedogs (see right).

5 The smoke hood of this black-leaded, cast-iron Edwardian register grate is decorated with thistles and other stylized organic motifs fashionable during the late 19th and early 20th centuries. The grate has a damper below the bars to regulate the draught and thus the rate of combustion.

6 The hearth of this late-19th-century black marble fireplace has a pair of brass-finialed firedogs designed for burning logs rather than coals. The primary purpose of the brass fender is to stop burning logs rolling onto the surrounding carpet.

7 Set in a 19th-century American Rococo Revival stone surround, which features exuberantly carved foliate motifs that are typical of the style, this arch-top, cast-iron register grate is fitted with its summer cover. The intricacy of the pierced foliatge motifs decorating the cover echoes those on the surround. *8 This late-Victorian, one-piece register grate and fire surround are made of cast iron, and burnished, rather than black-leaded, like the grate in 5.*

HEARTH ACCESSORIES
Since the Middle Ages, most hearths have been equipped with a basic set of tools – tongs, billets, shovels, brushes and bellows – that is used to prepare, manage and clean log and coal fires. However, a variety of other implements have also been sited in the hearth to make use of the heat. These include bottle and jug stands for warming wine and, as here, plate warmers made of tin, cast iron, brass or copper.

STOVES

During the course of the 18th century, enclosed wood-burning stoves made of cast iron became increasingly common in continental Europe, Scandinavia and America, although far less so in Britain. Throughout this period, most models were employed in houses with combined kitchen and living areas, and incorporated one or more hot plates for heating food and liquids. In this respect they supplanted earlier open-hearth methods of cooking, and were precursors of the more sophisticated cast-iron cooking ranges that gradually came into widespread use during the 19th century (see pp.152–3 and 158–9). While hot plates were retained on 19th-century stoves sited in kitchens, they were usually removed from models installed in other rooms for purely heating purposes. Further developments included a substantial increase in the number of stoves designed to burn coal (and, near the end of the 19th century, gas); the introduction of fireproof glazed doors; and a much greater emphasis on decorative detail, such as brass hinges and knobs, and moulded geometric and organic patterns and motifs.

3 Copied from a 19th-century French model, this reproduction fireplace heater can be fuelled by logs, coal or gas. Smoke and waste gases pass up the chimney flue via a domed ventilator on the top. The naturalistic plant-form imagery on the arched frame surrounding the glazed door is typically French, and is echoed in the splayed feet, which are modelled as stylized leaf forms.

5 Many Victorian heaters had elaborate cast-iron casings. Architectural in form, this reproduction model features a pair of engaged fluted pillars on the two "show" corners, and a stepped plinth edged with rope moulding and highly stylized palmettes. Further decoration derived from the classical vocabulary of ornament includes a string of husks on the doorframe and, above that, swags of foliage.

1 This reproduction, coal-burning English stove has a black-leaded, cast-iron casing with glazed doors. Features include a warming plate, double-doors with arched glazed windows, and a sliding soot and cinder tray on the underside. The duck motifs on the doors are typical of the floral and faunal decoration often applied to these stoves.

2 Late-19th-century, and also made of cast iron, this large, free-standing heater is designed to burn logs, although coals could also be used. Mounted on castors, it can be moved to anywhere in the room, provided that the flue can be set up to carry the smoke and waste gases up through the roof to the outside of the house.

4 Highly versatile, this American, black-leaded, cast-iron stove – known as a "potbelly" – could be enclosed in a hearth or inglenook, or placed out in a room, provided that the flue could be run through an opening cut in the roof. Either log or coal burning, most potbellies have a warming plate on top. This model has rather elaborate cabriole legs that are decorated with foliate motifs and end in paw feet.

136

RADIATORS

Central-heating systems, servicing rooms via a series of cast-iron radiators linked by hot-water pipes running from a coal-, wood- or gas-powered boiler, were first installed in grander American and European houses during the last quarter of the 19th century, but substantial installation and running costs meant they were beyond the means of most homeowners until after the Second World War. Consequently, in order to supplement coal- or wood-burning open fires or cast-iron stoves with central heating in houses built prior to the late 19th century, owners have had to compromise period authenticity for greater domestic comfort. The most visually effective and commonly used solution has been to disguise modern steel radiators with either purpose-built cabinets designed in the style of joinery, or pieces of carcass furniture (such as chiffoniers or window seats), appropriate to the period of the house. Many owners of late-19th-century, and later, houses have also adopted this practice, but today's greater availability of reproduction cast-iron radiators of the period has provided a more historically accurate option.

3 Made to simulate a Regency chiffonier, this painted wooden radiator cabinet features fluted pilaster jambs topped with shell motifs, and latticework door panels. Plainer and more decorative models are made in various other period styles from materials such as limed oak and mahogany.

4 Instead of being concealed in purpose-built cabinets such as 3, radiators can be disguised within the basic architectural features of a room. For example, in this corner of a late-19th-century, French neo-classical-style interior, a modern panel radiator has been made an integral part of the dado by framing it with simple wooden mouldings. The skirting board disguises the pipework; vertical panels, like those on the door, conceal the valves; and a dado rail-like shelf conceals its top, leaving the centre exposed as reeded dado panelling.

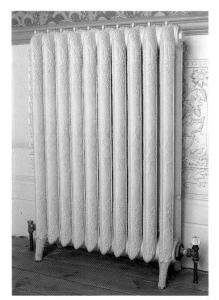

1 & 2 The two radiators shown above are made of cast iron. The one on the left dates to the early 20th century; the one on the right is a modern reproduction. They both display minor variations on a standard *design that has been employed on both sides of the Atlantic, but especially in Europe, since the turn of the 19th century. The earlier example is slightly more decorative, in that the individual pipes are* *moulded in low relief with stylized foliate motifs. Its feet, which supplement concealed wall brackets, are also more prominent and ornamental than those on the more recent model. A notable, and* *substantial, variation was the free-standing circular types first made at the beginning of the 20th century. These could be dismantled into two semi-circular halves designed to fit around a pillar or column.*

5 As an alternative to boxing-in and disguising radiators aesthetically ill-suited to pre-late-19th-century interiors, some contemporary architects and designers make a feature of them. This usually involves adapting the basic design to create a pastiche of a classical architectural form – the engaged fluted column or pilaster, as here. The success or otherwise of this approach invariably depends on the radiator's position – in other words, whether it is sited where one would normally expect to find a real column or pilaster.

OVERMANTEL MIRRORS

When the fashion for placing a mirror above a fireplace began in the late 17th century, most mirror-plates were produced from blown glass – a process that limited their size and made them very expensive. Consequently, until the second half of the 18th century, when the perfection of casting techniques facilitated much larger and cheaper plates, such mirrors were the preserve of the wealthy, and invariably took the form of a small centrepiece in a large architectural overmantel. The latter, made from wood, stone or plaster, usually consisted of an entablature and flanking columns or pilasters designed as an integral part of the fire surround beneath. Integrated, architectural-style overmantels with inset mirrors continued to be employed during the 19th and early 20th centuries, when they often incorporated shelves and niches for the display of artefacts. However, from the late 18th century onward, larger mirror-plates framed independently of the fire surround generally proved more popular. Fashionable shapes included rectangular, oval, round, cartouche (scroll-shaped) and convex. Framing materials – notably, gold, silver, copper, plaster and, more commonly, gilded, painted or polished wood – were fashioned in diverse styles, ranging from simple rectilinear mouldings to more elaborate compositions incorporating geometric, mythological or floral and faunal motifs primarily derived from the classical or Gothic vocabularies of ornament.

1 Made of painted wood and plaster, this elegant overmantel mirror is in a boudoir in a late-18th-century château in France. It illustrates the lingering influence of Rococo-style decoration during the early years of Louis XVI's reign (1774–92) – a period in which neo-classical styles of architecture and ornament gradually supplanted the Rococo. The latter is seen in the delicately carved flowers entwining the mirror-frame. However, the much plainer mouldings used to panel the fireplace wall establish the more austere rectilinear style of neo-classicism.

2 Surmounting an 1820s' neo-classical marble fire surround with herm jambs, this overmantel mirror is quintessentially Rococo style. Typically, the delicately carved flowers and foliage entwine a curvaceous giltwood frame that incorporates a series of S- and C-scrolls.

3 This 19th-century overmantel has a triptych-style mirror-glass, and a bronzed giltwood, pillared frame decorated with classical motifs, such as rope and egg-and-dart mouldings.

4 Giltwood overmantel mirrors framed with simple rectilinear mouldings of classical origin were fashionable throughout the 19th century, but particularly in earlier and later Victorian interiors.

138

5 *Sited above a carved-stone fireplace, this Baroque Revival-style overmantel mirror has a typically ornate and sculptural black-and-giltwood frame. The decoration is in the form of boldly carved S- and C-scrolls interspersed with flowers, foliage and berries. The artefacts in front include a bracket clock with temple-front portico case and a pair of torchères.*

5

6 *This 19th-century American giltwood overmantel displays many of the architectural forms and decorative motifs of the Gothic Revival. Notable features include pointed arches, tracery, a trefoil, finials, crockets and carved, naturalistic plant forms.*

7

7 *Carved from stone, the frame of this modern overmantel mirror draws on the Imperial Roman forms of architecture and ornament that were revived and adapted in the Empire style of the late 18th and early 19th centuries. It initially emerged in France under the patronage of Napoleon Bonaparte, and later spread throughout much of Europe and then to America. In addition to the wreaths of laurel or oak leaves on this frame, Empire style was characterized by the use of motifs such as lances, arrows, figures of Victory and Fame, chimeras, griffins, eagles, lions, winged torches, stars and anthemia.*

6

8 *Wall-hung, oval-shape overmantel mirrors first appeared in France during the 18th century. They were very popular in Regency interiors, but were also hung, as here, in many Victorian houses. This example*

has a flat mirror-glass. However, some were fitted with convex glass, and known as girandoles. Decoration of this giltwood frame includes bead moulding, strings of husks and a crest of scrolling foliage.

8

9

9 *During the second half of the 19th century, large overmantels became increasingly fashionable and remained so well into the 20th century. Usually architectural in form and modelled as an extension of the fire surround below it, they invariably incorporated a panel of mirror-glass. In this late-19th-century example, the inset mirror is framed by a pine surround. The latter features carved stylized floral motifs, a pair of turned pillars, and a pair of tabernacles (canopied niches) intended for the display of decorative artefacts.*

BATHROOMS

From the Middle Ages to the middle of the 19th century, very few houses had rooms specifically designed, or set aside, as bathrooms. Portable chamber pots were used inside the house, mainly in bedrooms, and toilets (privies) were usually sited in small wooden, stone or brick "houses of easement" above a cesspit at the end of the yard or garden. Everyday washing took place in bedrooms or dressing rooms, using jugs and basins, and bathing – infrequent by today's standards – was mostly carried out in portable hip baths placed in front of a fire (the baths were often hung on the back of a door when not in use). One of the main disadvantages of these facilities was that they were very time-consuming. Basins and bathtubs had to be filled by hand, with buckets of water either carried from a well or water butts outside the house or, more rarely, from crude wooden pipes that brought water, at very low pressure, into the ground floor or basement. Moreover, when hot water was required, it had to be first heated over the kitchen fire or range before being toted around the house. Equally arduous was the task of emptying basins and baths. However, it was not as as onerous as having to empty chamber pots into stinking cesspits that often overflowed after a heavy rainfall, and sometimes fouled the fresh-water supplies, causing diseases such as cholera (of which there were two major outbreaks in Europe during the mid-19th century).

Labour-intensive, and too often unhygienic, these sanitary arrangements became increasingly unacceptable to the rapidly expanding urban populations of the Victorian age. Fortunately, the widespread desire to improve standards of hygiene was matched by the necessary technological innovation, industry and prosperity to make it possible. The resulting series of major public and private works – initially in the towns and cities – from the second half of the 19th century onward saw the installation of extensive sewerage systems, the introduction of mains water under pressure (via lead and iron pipes) into many homes, and the development of more efficient methods of heating water – in the form of coal- and gas-fired geysers and boilers. Inevitably, these technological improvements were mirrored in the development of much-improved sanitary fixtures and fittings. Mass-produced, enamelled cast-iron baths (see pp.142–3) and ceramic basins (see pp.144–5) were plumbed into pressurized or gravity-fed hot-and-cold-water systems (controlled by reliable metal taps – see pp.148–9) and, like "self-flushing" toilets (see pp.146–7), could be emptied via waste pipes directly into the sewers. And, because it made ergonomic sense to run most of the internal waste and water pipes to one area of the house, all these fixtures and fittings were increasingly installed either in a single room – a bathroom – or in an adjoining bathroom and toilet.

As the vast majority of houses built prior to the second half of the 19th century had not been designed with such a room (or rooms) in mind, most early bathrooms were converted from existing bedrooms, dressing rooms or storerooms. Partly because of their original use, and partly to allay lingering Victorian fears about the hygienic merits of bringing toilets inside the home, they were often furnished as other rooms in the house, and the sanitary equipment "concealed" in furniture-like wooden encasements. The decorative convention of encasement lasted in many households for much of the second half of the 19th century (and enjoyed a number of revivals during the 20th century). However, as reticence to indoor toilets receded, and particularly after architects began to design houses with purpose-built bathrooms in the late 19th century, sanitary fixtures and fittings gradually came "out of the closet" and bathrooms acquired their own decorative genre. This could be characterized as a more streamlined, functional and hygienic look. Floors were covered with tiles or linoleum (see pp.94–7), rather than carpet; dadoes were tiled (see pp.116–17) or flat-painted; curtains were replaced with "frosted" glass; and the design and decoration of baths, basins, toilets, taps and accessories such as towel rails, toilet-roll holders and soap dishes (see pp.150–1) was governed by changing fashions and ease of cleaning in almost equal measure.

BATHS

Before the Victorian era, most domestic bathing took place in portable hip baths, made from sheet lead, copper, tin or zinc, placed in front of a bedroom, scullery or kitchen fire, or in an outhouse, and filled and emptied by bucket. However, during the course of the second half of the 19th century, hip baths were gradually supplanted by fixed baths which, following the introduction of pressurized mains-water supplies and improved drainage systems, were plumbed in and usually installed upstairs, in either a converted bedroom or in a bathroom. Although copper and zinc baths were still used, mass-produced, roll-top-rimmed, cast-iron baths increasingly became the preferred choice in most households. Lined with vitreous enamel, they were often encased in wooden frames. However, from the last quarter of the century onward, they were more often raised above the floor on ornamental feet, and their exposed sides either flat-painted (and often stencilled), or painted in imitation of marble or other decorative stones.

2 Finished in white porcelain, this late-Victorian, cast-iron, roll-top bath stands on elaborate ball-and-claw feet. These are modelled as harpies – the beasts of Greek and Roman mythology, with wings and claws of a bird, and the head of a woman.

3 This late-Victorian, cast-iron, roll-top bath is finished in vitreous enamel, and its exterior painted sage green. The ball-and-claw feet are caricatures of mythical birds, and highlighted with gold paint.

2

1 Combined bath-and-shower units began to be installed in some grander houses during the latter part of the 19th century, following the technical improvements made to hot-water boilers and pressurized water systems. The example shown here consists of a vitreous-enamelled, cast-iron, roll-top bath (on lion's-paw feet), plus an overhead douche, and a shower compartment – also vitreous-enamelled, fixed to the bath's rim and housing horizontal "needle" sprays. The douche, pipework and capstain-headed taps are all chromed, with the latter allowing the bather instantly to divert hot and cold water from the bath to the douche, or to the needle sprays or to both at the same time.

3

4 Before cast-iron baths became fashionable during the last quarter of the 19th century, most baths were made from sheet lead, copper or zinc. This French example is copper, has a roll-top rim and dates to the mid-19th century. Hot and cold water is supplied by a late-19th-century, wall-mounted, bath-shower mixer tap. This is made of brass, and has elegant, shell-shaped spouts.

1

4

5 Like baths 3 and 4 shown, this enamelled and painted, cast-iron bath is a "double-ended" turn-of-the-century reproduction. Positioned with one side, rather than one end, against a wall, double-ended baths receive their water supplies from taps or bath-shower mixers mounted on either the wall, an infill panel inserted between the bath and the wall or, as in example case, a flat section (a "deck") fashioned into the rim.

8 Fashionable painted finishes applied to the outside of 19th-century, enamelled, cast-iron baths included faux marbre and, as here, repeat motifs stencilled over a flat-painted monochrome ground.

9 The roll-top rims of Edwardian, enamelled, cast-iron baths – as on this reproduction model – were generally less bulbous than their Victorian counterparts.

6 The decorative convention, instigated by the Victorians, of encasing sanitary fixtures and fittings with joinery has been partly adopted in this modern bathroom to give it a period feel. In many Victorian bathrooms, the bath, basin and toilet would all have been encased; here, only the cast-iron bath is recessed within, and side-panelled to match, the painted sea-green wall panelling.

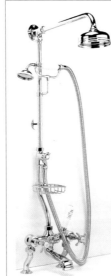

7 Portable hip baths were common up to the late 19th century. Designed with a high, sloping back to support the neck and shoulders, and a tapered end to save water, they were originally placed in front of a fireplace, and filled and emptied by bucket. However, this enamelled, cast-iron reproduction has a plumbed-in waste, and is filled via a floor-mounted bath-shower mixer tap.

SHOWER SETS

Combination bath-and-shower taps (or shower sets) evolved during the latter part of the 19th century, although their use was initially confined to those wealthier households, whose boiler was sufficiently powerful to pipe hot water to the faucets at roughly equal pressure as that of the cold water supplied from the tank. One of their main attractions was that they allowed the homeowner to bathe and shower in the same tub. They also helped reduce condensation in the bathroom by mixing the hot and cold water to a comfortable temperature before it was exposed to the atmosphere. Moreover, by linking a hand-held shower to the main body of the tap with a flexible, rubber-core, metal-link hose, they gave the bather complete control over the direction of the spray. The early 20th-century model shown here is particularly sophisticated, in that it combines the bath taps and hand-held shower with a fixed, overhead douche, and also incorporates a soap and sponge rack on the riser pipe. Examples of shower sets without overhead douches are shown above, opposite and on page 150.

BASINS

Plumbed-in washbasins were a rare luxury prior to the last quarter of the 19th century, and where they were installed – in only the grandest of houses – they often took the form of a small fountain recessed in a niche in the wall. In the vast majority of households, daily washing was carried out using ceramic basins and jugs, which were filled and emptied by hand and, together with various other bowls and dishes (designed to hold soap, perfumed water, toothbrushes and shaving equipment), were placed on top of washstands. Sited in a bedroom or dressing room, most washstands were made as free-standing wooden dressers, and were usually fitted with a durable marble top. However, following the introduction of pressurized water systems controlled by metal taps, and more efficient drainage systems, washstands, now made of wood or cast iron, were fitted with inset, plumbed-in, ceramic or enamelled-metal basins. Around the turn of the century, these were generally superseded by ceramic pedestal basins, which were screwed to the wall and further supported on columnar-like, ceramic plinths.

2 Many Victorian and Edwardian washbasins were wall-mounted on brackets, rather than being encased in a washstand. Here, white-painted, plain tubular brackets are used under a reproduction ceramic basin. Because of the preoccupation with hygiene during the late 19th and early 20th centuries, water and waste pipes were often left exposed to facilitate cleaning.

3 This architectural, cast-iron washstand is late Victorian, and has an inset, transfer-printed ceramic basin, and an integral shelf and mirror. It is embellished with moulded and painted floral motifs, primarily derived from the classical vocabulary of ornament.

1 Before the advent of separate bathrooms, and the installation of running hot-and-cold-water systems during the latter part of the 19th century, daily ablutions in most houses were carried out in bedrooms, using hand-filled jugs and basins. Here, in a bedroom at Ulysses S. Grant's house in Galena, Illinois,the Warwick china jug and basin are part of a set that also includes a slop pail, a chamber pot and various other toilet accessories. They are sited on and around a marble-topped, mahogany washstand, dated to c.1860.

4 Classical influence is also evident in the plain, columnar plinth and the serpentine profile of the leading edge of this reproduction Edwardian washbasin. As well as supporting the basin (which is additionally secured by screws to the wall), the hollowed-out plinth disguises the presence of the waste and water pipes.

5 Washstands with inset basins enjoyed a notable revival during the late 20th century, and are nowadays more usually referred to as vanity units. This example features chromed pillar taps, and consists of a top and basin made of synthetic marble, on a plinth-mounted cabinet with fielded-panel doors. Stylistically, it is broadly modelled on an encased Victorian washbasin. However, the gray-green tones of the distressed paint finish applied to the softwood cabinet are more in keeping with the colour schemes favoured during the second half of the 18th century.

5

8

6 While most Victorian ceramic, and enamelled-steel, washbasins were manufactured in plain white, cream or an ivory colour, brightly patterned models were also very fashionable, especially during the last quarter of the 19th century. Set in a marble-topped washstand, this reproduction ceramic basin is embellished with cherubs and sprigs of flowers and foliage.

6

7 Located in one of the bathrooms at the Rockcliffe Mansion in Hannibal, Missouri, this ceramic washbasin dates to 1898–1900. Neo-classical in style, it is supported on a pair of baluster legs, and features a serpentine-profile front, sides and rim-mounted splash-back. The taps, soap dishes, towel hook and waste and water pipes are all original.

7

8 Installed in a recently converted attic bath-room, this original Victorian washstand is made of cast iron, and has an inset ceramic basin. The latter features a raised back and sides, designed partly to stop soap sliding off onto the floor, and partly to protect the wall and floor from splashing.

9 This late-Victorian corner washstand is made of mahogany, inset with floral-pattern ceramic tiles, and has a matching splashback. Its ceramic basin is mounted on a pair of lugs set in the marble top. These allow the basin to be swivelled upside down so that water can be emptied into the waste pipe via a funnel in the cabinet.

9

145

TOILETS

Prior to the mid-19th century, most houses had outside privies, which were usually composed of a wooden seat placed over a shaft leading to an ash- or cesspit – the latter periodically cleared by labourers. Inside the house, chamber pots were used, and were sometimes built into a small piece of movable furniture, known as a "close stool", which, in large houses, could be permanently housed in a small closet. While chamber pots were retained in many bedrooms well into the 20th century in Europe, the introduction of pressurized mains-water supplies and improved sewerage systems during the Victorian era resulted in all other facilities being replaced by the internal, plumbed-in water closet (or toilet). Sited in its own room, or a bathroom, the toilet went through various stages of technical development, culminating in the 1890s in the perfection of the "wash-out" model. Still used today, it consisted of a ceramic bowl (with a fitted seat), the contents of which were flushed through an S-bend gas trap by a downrush of water from an overhead cistern – the latter usually operated by pulling a chain.

1 Encasing the toilet in a chair- or throne-like enclosure was common practice during the 19th century, and was largely done to help overcome initial reticence about installing toilets inside (rather than outside) the house. This grand reproduction enclosure is made of stained and polished oak. Notable features include turned pilasters, drop pendants, linenfold carving and, on the seat lid, a carved portrait roundel – all primarily modelled in the English Tudorbethan style of the late 15th and 16th centuries.

2 High-level cisterns, which produced a powerful downrush of water to flush the toilet, were introduced in the 19th century. Many were hidden behind panelling, but more decorative models, such as this striking, burnished cast-iron example, were specifically designed to be displayed on the wall.

3 In this Gothic Revival cloakroom, the columnar toilet bowl is flushed by a concealed high-level cistern – operated by pulling the chain handle in the arched niche in the wall panelling.

4

5

5 *While most ceramic Victorian toilet bowls were produced in plain white (like basins, see pp.144–5), transfer-printed-patterned models were also made. This original Victorian bowl displays a blue floral pattern on a white ground. The bold naturalistic flowers are typical of the mid-19th century; smaller, more delicate floral patterns were favoured during the late-Victorian period. The ceramic seat, which bears the maker's emblem, is bordered with bead and stylized floral motifs.*

4 *The toilet bowl in this original Edwardian bathroom suite is flushed by a high-level, chain-operated, ceramic cistern mounted on painted, cast-iron wall brackets. Ceramic cisterns became increasingly popular during the early 20th century, although cast-iron versions continued to be produced in great numbers during this period. Most were plain white, but some bore transfer-printed patterns. The finish on the down-pipe from the cistern is lacquered brass, and matches the towel rails and the taps on the bath and basin. The toilet seat is mahogany; other fashionable woods included oak and pine – the latter sometimes painted, usually white.*

6

7

6 & 7 *Both of these modern toilets are styled on Edwardian models. The one on the right has a separate cistern, which is mounted much lower on the wall than its high-level Victorian (and some Edwardian) predecessors (see 2 and 4). The example on the left, although Edwardian in profile, and also lever-operated, has a close-coupled cistern. These cisterns were introduced much later in the 20th century, and rely on a plunger rather than gravity to push water out through the holes under the rim of the bowl. Although not strictly authentic to Edwardian (and earlier) interiors, they are often used in them nowadays, as they allow the toilet bowl to be sited under a window.*

147

TAPS

Although crude taps made of wood or metal were in use before the 1850s, mechanically efficient metal taps were not perfected until the second half of the 19th century, when pressurized mains-water supplies, water-storage tanks, hot-water boilers and plumbed-in basins and bathtubs were introduced to ordinary households. Apart from various stylistic changes, which included numerous different designs and finishes, many of them being reproduced today by specialist suppliers, the basic types of tap developed by the Victorians have been employed ever since. These types include pairs of bibs and globes (connected to separate hot-and-cold-water pipes in the wall above a bath or basin); pairs of pillars (mounted on the rim of a bath or basin); mixer taps (wall- or bath/basin-mounted, and mixing hot and cold water in the body of the tap before delivery via a single spout); and combination bath-and-shower mixers.

1 Reproduced from a classic turn-of-the 19th-century utilitarian design, this pair of pillar taps supplies hot and cold water separately and are intended to be mounted on the rim of a basin. The taps have capstain handles and a nickel-plated finish. ("Antiqued" nickel-plated reproductions of these taps are also available.)

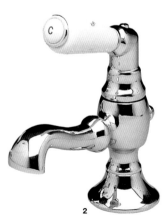

2 These pillar basin taps are finished in chrome, and have ceramic "quick-turn" lever handles and elegant curved spouts. Although they are reproduced from a mid-19th-century Victorian design, they are also stylistically compatible with late-18th-century Georgian and early 19th-century Edwardian bathrooms.

3 Basin-rim-mounted, these reproduction Victorian pillar taps are "antique" nickel-plated and have cross-head handles. Capstains and cross-heads have proved to be the most enduringly fashionable types of handle since the mid-19th century, despite the fact that lever handles are easier to operate.

4 This Edwardian-style, wall-mounted bath mixer with cross-head handles is finished in "antique" gold. Alternative finishes include chrome, nickel and gunmetal.

5 The nickel-plated globe tap shown here is modelled on a c.1890 prototype. Although its four-point capstain handle is a traditional Victorian design, its streamlined spout pre-empts Modernist 20th-century designs.

6 This basin mixer tap is early 20th century. Chrome-plated, it has a single spout (with an integral pop-up waste plunger) connected beneath the basin rim to a pair of capstain-headed mixer handles.

7 *This mono-bloc basin tap pre-mixes hot and cold water in the same way as the bidet tap shown below right. However, its truncated, swan's-neck spout is not adjustable. The finish is chrome, with contrasting brass detailing on the capstain handles, pop-up waste plunger and spout end. Mixed-metal styling such as this dates from the early 20th century.*

8 *In contrast to the basin mixer tap on 6, this polished-brass example has "quick-turn" lever handles (with ceramic inserts), and a swan's-neck spout. Brass taps have been popular since Victorian times. This is a modern reproduction, but a considerable number of restored 19th- and early 20th-century originals are still available through specialist suppliers.*

9 *Finished in burnished brass, this bath-shower mixer is a reproduction of a traditional Victorian design. The shower handle and the diverter lever (which diverts the flow of pre-mixed hot and cold water from the spout to the shower head, and vice versa) are ceramic, although many reproductions have plastic handles, and some Victorian originals had ebony or white- or black-painted wooden handles.*

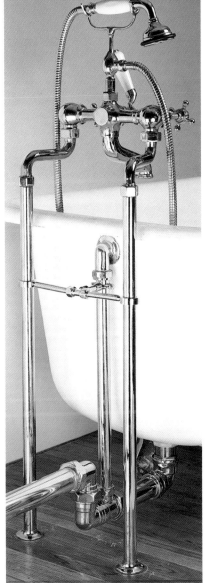

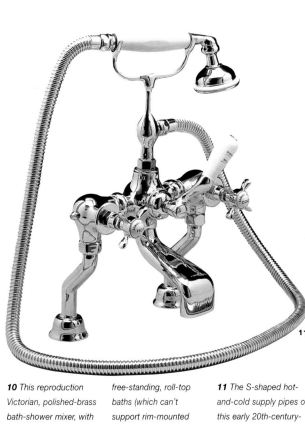

10 *This reproduction Victorian, polished-brass bath-shower mixer, with ceramic shower handle and diverter lever, is designed to be used with matching brass supply and waste pipes. This ensemble allows* *free-standing, roll-top baths (which can't support rim-mounted taps) to be sited in the centre of a room, or adjacent to a wall structurally unsuitable for mounting taps or concealing pipework.*

11 *The S-shaped hot-and-cold supply pipes of this early 20th-century-style "antique" chrome bath-shower set can be swivelled prior to fixing to adjust the position of the spout in relation to the rim of the bath.*

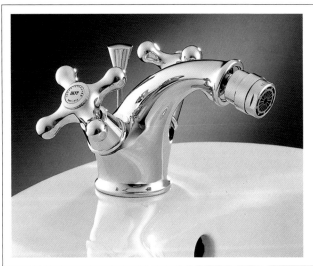

BIDETS

The bidet was first introduced during the early 18th century, in France. The earliest models took the form of portable, hand-pumped sprays. This more efficient, plumbed-in, chrome-finish bidet tap is a reproduction of an early 20th-century design. Known as a mono-bloc or centre-set bidet mixer, it has a pair of capstain handles, which allow the user to pre-mix the hot-and-cold-water supplies in the body of the tap, and an adjustable (swivel) spout for controlling the strength and arc of the spray. The back of the tap also accommodates a plunger which, via two connecting rods, operates a pop-up waste in the base of the ceramic bowl.

BATHROOM ACCESSORIES

A diverse range of bathroom accessories has been created for the convenience of bathers. Most of them were initially introduced by the Victorians during the latter part of the 19th century, especially after more and more houses had rooms (mostly bedrooms) either converted for use as bathrooms or, from around the turn of the century onward, were built with dedicated bathrooms. Notable examples include slatted racks, designed to hold soap, sponges and flannels, and be either wall-mounted next to baths or showers, or supported on the rims of baths; soap dishes, wall-mounted on metal brackets above basins or baths; wall-mounted and free-standing toothbrush holders; toilet-roll stands and holders; bathing-robe and dressing-gown hooks; adjustable mirrors; wall lights (*see* pp.168–9); and towel rails – the latter either free-standing, or floor- or wall-mounted, and either heated or unheated. Favoured materials for their manufacture have included, depending on the item, softwoods and hardwoods (the former often painted, the latter usually varnished, to insulate against moisture); glazed earthenware and porcelain; and various metals, notably brass, cast iron and chrome- (and even gold-) plated brass and steel. In terms of design, all of these accessories have been fashioned or embellished in a range of period styles, including the numerous Victorian and Edwardian classical and Gothic revivals, as well as the Art Nouveau and embryonic Modernist styles of the late 19th and early 20th centuries.

2 & 3 The majority of wall-mounted soap dishes are designed to be positioned above or next to washbasins, but they can also be sited over baths. The one on the left is a reproduction Edwardian model with a cut-crystal dish bearing stylized floral motifs and mounted on a chromed-metal holder. Also reproduction Edwardian, the example on the right is made of bone china, and set in a lacquered-brass holder. Both of these dishes can be instantly lifted and upturned to empty accumulations of water.

4 Floor-mounted, hot-water towel rails, piped into the central-heating system, became increasingly common during the early years of the 20th century, and were styled on the free-standing, unheated, wooden clotheshorses used in many Victorian bathrooms. This double-rail, with ball joints, is finished in lacquered brass. Single rails are also produced, and other popular finishes include polished brass, chrome, and painted or gold-plated iron.

1 Metal bathracks have been in use since the Victorian era, and are divided into a series of compartments (slatted for draining) designed to hold soap, shampoo, loofahs, sponges and various other cleansing paraphernalia. Rested on, rather than fixed to, the side rims of the bath, their position can be easily adjusted to provide optimum access to the contents. This example is chromed, but they are also available in lacquered-brass and gold-plated finishes, as well as in varnished hardwoods, such as beech or mahogany.

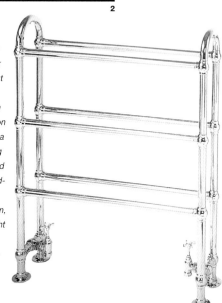

5 This chrome-finish, double-bathing-robe or dressing-gown hook is a reproduction of an Edwardian model, and is designed to be mounted on a wall or the back of a door. Single hooks are also available.

6 Unheated, chromed, and designed to be wall-mounted, this double-towel rail is reproduced from an Edwardian rail dated to c.1910. Its lower rail is projected further away from the wall than the upper rail in order to create a ventilation space between drying towels.

7 Designed to be mounted above a basin, extendable shaving mirrors are available in various sizes. They can be pushed flush to the wall when not in use and, unlike fixed wall mirrors, pulled out and swivelled to the most desirable position when shaving. This chromed model has a standard mirror on one side, and a magnifying mirror on the other.

8 Like bathracks (see 1), wall-mounted, slatted metal shower racks are employed to provide ease of access to soap, shampoo, flannels and sponges. This is a reproduction Edwardian model with an "antiqued" chrome finish.

9 & 10 Toilet-paper holders have been produced in numerous styles during the 19th and 20th centuries. The wall-mounted example on the left is late Edwardian, finished in chrome and designed to hold rolls of toilet paper. The chromed, floor-standing model on the right is reproduction Edwardian, and also designed to hold toilet rolls. Wall-mounted, "letter box" models are also made to hold wads of individual sheets of paper. The holders are available in polished or lacquered brass, gold plate and varnished soft- and hardwoods.

11 This reproduction Edwardian toothbrush and toothpaste holder is wall-mounted, and consists of a white bone-china tumbler set in a chrome-ringed bracket. The tumbler can be lifted out for cleaning. The bracket is also available in brass and gold-plated finishes.

12 Also reproduction Edwardian, this toothbrush stand is fitted with slotted ceramic discs mounted on an "antiqued", gold-plated stand with a decorative ball finial. It is intended for use on a washstand, or a shelf wall-mounted above the washbasin.

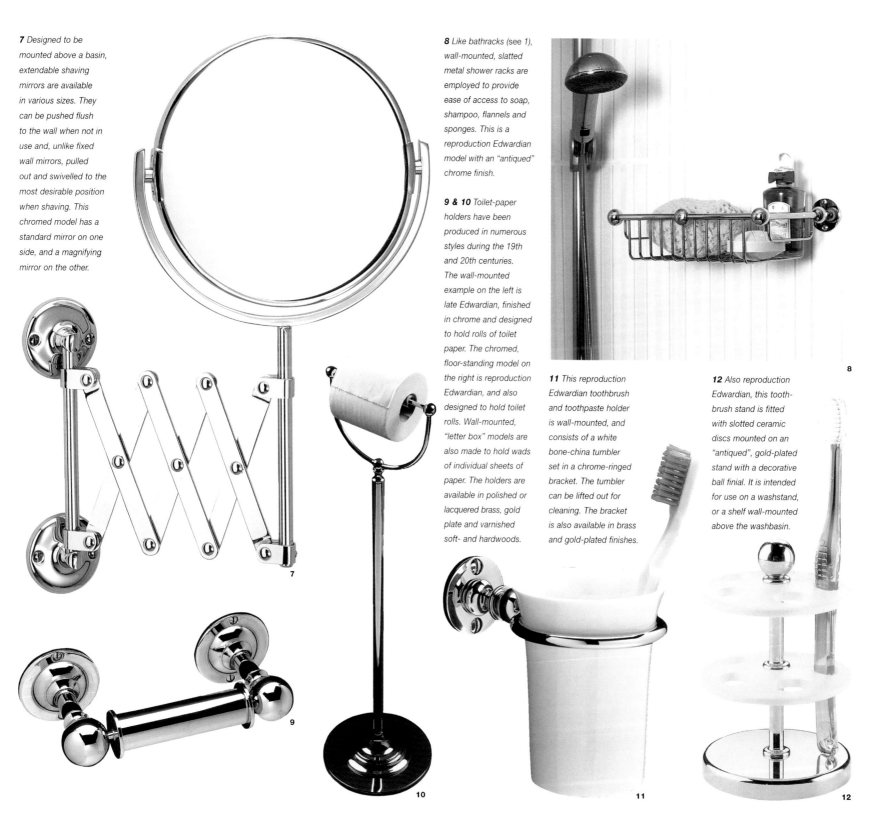

KITCHENS

Technology has had a more profound effect on the evolution of kitchen design than on any other room in the domestic interior. It touches every aspect of the preservation, preparation, cooking and presentation of food. Storage, working surfaces, the *batterie de cuisine*, the means of cooking and the efficient provision of water, fuel and ventilation are all vital considerations. Not only must the modern kitchen comply with a practical need, but it must also embody the kind of comfort and aesthetic character that make it the heart of the home.

Only in our very recent history have kitchens become the hub of the household, having both a social and decorative role. In the past, the kitchen was usually the servants' domain and a place of work, and hence the room was largely bereft of the frivolities of ornamentation. In grander houses, the kitchen was often placed in the basement. In 1570, the Italian architect, Andrea Palladio, described the service areas of the house as "the less comely parts", advocating that "somewhat underground, may be disposed the cellars, the magazines for wood, pantries, kitchens, servants' hall, wash-houses, ovens, and suchlike things necessary for daily use". His description illustrates how the kitchen environment was unlike the modern arrangement as we know it. Because most of the storage, preparation, cooking tasks and washing were carried out in side rooms, the main kitchen served as the central "engine room", and usually contained a huge work table, dressers for holding sets of china, serving plates, and mixing bowls, hanging racks for frequently used items, drying racks for plates, a pantry for storing food and a large and often cumbersome cooking range. In middle-class homes, all of these items would have been housed in only one or two rooms.

The evolution of cooking systems made slow progress in three principal steps, namely the open ("down") hearth, the open-fire range, and the enclosed ("closed") range. The basic "down hearth" served as the means of cooking until the use of coal necessitated the creation of a draft by containing the fuel in a metal basket that was raised over the fire. This developed into a more or less standard facility that was constructed with an arrangement of horizontal bars and vertical posts. From 1567, iron "jacks" had been installed in the chimney, which in time became a sophisticated mechanism based on up-draught or ratcheted wheels that provided a means of turning roasting meat. The hob grate, first introduced in the 1750s, ousted the less efficient basket grate, and the period between 1770 and 1820 saw an increase in the use of cast-iron stoves incorporating an oven into the roasting range, and a back-boiler for hot water. This "closed range" dominated cooking methods from the late 18th century, and was even used until the 1920s. Despite being at the cutting edge of technological invention when it was introduced, in reality this range was a nightmare – dirty, temperamental, and in daily need of dedicated servicing and polishing. The mid-19th century saw the arrival of the cast-iron gas stove and, while oil stoves remained popular, it took another 50 years before gas superseded the solid-fuel range. In turn, the first Edwardian electric stoves were deemed expensive, unglamorous and slow to heat up.

Over the centuries, there have been many influences on the kitchen's metamorphosis. Global trade brought wealth, cultural changes, and the introduction of new foods, and ways of using them. The Industrial Revolution resulted in a large urban population with related domestic needs. The inventiveness of the Victorians resulted in a plethora of ingenious kitchen equipment and labour-saving devices, and the two World Wars had a profound effect on the way food was produced on the kitchen's social environment.

The kitchen corner shown *left* is in a house in Rhode Island, and is the work of Stephen P. Mack (*see* page 187). Its unpolished stone sink, simple open shelves and rustic woodwork illustrate how historical reference to detail creates a characterful setting. In combination with today's technology and lifestyle, the kitchen has finally become a place of physical and spiritual nourishment at the centre of family life.

SINKS

Early 18th-century sinks were very basic: wide and flat, they were usually made of stone, or of lead sheeting over a wooden framework, with a large vessel (a copper) to heat water brought in from a well. From the early 19th century, water provision started to improve. A single tap, usually located on the wall above the sink, and fed by the public water supply or a tank, gave cold water, which was still heated in a copper. In America during the Federal period, only the grandest houses had running water; more modest houses continued to use well water that was brought inside. Sinks were usually made of stone or metal, and included a tap and a hand pump to pump in water. In Britain, shallow earthenware sinks began to be mass-produced in the Midlands in pottery towns. By the mid-19th century, wooden sinks lined in beaten lead or copper were popular, but too expensive for most households. The Victorians used a variety of sinks for specific jobs, installing them in the kitchen's "domestic offices" away from the main cooking area. These included porcelain-glazed sinks such as the Belfast, "pot", butler's and gamekeeper's sinks – so named because of their origin, shape or original uses. Teak sinks were used in the butler's pantry for washing fine glass and china. Arts and Crafts sinks were utilitarian, consistent with the movement's ideology. The early 20th century saw a vast improvement in hot-water systems, with the result that sinks were now supplied with hot and cold water.

2 *Here, an American Victorian tin butler's sink with an embossed front and accompanying pump is housed in a Palladian-style wooden framework. (The sink is in an 1830s house but it was installed during an update in 1850.) Details such as choice of "drab" paintwork, the old-fashioned faucets and soap holder, and the stone jars and other kitchen paraphernalia serve to enhance the style of the period.*

1 *This heavy, rough-stone sink, which needed to be supported on brick, stone or concrete piers, is of a type that would have been in general use in America during the 1820s. The sink is huge and shallow and has only very basic drainage. The large hand pump, sitting on what would now be employed as a draining board, was a great improvement on fetching water in a bucket from a well in the kitchen's yard.*

3 *This type of long, shallow, Victorian-style ceramic sink is usually known as a gamekeeper's sink for the obvious reason that it was roomy enough to deal with the cleaning of his catch. Its weight requires solid support, as here, where it is held up on brick piers. The front edge of the sink is embellished with a central roundel that is flanked with fluted mouldings. It is fed by a pair of hot-and-cold pillar taps. When such a sink is used in a modern, albeit period-style, kitchen, it has the advantage of being able to accommodate large pots and pans.*

4 *This reproduction Victorian Belfast sink has been installed on an attractive country-style pine base, leaving enough space underneath to display decorative cooking pots. It would be suitable in an informal kitchen that has free-standing mix-and-match units.*

5 *A huge "pot" sink is supported in the traditional manner on sculpted plaster piers, which give it presence, and provide a convenient storage cubbyhole beneath. The draining boards on either side of the sink have a sensible slope and overhang.*

6 *Traditional materials and modern convenience are brought together in the design of this space-saving ceramic sink, with its built-in Iroko-wood drainer and polished-chrome swan's-neck mixer taps.*

7 *This unusual double-"pot" sink, with its wall-mounted taps, would originally have been installed on plaster piers in the scullery, where all the washing-up was done. Here it takes pride of place set in the middle of simple yellow-painted cupboards with a cutaway front.*

8 *Set within a cutaway cupboard unit with wrought-iron hinges and handles, this butler's sink has brass swan's-neck mixer taps, which make an elegant contribution to the country style and period detailing.*

9 *This plain modern double-sink is housed in a wooden unit with rectilinear mouldings. The period-style taps and the plate rack above give it a more old-fashioned look. The sinks are flanked by teak drainers – teak being the most resilient wood for the purpose.*

155

TAPS

The majority of early sinks did not have taps; instead, water for washing dishes, utensils, and pots and pans was brought in from wells outdoors. The few taps in existence were primitive, and made of wood or metal, although in grander houses pumps brought in water to feed the sinks. In the mid-19th century, with the great improvement in the supply of water, taps became more common. From the Victorian era to the 1920s, X-head and capstain pillar taps were most frequently used, and these were usually wall-mounted in pairs. Mixer taps first appeared during the Victorian period, some with "quick-turn" lever handles.

1 This reproduction chrome tap with an X-head handle dates to the Victorian era, and is intended to be mounted on the rim of the sink.

2 A wall-mounted tap such as this chunky chrome copy of a mid-19th-century style is suitable where there is no available connecting hole in a sink.

3 This brass pillar mixer taps has porcelain handles and are a handsome choice for a period sink. This example has a swan's neck, which is a traditional style that has been employed since the 1850s. The high neck allows large pots to be cleaned or filled easily, and the lever handles can be pushed off with an elbow when both hands are occupied.

4 This elegant, polished-brass pillar mixer tap has a swan's neck, capstain handles, and traditional "hot"-and-"cold" tops.

5 Here, a brass mixer tap with a swivel nozzle has X-head handles for easy operation. It is is made to suit a period sink with a single outlet.

6 This unobtrusive wall-mounted flat-chrome mixer tap, with lever handles, goes well with the rustic decorative effect of pique-aisette ("crackle") tiles and granite sink surround.

7 Of classic American design, this wall-mounted mixer tap is especially suitable for older sinks that cannot use modern fittings.

8 Similar to 7, this tap has an upstanding mixer spout in chrome. Brushed or polished nickel and brass are alternative finishes.

WORKTOPS

Until the 19th century, kitchen furniture and work surfaces were kept to a minimum. As the century progressed, however, cooking methods became more elaborate, and there was a greater awareness of hygiene, resulting in the need for a variety of different types of working surfaces. The kitchen's mainstay was the central work table, usually made of pine, and standing quite low to aid kneading bread and pastry dough. The processing of dairy produce required an ultracool environment and, in the largest houses, marble, or even alabaster, were the favoured surfaces. Shelves would sometimes be made of slate with a marble trim; in modest households, stone would be used. The late-19th-century wet larder housed all the food not kept in the housekeeper's dry storeroom – meat, vegetables, bread, cheese and fruit. Shelves were made of slate and marble several inches thick, and embedded deep in the walls. Fish and vegetables, covered in muslin, would be laid on these cool slabs. Meat would be chopped on a strong wooden dresser, and there would be stone troughs for salting. The pastry area or room had marble slabs for kneading and rolling out dough.

1 This well-worn butcher's block mounted on a purpose-built console is an excellent work surface, and it also provides a warmly patinated quality that matches the decor of this kitchen. Butchers' blocks are traditionally made from maple or beech, and cut across the grain to ensure even wearing and minimize warping although, for decorative effect, the wear and tear is part of their charm.

2 Here, oak covers both the sink area and the dresser counter, and allows sufficient working space for the cook. The honeyed colour of this traditional wood gives this kitchen a special glow.

3 An unusual and attractive worktop can be made from ceramic or quarry tiles, providing a cool surface on which to work, and having the added bonus of being easy to clean. The tiles are edged with a wooden girdle for support. Their rustic quality and colour are well-suited to the kitchen's earthy tones and textures. The central table, as in traditional kitchens, is used to prepare food, but also for dining.

4 In this imaginative kitchen, a piece of marble has been cut to fit an old Gothic-style cupboard, and is used for preparing dough.

5 Oak and marble worktops make naturally good-looking partners in this period-style kitchen, and are a practical combination for food preparation. In this kitchen they take the place of the central work table.

RANGES, HOBS AND OVENS

The cooking stove has always represented the biggest single investment in the kitchen, and has certainly been the most exploited item in search of the perfect culinary performance. A *c.*1869 article in *American Woman's Home* enthusiastically describes a multipurpose cooking range that kept 17 gallons of water heated at all times, baked pies and puddings in a warm oven, heated flat irons under the one cover, boiled a kettle and a pot under another cover, baked bread in the oven, and cooked a turkey in the tin roaster, as well as providing a heated flat surface for cooking in pans. Although the cooking skills and implements improved in the Victorian era, the rudimentary design of the kitchen, with its massive black cast-iron range and basic furniture arranged to a rigid formula, remained little changed until the social modernization of the early 20th century. The builder's merchant was a great influence on commerce and fashion during the Victorian period, selling anything from pans to cooking ranges, illustrated in splendid catalogues, to the burgeoning building industry. The greatest influence on the development of the cooking range was the introduction of the "closed" range which, as the name suggests, had an enclosed fire grate, and was used in one form or another until the 1920s.

1 *Even in its most basic form, the solid-fuel range has a retrospective charm given the right setting. This early 20th-century English example is made of black-leaded cast iron, and has a single-domed hotplate. Its predecessor was invented by Count Rumford, who designed ranges with flues and a heavily insulated stove system. The idea of the "social kitchen" is a relatively recent one, and a traditional oven can help to enhance the room's place at the heart of family life.*

1

2

2 *In contrast to the utilitarian style of its 20th-century descendant, this majestic late-19th-century American cast-iron range has a more ornamented finish than its British counter-parts, and is typical of the Beaux Arts era. The American kitchen was generally less segregated from the living areas of the home than in Europe, and therefore warranted more embellishment.*

3

3 *This impressive modern version of the traditional range makes a design statement in its own right. Influenced by the early 20th-century concept of an island unit combined with the high-tech of professional ranges, this brass-and-enamel cooker has been set in the centre of the kitchen, taking the place of the traditional Victorian work table.*

4

4 *The Aga, which is synonymous with the traditional British country kitchen, was designed in the early 1920s by the Swedish scientist Gustav Dalen, and was first marketed in Britain in the 1930s in its solid-fuel form. Today, it can be run on oil, gas or electricity, and comes in different sizes and colours. Here it makes an appropriate choice for a period-style country kitchen.*

5 *This dark blue Aga is framed by ceramic and slate tiles, bricks, and limed wood. Agas have been adapted world-wide to suit many different domestic environments, and have been used not only in a romanticized rural setting, but also in the refined high-tech urban home. Their imposing and serviceable good looks make them perfect partners to a variety of kitchen materials and styles.*

6 *This 1920s' free-standing, vitreous-enamelled American gas cooker incorporates a large and a small oven, both thermostatically controlled, a four-ring hob, an overhead pot rack and a built-in splashback. Generally, the United States was well in advance of Britain in its kitchen-equipment designs, and their gas stoves had become more streamlined by this period. This example, however, has the gray finish and charmingly old-fashioned cabriole legs of earlier models. Similar cookers can still be found and adapted by experts to using modern gases, as is the case with this model, which has been professionally restored to its original condition.*

7 *Of an American utilitarian design, this old-fashioned and compact gas oven is in a galley kitchen in California. It has chrome-plated finishing detail and curved edges and corners.*

8 *The coming of the electrically ignited gas oven was a great advance in convenience and safety, and the introduction of a combined gas and electric range was the best of both worlds. The lean and clean lines of this example are reminiscent of earlier ovens.*

9 *The newest type of ovens very cleverly combine a deceptively old-fashioned body with a high-tech approach to cooking. This example is finished to look like black leading, and has a neo-classical in profile brass bar with finials, an arch-front door, and tap-style knobs. At the same time it offers forced-air cooking, variable grilling, a removable door and an integral cooling fan.*

10 *This heavy-duty version of 7 is similarly enamelled and has chrome door handles. Ename'ling came into widespread use in the early 20th century. The stove also has a four-ring cook top, twin ovens, and grill.*

KITCHEN ACCESSORIES

In Britain and America, the greatest development in kitchen equipment came after the mid-19th century, when the enclosed cooking range inspired more sophisticated cooking techniques. One of the first commercial fairs – the 1851 Great Exhibition in London – galvanized huge interest, resulting in the mass production of every kind of kitchen accessory. Until this period, cookware was made from cast iron, superseded by steel and aluminium, and, after 1840, enamelware or graniteware. Expensive copper pans lost popularity by the 1900s. In remote areas of Britain and America, traditional bakestones and griddles were used well into the 20th century, while the Pennsylvania Dutch fashioned decorative trivets, ornate tin workware, and carved hardwood spoons. Storage items included lockable tea caddies, earthenware or wooden salt holders, Victorian wirework egg baskets, American stencilled flour tins, plate and utensil racks, spice boxes, and more.

2 *The wall-mounted plate rack came into use in the late 18th century and has been employed ever since. It is practical to have the rack near the sink to dry and safely store crockery in constant use, while keeping the draining board uncluttered. It is also a decorative way of displaying a collection of plates. Usually found in pine, plate racks also look attractive when painted to harmonize with the kitchen style.*

1 *By the late-Victorian period, the batterie de cuisine had become extensive due to the elaborate cooking and presentation methods. Here, an eclectic collection of copper and brass equipment is hung decoratively from a rack over the kitchen table, an idea adopted from late-19th-century professional kitchens, where racks hung from hooks on a frame above the cooking range.*

3 *The Victorian kitchen usually had only open shelves and hanging racks around its walls, so that all the pots, pans and other cooking equipment were easily to hand. The same idea can be used today with a more decorative intention. The unpainted wooden rack shown here is crammed with brown-and-cream pottery storage jars and other colourful china.*

4 *A traditional pine display board, hung up against a background of old blue-and-white tiles, is the rustic version of an overhead hanging rack. Here, dried herbs and flowers, scissors, copper pans, sieves and graters are simply hooked onto nails hammered into a pine board that has a carved top.*

5 This 1920s' utensil rack, which also has a drip tray, would have held a set of three utensils. Earlier versions of the 1850s were made in wrought iron, then enamelled, and later, like this one, in stamped sheet aluminium. This example has echoes of Art Nouveau in its embossed design.

6 This food safe kept cheese, butter and bacon safe from vermin. Earlier meat safes were hung from the ceiling in a cool, well-aired place. Made in inexpensive softwood, this one would have been sold unpainted, and then painted at home.

7 On the right is a French c.1900 soda box, which held soda washing crystals. On the left is an allumette (match) container of the same period, which would usually have a striking strip on the top. Even such utilitarian objects have been finished with stamped decoration and bright enamelling.

8 Containers for precious spices were first made in the 17th century. As with this example, they were often in the form of small wooden cabinets with drawers, or a small chest-of-drawers, which stood on a table or were hung on the wall.

9 This Dutch spice container is of a type produced from the mid-19th century onward. With its naïve-painted decoration and unusual combination of spices, it may well have been made in a Dutch colony.

10 Beeswax candles have always been expensive items, and were often kept safe from damage by storing them in a sturdy wooden box hung in a convenient place. This 19th-century example has been converted to hold a roll of kitchen paper.

161

$\mathcal{L}$IGHTING

These days, we take our constant, clean and user-friendly electric light for granted. In comparison, the beeswax candle has historically been a luxury beyond the means of common man. Animal-fat tallow candles, oil or pitch, or rushes dipped in sheep fat sufficed during the 16th century. In the 17th century, ornate candelabra and chandeliers in brass, gilded wood and wrought iron, silver candlestands, and sconces on the wall were only for the wealthy.

In the Georgian period, lighting indicated status and wealth: grand reception rooms had low-hung chandeliers of wood, metal or glass, with three or more pairs of curved arms. Oil lamps – often whale oil in America – were confined to hallways and outdoors. Modest American houses were lit by rush lamps or Betty lamps that burned oil, lard or tallow. However, even these utilitarian items were sometimes touched by the elegant classicism of the period.

Progress in lighting was achieved by the invention, in 1784, of a colza (rapeseed) oil lamp by Aimé Argand, a Swiss physicist. The ventilated reservoir, wick cylinder and glass chimney produced a light ten times brighter than previous oil lamps, with no smoke. This lamp underwent many improvements after 1800, including a hanging-light version. Candlelight still remained the dominant lighting method, with the finest glass chandeliers being imported to America from Britain and France, neo-classical silver candelabra, and sconces with reflecting plates and *girandole* brackets either side of many grand chimney pieces. Lanterns for inside and out copied the delicate lines and ornamentation of the late-Georgian period. Paraffin's availability from the mid-19th century improved cleanliness and odour.

In Britain, Sir John Soane and Sir Walter Scott were among the first to install domestic piped gas in 1823–4, and it was generally available by the 1850s. The first gas lights – often large, clumsy creations – threw a savage light, much criticized for dulling diamonds, making complexions look sickly, and fading colours. Coloured-glass shades softened the light, and, by the 1830s, pulley systems and telescopic feeding mechanisms allowed easier access and positioning. The Victorians favoured many sources and styles of lighting in one room, and happily combined candle, paraffin, gas and, when available, electric light. The chandelier (*see* left) epitomizes the exuberantly elaborate fashion of the late 19th century, with its gilding and deeply fringed shades.

Although the American Thomas Edison had invented the incandescent electric light bulb in 1879, electricity was not generally domestically available until well into the 20th century. Early electric carbon filaments emitted a harsh, inefficient light that needed a shade to soften it: these were first made in copper and brass, and then in etched glass to diffuse the light, and pleated silk for shading. With improvements in filaments, flower- and flame-shaped bulbs were used without shades.

Louis Comfort Tiffany produced his first sensational stained-glass shades in 1895, with the intention of bringing "harmonized decoration" to the masses. Other Art Nouveau options included metal pendant fixings in sinuous imitation of plants, and pewter or copper sconces. Gas and electric light should have given creative scope, but designs were usually based on earlier gas lights or period styles such as Georgian candelabra or 17th-century lanterns, hall lanterns in the vernacular style of black metal with small panes of glass, and Georgian Revival sconces and glass bowl lights hung from chains for reception rooms. Dining did not require dazzling illumination, so pink-shaded wall lights and silver candlesticks with silk shades and beaded fringes were in vogue. From this period, light fittings acquired their own character. American fashion adopted many revivalist styles, promoting wrought- iron, wheel-like chandeliers, Georgian glass, Queen Anne brass or ornate branched chandeliers and Italian Renaissance bronze or gilded-metal chandeliers.

The early 20th century initiated a simplification and stylization of lines into clean-cut shapes, and this produced glass wall sconces in fan or shell shapes, vellum and parchment fixtures, and globe ceiling lights in chrome and glass.

CENTRAL LIGHTS

Providing a safe, long-lasting source of light in the communal areas of a house has always been an important consideration. When candles were the only lighting source, this was an impossibility, and so the introduction of oil lamps in the 1780s was a welcome innovation – even if the earlier types were inefficient, smelly and dirty. During the 19th century, candles and oil lights continued to be most commonly used, but toward the middle of the century new types of burners – using paraffin – and more efficient wicks and lamp chimneys were introduced. By the end of the century, gas "chandeliers" with glass-bowl diffusers were in common use, and these were made more convenient by their "rise-and-fall" mechanisms. The advent of electricity not only changed people's lives dramatically, but it also inspired designers to create new light fittings, which changed the way light was diffused, casting it downward where it was needed. Generally electric light was employed only in the communal areas, as early bulbs gave little more light than gas.

3

4

5

1 In the hallway of Lars Sjoberg's renovated c.1770 Swedish country house, this glass-and-metal candle-lamp hangs from the wooden ceiling. It is appropriate to the period and the situation of this rustic house, which retains many of the original features and decorations.

2 Oil lamps have been in general use since the middle of the Georgian period. They came in all shapes and guises, but the hanging light in this German house is typical of a continental design. The interior of the shade is white in order to reflect as much light downward as possible.

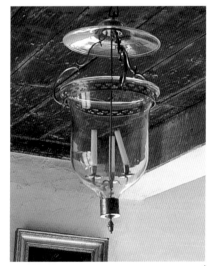

1

2

3 Of a classical rectilinear shape, this hanging lamp is in a small studio apartment in Greenwich Village, New York, that has been decorated in American Empire style.

4 The dining-room table of Thomas Calloway's mid-19th-century Los Angeles house, renovated in the Spanish Colonial style of Mexico, is lit by a simple paraffin hanging lamp of a type that was used through-out modest American homes of this period.

5 This paraffin lamp adds a touch of period authenticity to a recently refurbished French cottage. It is made of brass and opaque glass.

6

7

6 Here, a late-19th-century hanging globe is used in an American house of that period. It illustrates the Tiffany style of lamp, with a richly coloured leaded-glass shade, suspended by a chain.

7 The Edwardians favoured pendant lights with an opaque glass bowl and bronze chain and detailing, hung from a central ceiling rose. This reproduction has an acrylic diffuser and "antiqued" bronze trim.

8 This is a more ornate version of the pendant light shown in 7. The sinuously shaped opaque diffuser was designed to add extra illumination. This type of design would have been suitable for lighting the common parts of a house – the hallway or landing, for example.

9 Of the Art Nouveau period, this highly decorative light has geometric leaded stained glass, and is appropriate for lighting a dining-room table. Such lamps were known as "rise-and-fall" lights as they came with a pulley-and-weight mechanism for altering the height, making the manipulation of lighting much easier. This particular example does not have this mechanism, and hence it is hung low over the table.

10 This modern electrified version of a Victorian candle-lamp has a spring-clip holding mechanism attaching the shade. The etched, translucent "storm glass" allows the light to be moved safely from place to place around the house.

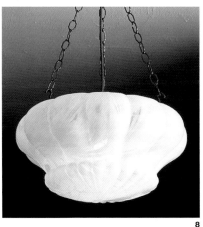

8

9

10

11

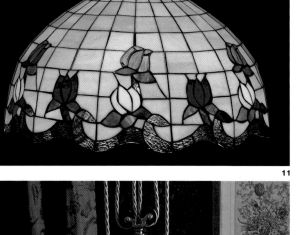

12

11 Tiffany shades were first sold in 1895, and were immediately fashionable. This fine copy of an original pendant light has hand-cut opalescent glass, held in place with copper foil and lead solder.

12 This reproduction of a "rise-and-fall" light has "antiqued" gold flex and rich red-silk pleated shades. It is suitable for use over a desk or table, where direct light is only occasionally required.

13

14

15

13 The introduction of electricity resulted in the production of a vast range of bulb-holding designs which could enclose the light bulb. This reproduction of a torchère "flame" is of the Edwardian period.

14 During the 1920s, lights were often hung from a decorative ceiling plate of brass, copper or silvered finish. Diffusers sometimes had tinted or marbled glass. This copy has an attractive cut-glass, acorn-shaped bulb holder.

15 The brass bobbin on this Edwardian reproduction contains the weight to counter-balance the rise and fall of the "coolie-hat" shade. This is a typical desk light of the period. Lamps over dining-room tables and desks often had many-branched, counterweighted lights.

CHANDELIERS

Chandeliers (from the French word for candleholder and the Latin *candelabrum*) have been a glorious expression of extravagance and exquisite craftsmanship throughout the centuries. They continue to maintain their appeal in today's interiors, working well as a foil where modern and antique styles meet. In the 17th and 18th centuries, chandeliers were made from carved and gilded wood, brass and wrought iron, and the grandest from rock crystal. Their use and ornate design demonstrated the owner's social and financial status, but they were usually only used on formal occasions – beeswax candles, their source of lighting, being a luxury. Certain types of chandelier have long enjoyed favour: the simplest swan's-neck metal form looks perfect in a Tudor, Edwardian vernacular or modern interior, for example. Candles have always remained the most appropriate means of lighting a crystal chandelier, but modern electric candle-bulbs have ensured that antique chandeliers have maintained their purpose in today's environment. Apart from a practical use, the chandelier can become a decorative device in its own right – a uniting visual focus, able to fill out an awkwardly barren vacuum in the middle of a tall room.

1

1 *This reproduction of a simple but elegant chandelier is of a type that is usually found in grand Tudor houses. The design of its metal body is so fashioned to reflect as much candle-light as possible.*

2 *With its branched candles and reflecting globe, this chandelier would fit equally well in a 17th-century hallway or a 20th-century formal dining room. Copies are available in different materials, including wood and brass. It is a good idea to disguise the chain with a casing – silk hangs best.*

3 *In the 18th century, chandeliers would only have been hung in the principal room and used on grand occasions. This magnificent French crystal chandelier hangs in the Swedish Room of the Château de Morsan, which was built c.1765 in Normandy, France, as a maison de plaisance or summerhouse.*

4 *The decorator Frédéric Méchiche makes an extravagant statement in his Paris residence by placing two 18th-century chandeliers side-by-side. The Directoire style to which they belong is characterized by neo-classical manner and detailing.*

2   3   4

5 *An Italian chandelier with characteristic "spun" branches illuminates a London dining room decorated in a Tuscan-inspired style. Such a fine piece becomes a decorative object in its own right – there is no need even to light the candles.*

6 *This classic design, with two tiers of branches, has been used since the Baroque period of the mid-17th century. However, the addition of electric candle-flame bulbs makes it much more convenient to use.*

7 *Although this chandelier has the same proportions as 6, it is from the American Victorian period, and has the characteristic loose-beaded "necklace" and inverted "crown" of glass drops.*

8 *This magnificent chandelier, which has more decorative glass than candlepower, graces the sumptuous Music Room of Richard Jenrette's American Empire-style house on the Hudson River, in New York State.*

9 *In contrast to the fixed glass chandeliers of earlier periods, this late-19th-century light has a complex system of weights and pulleys and a telescopic stem to give it versatility.*

5

8

10

6

10 *The High Victorian style of the Calhoun Mansion, in Charleston, South Carolina, is evident in the use of rich drapery, gilding and ornamentation. A pair of gas-converted chandeliers completes the room's decor..*

11 *English lead glass was considered most desirable for use in chandeliers. This elegant candlelit example, with its chains of glass beads, takes on a decorative role in a Rococo Revival-style drawing room.*

7

9

11

167

WALL LIGHTS

Wall lights have historically played an important part in illuminating interiors, and the mellow light projected from the sides of a room greatly enhances its ambience. Baroque sconces had reflective brackets to maximize precious candle-power – silver for the wealthiest only, but more usually brass and, later, mirror-glass. The *girandole* wall and mirror lights in Georgian houses complemented the sophisticated interior decor of the 18th century. Oil and then gas lights came in an abundance of different designs, and were sold through catalogues, but when electricity reached the masses, the designs remained broadly static until the 1920s.

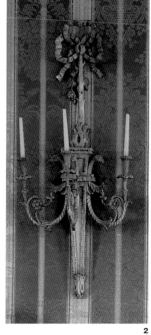

1 *The electrified torchère takes its design from the Greek flaming symbol of life. Using this type of classical reference was popular during the second decade of the 19th century.*

2 *This is a pretty example of a carved wooden French wall light with candles. It is of a type of design and lighting method that integrates extremely well with the Empire style of the room.*

3 *Fashioned like a miniature ceiling-hung chandelier, this side light has a fountain of glass drops on its central shaft and two slender candleholders.*

4 *Here is an example of an electrified Rococo-style sconce, carved from wood. The grandest house-holds would have had silver sconces to reflect the precious candlelight.*

5 *The early Georgian period saw the use of wall lights in brass, silver, and gilded or silvered wood in grander houses, and pewter or tin in poorer homes. This modernized brass version has two sets of elegant candle-flame bulbs, although three or more sets could be used.*

6 *The Edwardians preferred their electric lights to imitate earlier styles of candle lights. Pairs of wall brackets were a popular choice for selected rooms in the house, such as reception rooms and libraries. The invention of the fabric (as opposed to glass) shade helped to soften the light.*

7 *This "antique" satin-brass sconce, with its urn-shaped body and beading, echoes the dignified style of an Adam candle light, but it has been modernized with the use of fabric shades and electricity.*

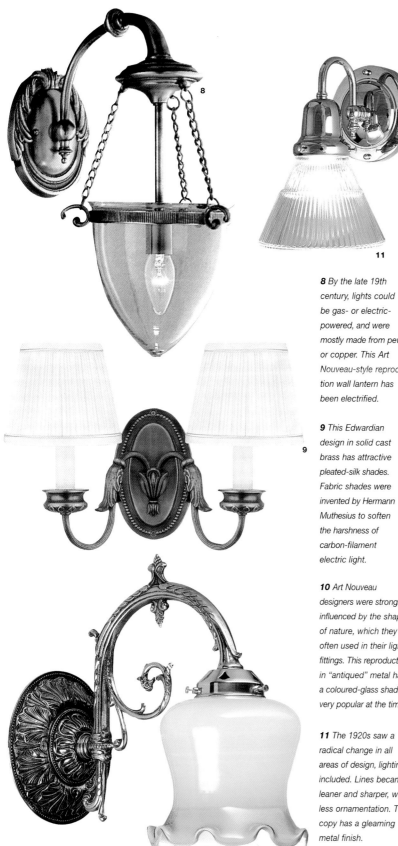

8

11

12

8 By the late 19th century, lights could be gas- or electric-powered, and were mostly made from pewter or copper. This Art Nouveau-style reproduction wall lantern has been electrified.

9 This Edwardian design in solid cast brass has attractive pleated-silk shades. Fabric shades were invented by Hermann Muthesius to soften the harshness of carbon-filament electric light.

10 Art Nouveau designers were strongly influenced by the shapes of nature, which they often used in their light fittings. This reproduction in "antiqued" metal has a coloured-glass shade – very popular at the time.

11 The 1920s saw a radical change in all areas of design, lighting included. Lines became leaner and sharper, with less ornamentation. This copy has a gleaming metal finish.

9

10

13

14

15

12 A feature of Victorian and Edwardian interiors was to use a pair of lights mounted as part of the overmantel mirror. These were often hinged for convenience, and they were easily converted from gas to electricity.

13 Uplighters give a pleasantly atmospheric glow to a room. This Art Deco-style wall light, which is encased in opaque glass, subtly diffuses the light up toward the ceiling.

14 Chrome swan's-neck globe wall lights were particularly popular in the 1930s. They are seen here flanking a bathroom mirror.

15 Picture lights, like this early 20th-century example, revolutionized the perception of the subtleties of detail and colour in paintings as never before.

169

TABLE LAMPS

Before the invention of the portable lamp, whether used in in oil or paraffin, ighting had limited effectiveness and practicality, as it was circumscribed by candlepower. The invention of the relatively efficient Argand (or colza) oil lamp by Aimé Argand in Geneva, Switzerland, in 1784, allowed those who were better off to gather around a well-lit large circular table as part of the evening's social entertainment. Safe, portable light was a huge step forward, despite the smell, dirt, unreliability and inconvenience of some lighting methods. In 1879, Thomas Edison invented the incandescent filament bulb – changing domestic lighting forever. Tiffany first produced electrified (geometric, leaded) table lamps in 1905, a time when electricity was not yet widespread. By 1920 in America, but later in Britain, electric lamps became much more common, and revolutionized the way people decorated their houses. This was because the lamps changed the way colours were perceived, defined the proportions and details of a room by illuminating every corner, and threw light in a directional path to create the *mise en scène*.

1

2

3

4

5

1 Of a type used in mid-19th-century America and Europe, this paraffin table lamp has a classic design. The glass flue and shade allowed portability and increased safety.

2 The Victorians were particularly fond of the ornate in the furnishings of their houses, as shown in this 19th-century candelabrum. It is truly a work of unabashed decoration, with its bronze stag and its "stalactite" glass pendants.

3 Unlike the Victorians, the Edwardians were much more traditional in design terms, preferring their lights to imitate the chandeliers and candlesticks of earlier years. The bronze Rococo-style base shown here is well matched by the muted tone of its pleated shade.

4 A vase, ginger storage jar or other china vessel can be used for the base of a table lamp. The pleated-silk shade is suitably formal for such an impressive example.

5 The animal theme of this 20th-century-vase-like lamp was inspired by the 18th-century Chinese blue-and-white export porcelain.

6 Bernd Goeckler's New York apartment is decorated and furnished in neo-classical style, to which this slender and elegant brass-column table lamp is most appropriate.

7 This original c.1880 electric table lamp has a bronze base and a shade made of glass with bronze mounts. It exemplifies the favoured design of an early electric lamp.

8 Here, an adapted French 19th-century vase lamp of ornate design perfectly suits the sumptuous colours and textures of its situation in the room.

9 Tiffany created a type of lighting that blended with the American and British Art Nouveau fashions of the late 19th century, although this lamp would suit Arts and Crafts and Gothic houses. Its bright green and golden-yellow geometric leaded-glass shade gives it a unique luminosity that greatly contributes to the atmosphere of the room.

10 The style of this reproduction 1920s' table lamp was influenced by the design principles of the American architect and designer Frank Lloyd Wright, who adopted geometric, clean-cut outlines.

6

8

10

7

9

CANDLES

This small sample of candlestick designs illustrates the candle's potential for decorative and aesthetic value. Historically, beeswax was always prohibitively expensive and, except for grand occasions, houses were illuminated with malodorous tallow candles. Despite all the advances in lighting, candles have remained in constant domestic use, being universally available, adaptable and decorative. For today's interiors, candlelight makes an inimitable contribution to providing a convivial and romantic atmosphere.

11

171

STANDARD LAMPS

Evolved from candlestands in the late 19th century, the standard lamp created a
new way of lighting a room, as it allowed a concentration of light to be focused
on a person or an object from an intermediate (and sometimes variable) height.
In addition, the standard lamp also had a profound effect on the balancing of light
at all levels in a room, and could therefore be teamed with overhead lights, wall
lights and table lamps to produce different lighting effects. Another advantage of the
standard lamp was that its slender dimensions do not occupy a great deal of space,
and thus it could be moved around without upsetting the distribution of furniture
or ornaments in a room. Decoratively, standard lamps are limited by the requirements
of proportion – a stable base, long "stem" and a capping shade. However, there
are certain designs that lend themselves to the lamps being placed as purely
ornamental features, given the right, uncluttered setting, such as in a hallway.

1

2

1 A stabilizing tripod
allowed illumination at
a higher level for the
lofty living hall of the
medieval dwelling.

2 Medieval candles
made of soft suet wax
were fixed on metal-
spiked cups. Instability
and mess meant that
a sand base was a
wise precaution.

3 A neo-classical
torchère-style bronze
lamp makes a fine and
practical companion
for a French tapestry-
covered chair.

3

4

5

6

7

8

4 This modern lamp
suits period or modern
interiors. Gold-leaf
finishing complements
the neat silk shade.

5 A minimalist lamp
in distressed bronze
echoes a French style
popular in the early
years of the 19th century.

6 Inspired by the
elegant lines of French
Empire style, this modern
lamp has brass casting
and an acrylic bowl.

7 This reproduction
standard lamp makes
an interesting feature in
a room with the strong
attenuated lines of its
"Etruscan" inspiration.

8 The ebonized wood
and classic gold-leaf
motifs and detailing
of the French Empire
period come together
in this dignified design.

LIGHT SWITCHES

Throughout history, lighting methods have involved the inconvenience of lighting and extinguishing each individual source separately. Not only was this time-consuming and frustrating, but it could also be highly dangerous as the fire risk of leaving a candle or lamp lit was obviously a threat. When Thomas Edison invented the incandescent electric light bulb in 1879, he presented the world with the precursor of modern sophisticated electric circuitry, which resulted in an immediacy and control of lighting that had not been previously experienced. To throw a switch and flood the room with light from different sources must have been a thrilling novelty indeed. As was expected after the proliferation of styles of lights and lamps over the years, design considerations have now even found their way into the utilitarian light switch. This is illustrated by the diversity of today's reproductions, which range from from wood to brass, and are in styles that are reminiscent of many different periods. Thus the humble light switch can be regarded as a design feature in itself and add to period authenticity.

1–4 These authentically reproduced "dolly" light switches re-create the period detail that adds character to today's renovated interiors. (1) A four-switch brass-and-mahogany combination. (2) A plain and simple brass switch. (3) An elegant fluted-dome switch. (4) A classic indented brass switch.

5 Manufacturers of reproduction switches have gone to a great deal of trouble to re-create period styling. This wooden plate has been hand-polished to enhance the natural figuring of the wood.

6 The sophistication of modern technology is combined with a period look in this discreet dimmer switch.

7–15 In many restored period homes, the decorations may be eclectic, which means that it is not always necessary to be a slave to authenticity. In fact, the adaptable style (and materials) of modern switch plates often makes such considerations irrelevant.

16-17 Two important considerations for choosing a switch are how suitable the plate material is to the interior style of the room, and how many lights it will need to supply. The switch on the left has neo-classical rope moulding, and is suitable for Georgian, Colonial and Federal interiors; the one on the right is plain, and appropriate for Georgian and minimalist interiors.

18-21 Push-button and dimmer switches are a modern convenience that greatly enhance the versatility of lighting effects.

22 The ubiquitous pull switch found in British bathrooms is here given added grace by using a decorative chrome ceiling attachment.

23-24 These "invisible" Perspex wall switches are invaluable when the decorative rhythm of wallpaper needs to be uninterrupted.

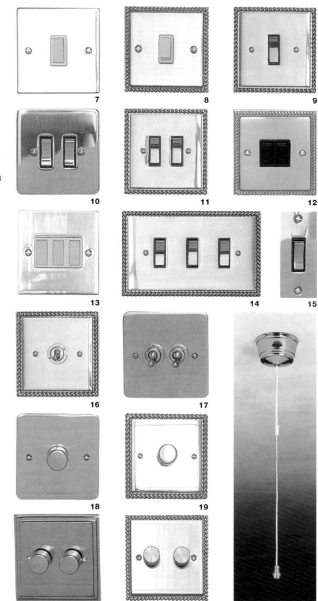

173

DIRECTORY

Photographs used in the book are credited at the end of the directory entries. The pages on which photographs appear are in brackets followed by the photograph number.

DOORS

Andy Thornton Architectural Antiques Ltd
Ainleys Industrial Estate
Elland
West Yorkshire
HX5 9PJ
TEL: 01422 375595
FAX: 01422 377455
E-MAIL:
ATAA@BTInternet.com

Restorers of original period furniture, architectural features and fittings and manufacturers of reproduction pieces. Doors, mantels, decorative ceiling and floor tiles, fretwork, balustrades and lighting, including Tiffany domes and pendant lights. Also decorative railings, gates and brass fittings and hand-carved copies of original wood columns, capitals, corbels and pediments.
(pp.60-1, 7; p.102, box; pp.104-5, box; pp.164-5, 11; pp.168-9, 10)

Architectural Components Ltd
4-8 Exhibition Road
London
SW7 2HF
TEL: (0171) 584 6800
FAX: (0171) 589 4928

Specialist suppliers of period door furniture, including locks, latches, security devices and handles. Also a wide range of cabinet and window fittings, ventilator and radiator grilles, electric switch and socket plates.

A Touch of Brass
210 Fulham Road
London
SW10 9PJ
TEL: (0171) 351 2255
OR: (0171) 352 5495

Suppliers of high-quality brass products, with a large range of interior and exterior door furniture to suit traditional and contemporary styles from the 16th century onward. Other finishes include chrome, black iron, bronze and verdigris. Also stock bathroom accessories, locks, curtain and electrical fittings.

Baileys Home and Garden
The Engine Shed
Station Approach
Ross-on-Wye
Herefordshire
HR9 7BW
TEL: (01989) 563015
FAX: (01989) 768172

Stockists of an extensive range of antique- and traditional-style fixtures and fittings, in brass and cast iron, including brackets, doorknobs and light fittings. Also stock tiles and fireplaces.
(pp.48-9, 8; pp. 154-5, 4)

J. D. Beardmore & Co. Ltd
17 Pall Mall
London
SW1Y 5LU
TEL: (0171) 670 1000
FAX: (0171) 670 1010

Manufacturers and suppliers of traditional hand-made ornamental brassware for doors, windows and cabinets. Supply a large range of reproduction pieces from the medieval through Elizabethan, Georgian and Regency periods to Art Deco.
(pp.48-9, 3, 4, 15, 16)

The Brass Knob
2311 18th Street NW
Washington DC 20009
USA
TEL: (202) 332 3370
FAX: (202) 332 5594
E-MAIL:
thebrassknob@juno.com
WEB SITE:
http://www.washington
post.com /YP/brassknob

Suppliers of architectural antiques, including chandeliers, sconces, mantels, fireplace accessories, tiles, ironwork and many other types of decorative architectural detail.

British Gates & Timber Ltd
Castleton's Oak Sawmills
Biddenden, Nr Ashford
Kent TN27 8DD
TEL: (01580) 291555
FAX: (01580) 292011

Makers of a range of traditional oak-ledged and boarded doors with original details and authentic hand finishes. Also supply other ranges of interior and exterior doors, frames and accessories.
(pp.56-7, 3; pp.64-5, 1)

Cinder Whit & Co.
SEE STAIRCASES
(P.180)

Comyn Ching (Sheffield) Ltd
7 Skylines Village
Limeharbour
London E14 9TS
TEL: (0171) 987 8787

Specialists in door furniture, locks, hinges, door closers and sliding door fixtures. Also supply a large range of black antique ironmongery.

County Hardwoods
Creech Mill
Mill Lane
Creech St Michael
Taunton
Somerset TA3 5PX
TEL: (01823) 443760
FAX: (01823) 443940

Manufacturers of made-to-measure traditional interior and exterior ledged and boarded doors and plank flooring in seasoned elm, oak and other hardwoods. Doors supplied either as ready to hang or in self-assembly kits.

Doverhay Forge Studios
Doverhay
Porlock
Minehead
Somerset TA24 8QB
TEL/FAX: (01643) 862444

Metalwork designs and wrought-iron railings, gates, street lights, staircases and domestic objects by award-winning blacksmith James Horrobin. His commissions include gates and railings for public buildings, such as the Victoria and Albert Museum and Canary Wharf.

The Fingerplate Company
1 Golygfa Dwyrain
Llandw
Cowbridge
Vale of Glamorgan
CF71 7NZ
TEL: (01656) 890691

Specialist manufacturers of quality reproduction fingerplates for period doors. Mainly handmade in brass or solid copper.

The Great Northern Architectural Antiques Co. Ltd
New Russia House
Chester Road
Tattenhall
Chester
CH3 9AH
TEL: (01829) 770796

Suppliers of period doors, fire surrounds, panelling, brassware, stained glass, spindles, newel posts, handrails and reclaimed timber. Also restoration of architectural woodwork.

Hallidays
The Old College
Dorchester-on-Thames
Wallingford
Oxfordshire
OX10 7HL
TEL: (01865)340028
FAX: (01865) 341149

Designers of period panelled rooms. Faithful reproduction door fittings of the Georgian and Regency periods by specialist craftsmen. Also specialize in wood-crafted Georgian and Regency mantelpieces and brass and cast-iron fireplace accessories.
(pp.58-9, 4)

Havenplan's Architectural Emporium
1 The Old Station
Station Road
Killamarsh
Sheffield
S31 8EN
TEL: (01742) 489972

Retailers of a full range of architectural items including staircases, doors, fire inserts and surrounds, cast-iron grates, railings and panelling.

Hendricks Woodworking
PO Box 139
Kempton
Pennsylvania 19529
USA
TEL: (610) 756 6187

Interior and exterior doors custom-made to period designs using traditional joinery techniques and made from solid woods. Radius woodwork for panelling, crown mouldings and arched doors is a speciality.
(pp.38-9, 9; pp.40-1, 9)

Heritage Oak Ltd
Unit V5
Dean Clough Industrial Park
Halifax
West Yorkshire
HX3 5AX
TEL/FAX: (01422) 348231

Restoration work carried out exclusively in English oak. Doors nailed and pegged, waxed and aged. Staircases reproduced from original patterns using traditional craft methods. Panelling and flooring as well as decorative panels, wainscots, screens and traditional and period-style floors.
(pp.36-7, 3; pp.84-5, 3, 9)

House of Brass
45-47 Milton Street
Nottingham
NG1 3EZ
TEL: (0115) 9475430

Specialists in classic hand-finished reproduction brassware. They also supply a wide range of door, window and cabinet furniture, electrical accessories, lighting, beds and headboards, locks and security devices, taps and mixers.
(pp.48-9, 5, 6, 10-14, 19-21; pp.64-5, 5, 6, 8, 9; pp.74-5, 1, 2, 4; p.173, 4, 7-21)

The House Hospital
9 Ferrier Street
Wandsworth
London SW18 15W
TEL: (0181) 870 8202

Specialists in second-hand period fireplaces, doors, basins, baths, WCs, cisterns, garden fencing and gates, brass door handles, brass taps and many other items of architectural salvage.

John Sambrook
Park House
Northiam
East Sussex
TN31 6PA
TEL: (01797) 252615

Specialist manufacturers of reproduction Georgian fanlights. Other products include reproduction Georgian metal skylights and bronze glazing bars for windows.
(pp.38-9, 2, 3; pp.40-1, 4, 5, 6)

Joseph Tipper (Hardware) Ltd
Century Works
Moat Street
Willenham
West Midlands WV13 1FZ
TEL: (01902) 608444
FAX: (01902) 608445

Manufacturers of wrought-iron door furniture reproduced to authentic historical designs. Includes knockers, pulls, knobs, letterplates, bolts and catches.

The London Architectural Salvage and Supply Co.
St Michael's Church
Mark Street
Shoreditch
London EC2A 4ER
TEL: (0171) 739 0448

Suppliers of a full range of quality interior and exterior materials, fixtures and fittings for the refurbishment and decoration of period buildings, including chimney pieces, panelling for rooms, fencing and gates, flooring, doors and joinery, flagstones and garden furniture.

Looking for Ages
East Hill
Parracombe
North Devon EX31 4PF
TEL/FAX: (01598) 763300

Suppliers of quality door fixtures and fittings, lighting, and other items for the period home. Sole manufacturers of traditional Domus doorbells consisting of brass bell, bell pull and wood plaque mount.
(pp.74-5, 1, 2, 4)

Nostalgic Warehouse Inc.
701 E. Kingsley Road
Garland
Texas 75041
USA
TEL: (972) 271 0319
FAX: (972) 271 9726
E-MAIL:
nostalgicw@aol.com

Suppliers of solid brass reproduction doorplates, hinges and knobs from the Victorian period through to Art Nouveau and Art Deco styles.
(pp.64-5, 7)

The Original Choice
1340 Stratford Road
Birmingham
B28 9EH
TEL: (0121) 778 3821

Suppliers of reproduction doors, tiles and antique fixtures, including Victorian and Edwardian stained-glass and leaded windows. Also specialize in antique fireplaces.

Robert Thompson's Craftsmen Ltd
Kilburn
York
YO6 4AH
TEL: (0870) 5666222

Manufacturers of individually crafted items in seasoned English oak, including doors, staircases and panelling.

Sabrina
Alma Street
Mountfields
Shrewsbury
Shropshire
SY3 8QL
TEL: (01743) 357977

Manufacturers of hand-crafted, traditional oak doors.

Samuel Heath & Sons Plc.
Cobden Works
Leopold Street
Birmingham
B12 0UJ
TEL: (0121) 772 2303
FAX: (0121) 772 3334
E-MAIL:
mail@samuel-heath.com

Manufacturers of marine brass-ware for doors, including knobs, handles, knockers, letterplates, bolts and sockets. And fasteners and fittings for windows.
(pp.64-5, box; pp.148-9, 2, 3, 11; pp.150-1, 7)

Solopark Ltd
The Old Railway Station
Station Road
Nr Pampisford
Cambridge
CB2 4HB
TEL: (01223) 834663

Suppliers of traditional building materials and other architectural items, including bricks, roofing tiles, slates, oak beams, staircases, window frames, panelling, mouldings, internal and external doors.

Verdigris Art Metalwork Restorers
Arch 290
Crown Street
London SE5 0UR
TEL: (0171) 7038373

Repairs, fine patinas, French gilding. Also metal colouring and lacquering. All carried out by experts on antique and modern metalwork in brass, bronze, copper and pewter.

The Victorian Ironmonger
The Old Garage
Fosseway
Brinklow
Rugby
Warwickshire CV23 0LN
TEL: (01788) 832292

Stockists of a range of original period house fittings, including fixtures for interior and exterior doors.

Winther Browne & Co. Ltd
Nobel Road
Eley Estate
Edmonton
London N18 3DX
TEL: (0181) 803 3434
FAX: (0181) 807 0544
E-MAIL:
sales@wintherbrowne.co.uk

Suppliers and manufacturers of fine wood features for the period home, including authentic-styled doors, staircases, beams, windows and mouldings. Pieces available in dark oak, light oak, gray or unstained finishes. Also supply aluminium screening panels and radiator cabinets.
(pp.104-5, 2, 8, 14; pp. 112-13, 12-15; pp.116-17, 9-15, 18-23)

Worthington
PO Box 868
Troy
Alabama 36081
USA
TEL: (1800) 872 1608
FAX: (334) 566 5390
WEB SITE:
http://www.architectural-details.com

Manufacturers of a wide range of quality decorative architectural features, including columns, capitals, mouldings, mantelpieces, cartouches, pediments and pilasters for interior and exterior decoration. Also provide technical advice.
(pp. 36-7, 5; pp.104-5, 5)

WINDOWS

Andy Thornton Architectural Antiques Ltd
SEE DOORS (P.174)

Architectural Heritage Ltd
Taddington Manor
Taddington
Nr Cutsdean
Cheltenham
Gloucestershire
GL54 5RY
TEL: (01386) 584414
FAX: (01386) 584236
E-MAIL:
puddy@architectural-heritage.co.uk
WEB SITE:
http://www.architectural-heritage.co.uk
SEE EXTERIORS
(P.186)

Arts & Crafts Period Textiles
5427 Telegraph Avenue W2
Oakland
California 94609
USA
TEL/FAX: (510) 654 1645

*Soft furnishings and textiles
from the studio of Dianne Ayres
using turn-of-the-century
techniques: hand embroidery,
appliqué and hand stencilling.
Pillows, table linens, curtains,
bedspreads and embroidery
kits available. Accepts
commissions.*

J. D. Beardmore & Co. Ltd
SEE DOORS
(P.175)

Bradley Collection Ltd
Lion Barn
Maitland Road
Needham Market
Suffolk
IP6 8NS
TEL: (01449) 722724
FAX: (01449) 722728
E-MAIL:
info@bradleycollection.co.uk
WEB SITE:
http://www.bradleycollection.
co.uk

*Designers of bespoke
curtain poles, finials and
accessories. Ranges in wood,
steel and resin, variously
made, finished and decorated
by hand. Also supply a range
of coordinating hold backs,
brackets, rings and hooks.
(pp.74-5, box)*

J. R. Burrows & Co.
PO Box 522
Rockland
Massachusetts 02370
USA
TEL: (781) 982 1812
FAX: (781) 982 1636
E-MAIL:
merchant@burrows.com
WEB SITE:
http://www.burrows.com

*Small company making
Victorian and Arts and
Crafts movement design lace
curtains in cotton/polyester mix.
Also hand-printed art
wallpaper.*

Copycats
The Workshop
29 Maypole Road
East Grinstead
West Sussex
RH19 3QN
TEL/FAX: (01342) 826066

*Master craftsman joiner John
Draper specializes in replica
replacements for original box
sash windows. Repair service
and exact copies of any style
window, single or double glazed.
(pp.70-1, 10)*

**The Cotswold Casement
Co. Ltd**
Fosse Way Industrial Estate
Stratford Road
Moreton-in-the-Marsh
Gloucestershire GL56 OHH
TEL: (01680) 650568

*Specialists in period-style
windows in steel and aluminium.
Also repairs and refurbishment.*

Crittal Windows Ltd
Springwood Drive
Braintree
Essex CM7 7YN
TEL: (01376) 324106
FAX: (01376) 349662
E-MAIL:
hq@critall-windows.co.uk
WEB SITE:
http://www.critall-windows.
co.uk

*Manufacturers of steel, UPVC
and aluminium windows and
doors. Steel windows in traditional Georgian styles with
hinged openings for the refurbishment of period buildings.
(pp.68-9, 10)*

Goddard & Gibbs Studios
41 Kingsland Road
Shoreditch
London
E2 8AD
TEL: (0171) 739 6563

*Installers of stained and
decorative glass, ranging from
windows, interior panels and
murals to domes and rooflights
using dalles-de-verre, acid
etching and sandblasting
techniques. Design service.*

The Iron Design Company
Summer Carr Farm
Thornton-le-Moor
Northallerton
North Yorkshire DL6 3SG
TEL: (01609) 778143

*Suppliers of a range of metal
furniture and artefacts, including
chairs, sofas, curtain poles
and beds.*

James Hetley & Co. Ltd
Glasshouse Fields
London
E1 9JA
TEL: (0171) 790 2333
FAX: (0171) 790 0201
E-MAIL:
tad@idesglass.co.uk
WEB SITE:
http://www.hetleys.co.uk

*Stockists, distributors and
exporters of antique glass,
including a full range of
Pilkington, laminated and
silvered float glass, hand-
blown and reproduction bullions,
glass lampshades in Art
Nouveau, Art Deco and
Tiffany styles; also antique
and rolled glass. Sell pattern
books and do-it-yourself
equipment.*

Looking for Ages
SEE DOORS (P.175)

Mumford & Wood Ltd
Hallsford Bridge Industrial
Estate
Ongar
Essex
CM5 9RB
TEL: (01621) 818155

*Manufacturers of ovolo
moulded double-hung sash
windows, doors and French
doors with many frame options
in period Georgian, Victorian
and Regency styles. Offer
technical advice on individual
projects requiring items
such as casements, bullseye
or shaped. Single and double-
glazing ranges.*

**The Original Box Sash
Window Company**
The Joinery
Unit 10
Bridgewater Way
Windsor
Berkshire
SL4 1RD
TEL: (01753) 858196
FAX: (01753) 857827

*Manufacturers of box
sash windows in traditional
designs made with pulleys
and sash cords; also
casement windows, with
single or double-glazing.
Finishes include wax,
stain or white paint.
Also oak doors.
(pp.38-9, 7, 8; pp. 40-1, 3)*

Samuel Heath & Sons Plc.
SEE DOORS
(P.175)

**The Sash Window
Workshop Ltd**
Mayfield Farm Industrial
Estate
Hatchet Lane
Winkfield
Windsor
Berkshire
SL4 2EG
TEL: (01344) 882008
FAX: (01344) 893034

*Restorers and makers
of traditional sash
windows.
(pp.42-3, 4;
pp.70-1, 9)*

J. Scott (Thrapston) Ltd
Bridge Street
Thrapston
Northamptonshire
NN14 4LR
TEL: (01832) 732366
FAX: (01832) 733793
E-MAIL:
100676.230@compuserve.
com

*Bespoke joinery company
providing sensitive
reproduction wooden windows
and doors for a wide range
of period homes - from
Georgian and Victorian
town houses to country
cottages.
(pp.50-1, 7; pp.70-1, 8)*

Winther Browne & Co. Ltd
SEE DOORS
(P.175)

FLOORS

Bruce Hardwood Floors
(Division of Triangle Pacific Corp)
16803 Dallas Parkway
Dallas
Texas 75248
USA
TEL: (800) 722 4647

Manufacturers of hardwood floors in an assortment of colours and patterns in traditional and country styles.
(pp.90-1, 5)

Campbell Marson & Co. Ltd
Unit 34
Wimbledon Business
  Centre
Riverside Road
London
SW17 0BA
TEL: (0181) 879 1909
FAX: (0181) 946 9395

Specialists in supplying and laying hardwood flooring, such as strip, strip overlay, tongue-and-groove, mosaic panels, parquet and cork tiles.

Candy & Co.
Heathfield
Newton Abbot
Devon
TQ12 6RF
TEL: (01626) 832641

Manufacturers of ceramic wall tiles, frost-proof vitrified floor tiles and terracotta floor tiles.

Castlenau Tiles
175 Church Road
Barnes
London
SW13 9HR
TEL: (0181) 741 2452
FAX: (0181) 741 5316

Suppliers of marble, terracotta and Mexican floor tiles. Also a wide choice of Italian and French tiles for walls and floors.

Chatsworth Carpets
227 Brompton Road
London
SW3 2EP
TEL: (0171) 584 1386

Suppliers of carpets, particularly 19th-century designs.

County Hardwoods
SEE DOORS
(P.174)

Criterion Tiles Ltd
SEE WALLS
(P.178)

Domus Tiles Ltd
33 Parkgate Road
London
SW11 4NP
TEL: (0171) 223 5555
FAX: (0171) 9242556

Suppliers of glazed and unglazed floor and wall ceramic tiles. Including refined porcelain stoneware, frost-proof heavy-duty tiles, polished finishes, anti-slips, step treads and skirtings.

Elon
Showroom:
66 Fulham Road
London SW3 6HH
TEL: (0171) 460 4600
FAX: (0171) 460 4601
Main address:
12 Silver Road
London W12 7SG
TEL: (0181) 932 3000
FAX: (0181) 932 3001

A range of terracotta, slate and glazed floor and wall tiles.

Fired Earth Plc.
Twyford Mill
Oxford Road
Adderbury
Oxon OX17 3HP
TEL: (01295) 812088
FAX: (01295) 810832
E-MAIL:
enquiries@firedearth.com

Manufacturers of ceramic tiles using traditional methods. Also reproduction early English delft tiles, natural floor coverings, tribal rugs and kilims.
(pp.94-5, 8)

Francis N. Lowe Ltd
The Marble Works
New Road
Middleton-by-Wirksworth
Derbyshire DE4 4NA
TEL: (01629) 822216
FAX: (01629) 824348

Specialist designers and manufacturers of architectural features in natural marble, granite and slate for commercial and private properties. Includes fireplaces, floors and skirtings.
(pp.92-3, 7, 10)

Froyle Tiles Ltd
Lower Froyle
Nr Alton
Hampshire
GU34 4LL
TEL: (01420) 23693

Producers of hand-made stone tiles suitable for interior and exterior areas in a wide variety of colours.

Heritage Oak Ltd
SEE DOORS (P.174)

Heritage Woodcraft
Heritage House
Wheatfield Way
Hinckley Fields Industrial
  Estate
Leicestershire LE10 1YE
TEL: (01455) 890800
FAX: (01455) 890700

Manufacturers and suppliers of all types of hardwood flooring. They maintain a large stock of reclaimed woodblock flooring, strip flooring and planking. Hardwood flooring is machined to customers' individual requirements.

H. & R. Johnson Tiles Ltd
Highgate Tiles Works
Tunstall
Stoke-on-Trent
Staffordshire ST6 4JX
TEL: (01782) 575575

Manufacturers of encaustic and geometric tiles for the restoration of 19th-century floors. Also supply the Minton Hollins Victorian range of wall tiles.

Junckers
Wheaton Court Commercial
  Centre
Wheaton Road
Witham
Essex
CM8 3UJ
TEL: (01376) 534705
FAX: (01376) 514401
E-MAIL:
mkt@juk.derxon.co.uk
WEB SITE:
http://www.junckers.com

Leading European producer of solid hardwood flooring, includes broad oak planking to recreate the flooring of period homes.
(pp.88-9, 8)

The North Wing
SEE WALLS (P.179)

Original Style Ltd
Stovax Ltd
Falcon Road
Sowton Industrial Estate
Exeter
Devon
EX2 7LF
TEL:(01392) 474000
FAX:(01392) 219932
E-MAIL:
info@stovax.com

Manufacturers of Victorian-style floor and wall tiles. Traditional clay colour stains re-create the elegant geometric and decorative patterns of late-19th-century tiles for hallways, bathrooms, kitchens, conservatories, exterior paths and porches. Also hand-decorated and Art Deco designs.

The Reject Tile Shop
178 Wandsworth Bridge Road
Wandsworth
London
SW6 2UQ
TEL: (0171) 731 6098
FAX: (0171) 736 3693

Specializes in second-hand quality discontinued tiles, particularly those from the Edwardian and Victorian periods, for floors, walls, worktops and fireplaces. Many of the tiles are exclusive to The Reject Tile Shop.

Rye Tiles
The Old Brewery
Wishward
Rye
Sussex
TN31 7DH
TEL: (01797) 223038

Hand-decorated wall and floor tiles made to order.

Stark Carpet Corporation
Represented in the UK by:
Afia Carpets
Chelsea Harbour Design Centre
Lots Road
London SW10 0XE
TEL: (0171) 351 5858
FAX: (0171) 351 9677
WEB SITE:
http://www.starkcarpetcorp.com

Makers of classically inspired carpet designs, woven by craftsmen in the finest wool. Includes hand-made rugs made to custom colours, sizes and textures and Chinese needlepoint rugs. Also fabric and furniture.
(pp.96-7, 6)

Stone Age
19 Filmer Road
London
SW6 7BU
TEL: (0171) 385 7954/5
FAX: (0171) 385 7956
WEB SITE:
http://www.stone-age.co.uk

*Suppliers of natural stone
flooring, specializing in
limestone and sandstone,
for kitchens, halls,
conservatories, bathrooms.
Also advice on fixing,
protecting and cleaning
stone floors. Stone accessories
made to order.
(pp.92-3, 5, 6)*

Stuart Interiors
SEE WALLS (P.179)

Tomkinsons Carpets Ltd
PO Box 11
Duke Place
Kidderminster
Worcestershire
DY10 2JR
TEL: (01562) 820006
FAX: (01562) 820030

*Manufacturers of the
Mr Tomkinson range
of carpets. Broad range of
plain carpets of all colours
with optional decorative
borders. Patterned items
include tartans, country styles
and Regency- and Victorian-
inspired designs.*

Treework Flooring
Treework Services Ltd
Cheston Combe
Church Town
Backwell
BS19 3JQ
TEL: (01275) 464466
FAX: (01275) 463078

*Manufacturers and fitters of
machined floorboards from oak,
ash, elm and other sustainable
timbers for restoration and new
building works. An ecological
commitment is central to their
activities. Associated products
include skirting boards, doors
and staircases.
(pp.88-9, 7)*

Wicanders
Star House
Partridge Green
West Sussex
RH13 8RA
TEL: (01403) 710001

*Suppliers of a wide range
of cork-based materials
to the specialist floor trade,
working with interior
designers.*

Angus Williams
10 Worthington Road
Surbiton
Surrey
KT6 7RX
TEL: (0181) 399 8563

*Hand-woven linen floor coverings,
hand-dyed to any colour and
reversible. Accepts commissions.*

WALLS

Aristocast Originals Ltd
49a Ogreave Close
Doorhouse Industrial
    Estate
Hansworth
Sheffield
S13 9NP
TEL: (0114) 269090

*Suppliers of Georgian-style
original feature plasterwork,
including mouldings, niches,
ceiling centres, fire surrounds
and stained glass.*

Baileys Home and Garden
SEE DOORS
(P.174)

G. P. & J. Baker
SEE WALLPAPERS
AND FABRICS
(P.179)

Copley Decor Ltd
Leyburn
North Yorkshire
DL8 5QA
TEL: (01969) 623410
FAX: (01969) 624398

*Manufacturers of architectural
mouldings in hard cellular
resin. Range includes
cornices, picture rails and
panel mouldings. Also dado
rails, architraves and
skirtings.
(p.103, 3, 6-8; pp.104-5, 7)*

Criterion Tiles Ltd
196 Wandsworth Bridge Road
London
SW6 2UF
TEL: (0171) 736 9610
FAX: (0171) 736 0725

*A range of English and
Continental ceramic tiles
with a variety of finishes and
effects, including hand-applied
transfer and stencilling, relief
moulding, in-glaze, hand-
painting and screen printing.
Also fine terracotta, slate
and large quarries both
glazed and unglazed.
Creative advice given.*

Crown Berger Ltd
PO Box 37
Crown House
Hollins Road
Darwen
Lancashire
BB3 0BG
TEL: (01254) 704951
FAX: (01254) 774414

*Manufacturers of Anaglypta
paints and relief wall coverings.
Ranges include lightly textured
patterns to heavily embossed
vinyl, complemented by toning
dados and borders. Also peel 'n'
stick coverings and ranges made
exclusively from recycled paper.
(pp.168-9, 3)*

Crowther of Syon Lodge
SEE FIREPLACES AND
STOVES (P.181)

**Davies Keeling
Trowbridge Ltd**
3 Charterhouse Works
Eltringham Street
London SW18 1TD
TEL: (0181) 874 3565
FAX: (0181) 874 2058

*Specialist decoration including
marbling, stippling, graining,
stoneblocking, plaster effects,
trompe l'oeil, murals and
stencilling.*

Elon
SEE FLOORS (P 177.)

Fired Earth Plc.
Twyford Mill
Oxford Road
Adderbury
Oxon OX17 3HP
TEL: (01295) 812088
FAX: (01295) 810832
E-MAIL:
enquiries@firedearth.com
SEE FLOORS (P.177)

Gillespie UK Ltd
Alma House
38 Crimea Road
Aldershot
Hampshire
GU11 1UD
TEL: (01252) 323311

*Specialists in suspended and
decorative ceilings, screens and
space-dividers, sculptures, murals,
crests and emblems, domes, Islamic
decoration, architectural features
and textured cladding.*

Hallidays
The Old College
Dorchester-on-Thames
Oxfordshire
OX10 7HL
TEL: (01865) 340068

*Specialists in Georgian
panelling and fireplaces,
particularly carved-pine
mantelpieces.*

H. & R. Johnson Tiles Ltd
SEE FLOORS
(P.177)

Hayles & Howe
SEE CEILINGS
(P.180)

Heritage Oak Ltd
SEE DOORS
(P.174)

**Jacqueline Bateman
Murals**
7 Rylett Crescent
London
W12 9RP
TEL/FAX: (0181) 749 3596

*Designers of murals, trompe
l'oeil, stencils, friezes and
pastiche. Interior and exterior
work undertaken.*

**The London Architectural
Salvage and Supply Co.**
SEE DOORS
(P.175)

The North Wing

Southover Grange

Southover Road

Lewes

East Sussex

BN7 1TP

TEL: (01273) 476761

FAX: (01273) 479565

Designer-makers of ceramic tiles. Also murals and signage and special commissions. Notable are reproductions of Victorian tiles and William Morris and William de Morgan designs.

Oakleaf Reproductions Ltd

Ling Bob

Main Street

Wilsden

Bradford

BD15 0JP

TEL: (01535) 272878

FAX: (01535) 275748

Reproduction timber in traditional and period styles, including simulated oak ceiling beams, panelling and embellishments, all manufactured in rigid cellular resin, moulded and hand-stained. Design service offered. (pp.104-5, 1, 4, 6; pp.112-13, 7-10; pp.116-17, 8, 16, 17)

Original Style

SEE FLOORS

(P.177)

The Reject Tile Shop

SEE FLOORS

(P.177)

Stuart Interiors

Barrington Court

Barrington

Illminster

Somerset

TA19 0NQ

TEL: (01460) 240349

FAX: (01460) 242069

Specialists in all aspects of period design, from medieval times to the 18th century, from concept and design through to manufacture and installation. Gothic-, Elizabethan- and Stuart-style furniture, architectural joinery, fabrics, lighting, pewter and brassware. (pp.58-9, 1; pp.62-3, 2; pp.78-9, 1; pp.82-3, 1; pp.108-9, 2; pp.146-7, 1; pp.166-7, 1)

Paintability

c/o Hillbury Press Ltd

Cranburne Industrial Estate

Potters Bar

Hertfordshire

EN6 3JN

TEL: (01707) 658948

A range of pre-cut stencil designs inspired by ancient ornaments, decorative stucco and plasterwork, trompe l'oeil and grisaille painted decoration.

Wheatley Plasterwork Ltd

SEE CEILINGS

(P.180)

Winther Browne & Co. Ltd

SEE DOORS

(P.175)

WALLPAPERS & FABRICS

Anna French

343 King's Road

London SW3 5ES

TEL: (0171) 351 1126

FAX: (0171) 274 8913

web sites:

http://www.decorex.com./index.html and http://www.thedesignstudio.com

Designers and suppliers of vinyl wall coverings, fabrics for curtains and upholstery and a range of matching trimmings, quilts and accessories.

Bentley & Spens

1 Mornington Street

London NW1 7QD

TEL: (0171) 387 7374

Fabric and wall-covering specialists.

Bernard Thorpe & Co. Ltd

53 Chelsea Manor Street

London

SW3 3ST

TEL: (0171) 352 5745

Carpet specialists.

Bradbury & Bradbury

PO Box 155

Benicia

California 94510

USA

TEL: (707) 746 1900

US wall-covering designers, distributed in the UK by Hamilton Weston Wallpapers.

Brunschwig & Fils

10 The Chambers

Chelsea Harbour Drive

London

SW10 0XF

TEL: (0171) 351 5797

FAX: (0171) 351 2280

Designers and manufacturers of an extensive range of more than 17,000 fabrics and 1,000 wall coverings, ranging from fine reproductions to striking contemporary New England designs. Also upholstered furniture, wall, table and hand-painted lamps, tables and trimmings.

Colefax and Fowler Group Plc.

19-23 Grosvenor Hill

London

W1X 9HG

TEL: (0181) 874 6484

Suppliers of a traditional English chintzes and wallpapers.

David Hartwright Ltd

Heraz Shop

2 Halkin Arcade

Motcomb Street

London

SW1X 8JT

TEL: (0171) 245 9479

Suppliers of antique oriental, needlework and European carpets, tapestries and textile cushions. Also offer specialist cleaning and restoration.

G. P. & J. Baker

PO Box 30

West End Road

High Wycombe

Bucks

HP11 2QD

TEL: (01494) 467467

FAX: (01494) 474771

Designers and manufacturers of soft furnishings, fabrics, upholstery, trimmings, wallpapers and accessories.

Guy Evans

96 Great Titchfield Street

London

W1P 7AG

TEL: (0171) 436 7914

Stockists of a range of soft furnishings and fabrics.

Hamilton Weston Wallpapers Ltd

18 St Mary's Grove

Richmond

Surrey

TW9 1UY

TEL: (0181) 940 4850

FAX: (0181) 332 0296

Architectural historians and designers who specialize in reproducing authentic wallpapers for the restoration and refurbishment of period interiors. Also borders and fabrics. Design consultation.

Ian Mankin

109 Regents Park Road

Primrose Hill

London

NW1 8UR

TEL: (0171) 722 0997

FAX: (0171) 722 2159

Pioneers of the use of utility fabrics, such as calicos, butchers' stripes and tickings, stylishly used for curtaining and soft furnishings. Around 300 natural fabrics in stock, from well-established English mills or hand-woven in India.

Interior Vision in the Craftsman Style

23 Oak Shore Ct

Port Townsend

West Virginia 98368

USA

TEL: (360) 385 3161

FAX: (360) 385 4874

Interior designers specializing in historic restoration of Arts and Craft-style interiors, such as stairways, porches, wood flooring, wainscotting. (pp.42-3, 8; pp.84-5, 10)

Jane Churchill

151 Sloane Street

London

SW1X 9BX

TEL: (0171) 730 9847

Designers of a range of quality fabrics for upholstery and curtains. Also wallpapers. Specialists in 18th- and 19th-century designs.

Mary Fox Linton

Chelsea Harbour Design Centre

London SW10 0XE

TEL: (0171) 351 9908

Fabric specialists. Also distribute Dedar, Glant and Jim Thompson designs.

Stuart Interiors

SEE WALLS (P.179)

Tissunique Ltd

Chelsea Harbour Design Centre

London SW10 0XE

TEL: (0171) 349 0096

Wholesalers and importers of furnishing fabric and wallpapers, braids and trimmings. Specialists in historic house reproduction work. Also producers of the National Trust Collection of Traditional Chintzes and the Historic Print Collection.

Zoffany

Showroom:

63 South Audley Street

London W1Y 5BF

TEL: (0171) 495 2505

FAX: (0171) 493 7257

Head office:

Talbot House

17 Church Street

Rickmansworth

Hertfordshire WD3 1DE

TEL: (01923) 710680

FAX: (01923) 710694

Designers and manufacturers of quality wallpapers, fabrics, carpets and trimmings based on authentic 17th-, 18th- and 19th-century designs and colours to fit the ambience of English country-house style.

CEILINGS

Andy Thornton Architectural Antiques Ltd

SEE DOORS (P.174)

Aristocast Originals Ltd

SEE WALLS (P.178)

Clark & Fenn Ltd
(Incorporating G. Jackson & Sons)

Unit 19

Mitcham Industrial Estate

Streatham Road

Mitcham, Surrey

CR4 2AP

TEL: (0181) 648 4343

FAX: (0181) 640 1986

Manufacturers and installers of a wide range of classical plaster cornices, friezes, ceiling centres, capitals and other decorative elements.

Hayles & Howe

Picton House

25 Picton Street

Montpelier

Bristol

BS6 5PZ

TEL: (01272) 246673

FAX: (01272) 243928

Restorers of plasterwork in historic and listed buildings. Specialists in making new, and in restoration of antique, scagliola. Design and execute bespoke ceilings and produce a large range of mouldings, cornices, columns, capitals and niches.

Raymond Enkeboll Designs

16506 Avalon Boulevard

Carson

California 90746

USA

TEL: (310) 532 1400

FAX: (310) 532 2042

WEB SITE:

http://www.enkeboll.com

Makers of an extensive array of architectural features in carved wood, including capitals, corbels, mouldings and inlays. Available in hard maple or red oak.

Stevensons of Norwich Ltd

Roundtree Way

Norwich

Norfolk

NR7 8SQ

TEL: (01603) 400824

FAX: (01603) 405113

Specialists in the design, manufacture and installation of standard and custom-made mouldings for interior decoration. Products include cornices, ceiling roses, columns, arches and fireplaces.

Wheatley Plasterwork Ltd

Avonvale Studio Workshops

Avonvale Place

Batheaston

Bath

BA1 7RF

TEL: (01255) 859678

FAX: (01255) 859678

Manufacturers of plaster patterns and moulds, including cornices, ceiling centres, niches, plaques, dados, fireplaces, corbels, columns and pilasters.

STAIRCASES

Chelsea Decorative Metal Company

9603 Moonlight

Houston

Texas 77096

USA

TEL: (713) 721 9200

FAX: (713) 776 8661

WEB SITE:

http://www.thetinman.com

Specialists in traditional pressed-tin ceilings, walls and cornices. Tin sheets are fashioned to traditional decorative designs ranging from Victorian to Deco.

Cinder Whit & Co.

753 Eleventh Ave South

Wahpeton

ND 58075

USA

TEL: (800) 527 9064

FAX: (701) 642 4204

Restorers and creators of replica and custom-designed cedar wood-turned porch posts and newel posts, balustrades, spindles and rails for staircases.

Clark & Fenn Ltd
(Incorporating G. Jackson & Sons)

SEE CEILINGS

(P.180)

Cottage Craft Spirals

The Barn

Gorsty Low Farm

The Wash

Chapel-en-le-Frith

Via Stockport

SK23 0QL

TEL: (01663) 750716

FAX: (01663) 751093

Producers of fine-quality cast-aluminium and wood spiral staircases. Modern materials and techniques are used to faithfully reproduce original Victorian designs and period tread patterns. All handrails are hand-crafted.

D. S. Nelson Co. Inc.

115 Airport St Quancit Point

N. Kingston

Rhode Island 02852

USA

TEL: (401) 267 1000

FAX: (401) 295 4756

WEB SITE:

http://www.dsnelson.com

Designers of custom-made curved staircases in wood, metal and glass. Complete design service available.
(pp.80-1, 1)

Havenplan's Architectural Emporium

SEE DOORS

(P.174)

Robert Coles Furniture and Architectural Joinery

Church House

Broad Street, Congresbury

Avon BS19 5DG

TEL: (01934) 833660

Designers and creators of hand-crafted, quality wooden furniture and architectural features, including staircases.
(pp.78-9, 6; pp.84-5, 7)

Solopark Ltd

SEE DOORS (P.175)

Spiral Manufacturing Inc.

17251 Jefferson Highway

Baton Rouge, Louisiana 70817

USA

TEL: (504) 753 8336

FAX: (504) 753 8351

Web Site:

http://www.spiralstair.com

Manufacturers of wooden spiral, curved and straight stairs and suppliers of stair parts and metal spiral kits.

Treework Flooring

SEE FLOORS (P.178)

Weller Patents Developments

1 Grand Parade Mews

Upper Richmond Road

London, SW15 2RF

TEL: (0181) 788 6684

Specialist manufacturers of internal and external architectural metalwork, including balustrades, gates, balconies and staircases. Made to client requirements to original designs or as authentic reproductions.

Winther Browne & Co. Ltd
SEE DOORS
(P.175)

Worthington
SEE DOORS
(P.175)

FIREPLACES & STOVES

Acquisitions (Fireplaces) Ltd
Acquisitions House
24-26 Holmes Road
London
NW5 3AB
TEL: (0171) 482 2949
FAX: (0171) 267 4361
E-MAIL:
sales@acquistions.co.uk
WEB SITE:
http://www.acquistions.co.uk

Manufacturers of reproduction Victorian and Edwardian fireplaces and accessories. Includes cast-iron, wood and marble surrounds, inserts, grates, fenders, coal buckets, hand-painted, embossed tiles to Victorian and Edwardian designs. All fireplaces suitable for solid fuel or decorative fuel-effect fires.
(pp.120-1, 1; pp.126-7, 1, 3; pp.130-1, 4, 10; pp. 132-3, 7)

Aga-Rayburn
PO Box 30
Ketley
Telford
Shropshire TF1 4DD
TEL: (01952) 642000
FAX: (01952) 641961

Manufacturers and retailers of traditional cast-iron stoves. Aga, Rayburn and Coalbrookdale cooker models can be run from oil, gas, solid fuel or off-peak electricity.
(p.136, 1; pp.158-9, 5)

Amazing Grates Fireplaces Ltd
61-63 High Road
East Finchley
London N2 8AB
TEL: (0181) 883 9590
FAX: (0181) 365 2053

Makers of quality British-made mantels faithfully following original 18th- and 19th-century designs. Also grates and gas fire inserts.
(pp.120-1, 5, 8; pp.138-9, 7)

Andy Thornton Architectural Antiques Ltd
SEE DOORS (P.174)

Architectural Antiques Ltd
351 King Street
Hammersmith
London W6 9NH
TEL: (0181) 741 7883
FAX: (0181) 741 1109

Specialists in architectural antiques, such as fireplace surrounds in wood, cast iron and marble. Also tiled fire inserts, accessories, doors with stained-glass or leaded panels, gates and railings. Restoration and repair service available.

Architectural Components Ltd
SEE DOORS (P.174)

Baxi Heating Ltd
Brownedge Road
Bamber Road
Preston
Lancashire PR5 6SN
TEL: (01772) 695555
FAX: (01772) 695410

Manufacturers of gas and solid-fuel domestic heating appliances. (pp.138-9, 4)

Bisque Radiators
15 Kingsmead Square
Bath BA1 2AE
TEL: (01225) 469244
FAX: (01225) 444708

Extensive range of radiators in a variety of colours and finishes. Heated towel rails, classic pieces, hot coils and panel heaters.
(p.137, 5)

The Brass Knob
SEE DOORS (P. 174)

Chesney's Antique Fireplace Warehouse
194-202 Battersea Park Road
London SW11 4ND
TEL: (0171) 627 1410
FAX: (0171) 622 1078
Extensive stock of antique and reproduction marble and stone fireplaces incorporating 18th- and 19th-century English and Continental designs. Bespoke masonry service and installation grates and gas-effect fires.
(pp.120-1, 4; pp.124-5, 4, 6; pp.126-7, 4; pp.134-5, 4)

The Chiswick Fireplace Company
68 Southfield Road
Chiswick
London
W4 1BD
TEL: (0181) 995 4011
FAX: (0181) 995 4012

Specialists in Victorian, Edwardian and Art Nouveau original fireplaces, marble, stone and wood mantels and comparatively rare cast-iron registers. Also baskets and grates and radiator covers. Offer a restoration and installation service for most types of fireplace and custom-made gas fires to suit all grates.
(pp.132-3, 4; pp.134-5, 8)

Crowther of Syon Lodge
Syon Lodge
Busch Corner
London Road
Isleworth
Middlesex TW7 5BH
TEL: (0181) 560 7978/7985
FAX: (0181) 568 7572
E-MAIL:
crowther.syon-lodge@virgin.net
WEB SITE:
http://www.crowther-syon-lodge.co.uk

Stockists of fine antiques for gardens and interiors. Items include Georgian architectural features, such as oak and pinewood panelling, stone and marble chimney pieces. Offer a complete panelling service. Stockists of an impressive range of antique garden ornaments, such as sundials and fountains.
(pp.100-1, 4; pp.108-9, 4, 7; pp.118-19, 6; pp.124-5, 3)

Dovre Castings Ltd
Unit 1
Weston Works
Weston Lane
Tyseley
Birmingham
B121 3RP
TEL: (0121) 7067600
FAX: (0121) 7069182
E-MAIL:
enquiries@dovre.co.uk
WEB SITE:
http://www.dovre.co.uk

Manufacturers of traditional cast-iron gas, electric, multi-fuel and wood-burning stoves in a range of enamelled colours.

Dowding Metalcraft Ltd
Mulberry Road
Canvey Island
Essex
SS8 0PR
TEL/FAX: (01268) 684205

Manufacturers of fireplace fenders in brass and steel, including 18th-century-style club fenders with leather seats. Also firedogs and reproduction grates for solid-fuel or solid-fuel-effect fires in a mix of classic French and English styles, fitted and finished by skilled craftsmen.

Dunedin Antiques Ltd
4 North West Circus Place
Edinburgh
EH3 6ST
TEL: (0131) 220 1574

Stockists of a large range of period chimney pieces and architectural items.

Emsworth Fireplaces Ltd
(The Robert Lyman Collection)
Unit 3
Station Approach
Emsworth
Hampshire
PO10 7PN
TEL: (01243) 373431
FAX: (01243) 371023
E-MAIL:
info@emsworth.co.uk

Producers of fine reproduction English and French style mantels available in solid timber: pine, mahogany, oak, other wood and white-painted finishes to order and in a choice of 90 different marbles.
(pp.124-5, 2; pp.128-9, 7; pp.130-1, 1, 7)

Faral Radiators
Tropical House
Charlswood Road
East Grinstead
West Sussex
RH19 2HJ
TEL: (01342) 315757
FAX: (01342) 315362

Suppliers of radiators, towel rails and accessories from Europe's leading manufacturers. Also a range of die-cast aluminium, steel-column and cast-iron radiators.
(p.137, 2)

Firestyle Chimneypieces
158 Upminster Road
Upminster
Essex RM14 2RB
TEL: (01708) 456895

Hand-crafted marble chimney pieces in classical period designs, also fireplace inserts. Fitting service available.

Flamewave Fires

The Farmyard

Pearson's Green

Brenchley

Tonbridge

Kent

TN17 7DE

TEL: (01892) 724458

FAX: (01892) 724966

E-MAIL:

nod@flamewavefires.co.uk

WEB SITE:

http://www.flamewavefires.

co.uk

Manufacturers of Tortoise
convection fires and importers
of the All Black range of stoves.
(p.136, 4)

Franco Belge

Manufacturers of traditional
stoves, distributed by Dovre
Castings. (p.136, 3)
SEE DOVRE CASTINGS
ENTRY ABOVE

Hallidays

The Old College

Dorchester-on-Thames

Wallingford

Oxfordshire

OX10 7HL

TEL: (01865)340028

FAX: (01865) 341149

Designers of period panelled
rooms. Specialists in wood-
crafted Georgian and Regency
mantelpieces and brass and
cast-iron fireplace accessories.
Faithful reproduction door
fittings of the Georgian and
Regency periods by specialist
craftsmen.
(pp.58-9, 4)

The House Hospital

SEE DOORS

(P 175.)

Manorhouse Stone

School Lane

Normanton-le-Heath

Leicestershire

LE67 2TH

TEL: (01530) 262999

FAX: (01530) 262515

Designers and manufacturers
of a specialist range of quality
reconstructed architectural
stonework for the restoration
and renovation of period
buildings. Includes fireplaces,
door surrounds, Aga shelves,
mullion windows made from
French limestone, Bramley
sandstone and dark Portland
gray. Also reclaimed bricks
and flagstones.

Marble Hill
Fireplaces Ltd

70-72 Richmond Road

Twickenham

Middlesex

TW1 3BE

TEL: (0181) 892 1488

FAX: (0181) 891 6591

Producers of reproduction
fireplaces, including
English stone mantels
to Victorian and Georgian
styles and a range of
stone mantels in Louis XV
and XVI styles, hand-crafted
in France. Stockists of a large
range of antique French
chimney pieces.
(pp.120-1, 7;
pp.122-3, 1)

Nevers Oak Fireplace
Mantels

312 N Hwy 101

Encinitas

California 92024

USA

TEL: (760) 632 5808

FAX: (760) 749 3990

Makers of hand-carved wooden
mantels in a range of woods,
including ash and poplar.

The Original Choice

SEE DOORS (P.175)

Oxley's Furniture

Lapstone Farm

Westington Hill

Chipping Campden

Gloucestershire GL55 6UR

TEL: (01386) 840466

FAX: (01386) 840455

Makers of solid aluminium
furniture. Pieces range from
classical to contemporary styles
and are all hand-made to order.

Robert Aagaard & Co.

Frogmire House

Stockwell Road

Knaresborough

North Yorkshire HG5 0JP

TEL: (01423) 864805

FAX: (01423) 869356

Reproduction hand-carved mantels,
made to authentic designs and emu-
lating original processes. Fire sur-
rounds based on originals dating back
to the 17th century, complemented
by granite, hand-painted tiles.
(pp.128-9, 4)

Stevensons of Norwich Ltd

SEE CEILINGS (P.180)

Stovax Ltd

Falcon Road

Sowton Industrial Estate

Exeter

Devon

EX2 7LF

TEL: sales (01392) 474000

FAX: (01392) 219932

E-MAIL:

info@stovax.com

Manufacturers of finely
reproduced 19th-century
cast-iron fireplaces. Hand-
cast and finished with period
details, the range embraces
fireplaces for solid-fuel and
gas-effect fires from the
Victorian, Georgian and Art
Nouveau periods. Also extensive
range of decorative hearth and
fireplace tiles and fireplace
surrounds in wood and
cast iron.
(pp.86-7; pp.94-5,
1, 2, 6; pp.116-17, 4)

THS Distribution

53-55 High Street

Uttoxeter

Staffordshire

ST14 7JQ

TEL: (01889) 565411

FAX: (01889) 567625

Importers of several makes
of multi-fuel stoves.
(p.136, 5)

Walney

Stanton Square

Stanton Way

London SE26 5AB

TEL: (0181) 659 3430

FAX: (0181) 659 1017

Manufacturers of radiator
cabinets and tubular steel
column radiators in range of
colours. Radiator cabinets are
made from top-grade Medium
Density Fibreboard (MDF) with
a range of grilles and timber
veneers. Traditional brass
radiator valves also available,
plus range of bathroom units
for basins, in wood or ceramic.
(p.137, 3)

BATHROOMS

A Touch of Brass

SEE DOORS (P.174)

Barber Wilsons & Co. Ltd

Crawley Road

Westbury Avenue

Wood Green

London N22 6AH

TEL:(0181) 888 3461

FAX:(0181) 888 2041

Range of taps ideal for those
seeking to re-create an authentic
period look. Each fitting is
manufactured to an original
design from a portfolio stretching
back to 1905 when the Company
was founded. Choice of finishes:
inca brass, chrome, nickel, satin
and polished brass.
(pp.148-9, 1, 5, 10; p.156, 1, 2)

Black Country
Heritage Ltd

Britannia House

Mill Street

Brierley Hill

DY5 2TH

TEL: (01384) 480810

FAX: (01384) 482866

Producers of every
conceivable bathroom
accessory and low-energy
towel warmers in three
ranges that reflect Edwardian
England, 1920s New York
and Art Deco styles. Hand-
made in solid brass with
antique-gold, polished- or
satin-nickel and chrome-
plate finishes.
(pp.150-1, 2, 3, 5, 6,
8, 9, 11)

Brass & Traditional
Sinks Ltd

Devauden Green

Chepstow

Monmouthshire

NP6 6PL

TEL: (01291) 650738

FAX: (01291) 650827

E-MAIL:

sales@sinks.co.uk

WEB SITE:

http://www.sinks.co.uk

Leading suppliers of traditional
and modern fireclay sinks.
(pp.150-1, 10)

Caradon Plumbing Solutions

Launton Road

Alsager

Stoke-on-Trent

ST7 2DF

Tel: (0870) 8400035

Manufacturers of a full range of bathroom products made from vitreous china. Also steel and acrylic baths, taps, fittings and accessories. Makers of Twyford and Doulton bathroom ranges and Mira showers.

Chadder & Co.

Blenheim Studio

Lewes Road

Forest Row

East Sussex

RH18 5EZ

Tel: (01342) 823243

Fax: (01342) 823097

Web Site:

http://www.pncl.co.uk/chadder

Specialists in antique and traditional baths, showers, toilets and accessories, featuring hand-cast metal, ornate brackets, chrome, nickel and antique gold pipes and porcelain handles.
(pp.146-7, 2)

Colourwash Bathrooms

165 Chamerlayne Road

London

NW10 3NU

Tel: (0181) 459 8918

Suppliers of wide range of stylish bathroomware, including Art Deco styles. Provide a consultation and installation service.

Czech & Speake

244-254 Cambridge

Heath Road

London

E2 9DA

Tel: (0181) 980 4567

Fax: (0181) 981 7232

Designers of stylish kitchen sink mixers and accessories for bathrooms and kitchens in traditional designs. Includes an Edwardian range, also towel rails, shower hoses, mahogany toilet seats. Metalware in chrome, nickel and no-tarnish brass. Showrooms in London's Jermyn Street and Fulham Road.
(pp.142-3, 9; pp.150-1, 4; p.156, 4, 5)

Doulton

Caradon Plumbing Solutions

Launton Road

Alsager

Stoke-on-Trent

ST7 2DF

Tel: (0870) 8400035

(pp.146-7, 6)
SEE CARADON
PLUMBING SOLUTIONS
ENTRY ABOVE

C. P. Hart & Sons Ltd

Keats Road

Belvedere

Kent

DA17 6BX

Tel: (0171) 902 1000

Fax: (0171) 902 1001

Manufacturers of glazed ceramic sanitaryware for bathrooms. Period and contemporary styles; all white, with matching taps and complementary accessories.

Heritage Bathrooms Plc.

Unit 1a

Princess Street

Bedminster

Bristol

Avon BS3 4AG

Tel: (0117) 9639762

Fax: (0117) 9231078

Manufacturers of traditional-style English bathroom suites, stand-alone pieces, brassware, furniture and metal and ceramic accessories. Includes cast-iron baths and heated towel rails.

Ideal-Standard UK

The Bathroom Works

National Avenue

Kingston-upon-Hull

HU5 4HS

Tel: (01482) 346461

Fax: (01482) 445886

A wide range of traditional-style baths and basins, shower fittings, taps and other accessories.
(pp.142-3, 6; pp.144-5, 4; pp.148-9, box)

Lefroy Brooks Midland Ltd

Unit 3

Marsten Road Industrial Estate

Marsten Road

Wolverhampton WV2 4LX

Tel: (01902) 421922

Fax: (01902) 427109

Quality English bathroomware and accessories, including an Edwardian range. Taps made in solid brass and cast, polished and assembled entirely by hand. Items include cast-iron baths, towel warmers, shower rails.
(pp.142-3, 5, box; pp.146-7, 7; pp.148-9, 4; pp.150-1, 12)

Old Fashioned Bathrooms

Little London Hill

Debenham

Stowmarket

Suffolk

IP14 6PW

Tel: (01728) 860926

Fax: (01728) 860446

Suppliers of reproduction and original Victorian and Edwardian period and traditional sanitaryware and bathroom accessories.

Original Bathrooms

143-145 Kew Road

Richmond

Surrey

TW9 2PN

Tel: (0181) 940 7554

Suppliers of bathroom sanitaryware and accessories.

Pipe Dreams of Kensington Ltd

72 Gloucester Road

London

SW7 4QT

Tel: (0171) 225 3978

Fax: (0171) 589 8841

London dealers in antique baths, basins and accessories in Art Deco, Victorian and other period styles.
(pp.92-3, 8; pp. 142-3, 2, 8; pp.144-5, 5, 6)

Samuel Heath & Sons Plc.

SEE DOORS

(P.174)

Silverdale Ceramics Ltd

Silverdale Road

Newcastle-under-Lyne

Staffordshire

ST5 6EL

Tel: (01782) 717175

Fax: (01782) 717166

Manufacturers of bathroom sanitaryware.

Smallbone of Devizes

SEE KITCHENS (P.184)

Stiffkey Bathrooms

Stiffkey

Wells-Next-Sea

Norfolk

NR23 1AJ

Tel: (01328) 830460

Fax: (01328) 830005

Restored bathroom fittings and period sanitaryware, all reconditioned. Includes Victorian shower baths, marble basins and Edwardian towel warmers. Also taps and shower mixers and other original and reproduction accessories, such as mirrors and soap dishes.
(pp.146-7, 4)

Swadling Brassware

23 Arnside Road

Waterlooville

Portsmouth

Hampshire

PO7 7UP

Tel: (01705) 255536

Fax: (01705) 254388

Manufacturers of quality water fittings. Taps for baths, basins and kitchen sinks in Victorian and Edwardian styles. Made in brass, nickel and chrome.

Water Front Ltd

9 The Burdwood Centre

Station Road

Thatcham

Berkshire

RG19 4YA

Tel: (01635) 872100

Fax: (01635) 872200

E-Mail:

waterfront@btconnect.com

Web Site:

waterfront.ltd.uk

Classic quality bathroom accessories in a range of finishes.
(pp.150-1, 1)

The Water Monopoly

16/18 Lonsdale Road

London

NW6 6RD

Tel: (0171) 624 2636

Fax: (0171) 624 2531

Feature quality antique baths and basins and period accessories. Items date from 17th century to Victorian era.
(pp.142-3, 1, 7)

Watercolors Inc.

Garrison-on-Hudson

New York 10524

USA

Tel: (914) 424 3327

Suppliers of traditional and contemporary bathroom accessories in brushed and polished nickel, chrome, brass, gold and baked enamel in a range of colours. In addition to washbasin and shower sets, provide mirrors, shelf units and armchairs.
(pp.148-9, 6-9; p.156, 7, 8)

KITCHENS

Aga-Rayburn
SEE FIREPLACES AND
STOVES (p.181)

Crabtree Kitchens
The Twickenham Centre
Norcutt Road
Twickenham
Middlesex
TW2 6SR
TEL: (0181) 755 1121
FAX: (0181) 755 4133

*Designers and manufacturers
of hand-made fitted kitchens
in maple, oak, limed oak and
ash. Styles include Georgian,
Victorian, Shaker and
Mackintosh. Specialists in
hand-painted finishes:
stippling, distressing, sponging
and dragging.*

Harcourt Designs Ltd
4 Harcourt Road
Redland
Bristol
Avon BS6 7RG
TEL: (0117) 9756969
FAX: (0117) 9756675

*Designers and fitters of
kitchen furniture with a
range of made-to-measure
units in pine, hardwood or
composite materials, finished
in stain, colourwash or with
painted decoration. Also free-
standing furniture in any wood
and constructions, such as
conservatories and porches,
designed, built and fitted.
(pp.154-5, 8)*

**John Lewis
of Hungerford Plc.**
Park Street
Hungerford
Berkshire
RG17 0EA
TEL: (01488) 682066
FAX: (01488) 686660

*Suppliers of the Artisan
kitchen and furniture fittings
in a range of woods and
finishes.*

**Lansdowne Kitchen
Sinks and Taps**
Showroom:
Elon
66 Fulham Road
London SW3 6HH
TEL: (0171) 460 4600
FAX: (0171) 460 4601
Main address:
12 Silver Road
London W12 7SG
TEL: (0181) 932 3000
FAX: (0181) 932 3001

*Manufacturers of fine
fire-clay ceramic kitchen sinks,
complemented by a range
of taps in nickel, brass and
chrome.
(pp.154-5, 6)*

Lockhurst Kitchen Design
8-12 Lockhurst Lane
Coventry
CV6 5PD
TEL: (01203) 668141

*Manufacturers of kitchen
furniture. Also offer full
installation service.*

NCR Refrigeration Ltd
Vaux Road
Finedon Road Industrial Estate
Wellingborough
Northampshire
NN8 4TG
TEL: (01933) 272222
FAX: (01933) 279638

*Importers of American Amana
fridge freezers for built-in or
free-standing applications in
stainless steel and a choice
of colours.*

Neff (UK) Ltd
Grand Union House
Old Wolverton Road
Wolverton
Milton Keynes
MK12 5TP
TEL: (01908) 328300
FAX: (01908) 328399

*Innovative built-in appliances
for kitchens. Manufacturers of
single and double-ovens, cooker
hoods, hobs, fridges and freezers,
dishwashers and washing
machines using recyclable
materials.
(pp.158-9, 9)*

Polished Metal Products Ltd
Devauden Green
Chepstow
Monmouthshire
NP6 6PL
TEL: (01291) 650455
FAX: (01291) 650827
*Manufacturers of stainless-steel
undermounted kitchen sinks
and a range of traditional and
contemporary taps. Settings
in granite, slate or wood.*

Rencraft Ltd
Unit 9
Chart Farm
Styants Bottom Road
Seal Chart
Sevenoaks
Kent TN15 0ES
TEL: (01732) 762682
FAX: (01732) 762535

*Manufacturers of traditional,
hand-crafted kitchen units,
available in pine and oak.*

Robinson and Cornish Ltd
Southay House
Oakwood Close
Roundswell
Barnstaple
Devon EX31 3NJ
TEL: (01271) 329300
FAX: (01271) 328277
*Designers of bespoke wooden kitchens
for the period and contemporary home.
Exclusive suppliers of a range of hand-
made kitchen tiles. Also bathrooms
and free-standing furniture.*

Romsey Cabinetmakers
Greatbridge Business Park
Budds Lane
Romsey
Hampshire SO51 0HA
TEL: (01794) 522626
FAX: (01794) 522451

*Designers and makers of
bespoke kitchens for over 20
years. Styles and finishes reflect
a range of periods and are
available in painted finishes or
solid timber: oak, cherry and
ash.
(pp.56-7, 8; pp.154-5, 9)*

SieMatic UK
Osprey House
Rookery court
Primett Road
Stevenage
Hertfordshire SG1 3EE
TEL: (01438) 369251
OR: (01438) 369327
FAX: (01438) 368920

*UK branch of German
manufacturer's range of fitted
kitchens. A broad range of styles
and designs, including classic
farmhouse and country kitchens.
(pp.158-9, 3)*

Smallbone of Devizes
The Hopton Workshops
London Road
Devizes
Wiltshire SN10 2EU
TEL: (01380) 728000

*Designers of quality hand-made
kitchen furniture in English oak
and antique pine. Hand-painted
units with decorative detail are
complemented by free-standing
pieces such as dressers, plate
racks and china cupboards.*

Sutton Kitchens
30 Beacon Grove
High Street
Carshalton
Surrey SM5 3BA
TEL: (0181) 241 2002

*Designers and refurbishers of
kitchens in period homes from
the 16th century. Doors are
hand-crafted in reclaimed antique
oak and pine. Also specialist
paint finishes, including
marbling and stencilling.*

Underwood Kitchens Ltd
Lawn Farm Business
Centre Grendon Underwood
Buckinghamshire
HP18 0QX
TEL: (01296) 770043
FAX: (01296) 770412

*Manufacturers of an
exclusive range of
hand-crafted kitchens in
solid English oak and elm,
Canadian maple, European
beech and limed ash. Styles
include traditional American,
Edwardian elegance and
incorporate hand-painted
finishes and dark granite
worktops. Provide a
consultation and design service.
(p.157, 5)*

LIGHTING

**Andy Thornton
Architectural Antiques Ltd**

SEE DOORS
(p.174)

The Antique Lamp Shop
600 King's Road
London
SW6 2DX
TEL: (0171) 371 0077
FAX: (0171) 371 3507

SEE CHRISTOPHER
WRAY ENTRY BELOW

Arroyo Craftsman

4509 Little John Street

Baldwin Park

California 91706

USA

TEL: (626) 960 9411

FAX: (626) 960 9521

Arts and Crafts movement-inspired lighting. Elegant table, wall and ceiling lamps incorporating design principles of Gustav Stickley and Frank Lloyd Wright for interior and exterior use.
(pp.52-3, 11; pp.170-1, 10)

Bella Figura

Decoy Farm

Old Church Road

Melton

Suffolk IP13 6DH

TEL: (01394) 461111

FAX: (01394) 461199

Specialists in distressed Florentine chandeliers and sconces in painted metal.

Bradley Collection Ltd

SEE WINDOWS (P.176)

Brooklands Brass Lighting

Units A+B

15 Wintersells Business Park

Brooklands

Surrey KT14 7LF

TEL: (01483) 267474

FAX: (01483) 267863

Manufacturers of quality solid-brass lighting fittings in classical designs. Includes lanterns and wall, table, desk and standard lamps.

Chelsea Lighting Design Ltd

Unit 1

23A Smith Street

Chelsea

London

SW3 4EJ

TEL: (0171) 824 8144

FAX: (0171) 823 4812

Makers of an exclusive range of pendant lighting bowls in natural alabaster. Pieces range in size and metalwork finishes. Offer a design and advisory service.

Chelsom Ltd

Heritage House

Clifton Road

Blackpool

Lancashire

FY4 4QA

TEL: (01253) 831400

FAX: (01253) 698098

Designers and manufacturers of a wide range of stylish light fixtures, including table and floor lamps, corridor, bathroom, architectural and exterior lighting. Also have a range of reproduction Georgian and Regency lanterns.
(pp.52-3, 10, 12, 13; pp.164-5, 7, 10, 13; pp.168-9, 5-9, 14; p.172, 4-8; p.173, 5)

Christopher Wray Lighting

591-593 King's Road

London

SW6 2YW

TEL: (0171) 736 8434

FAX: (0171) 731 3507

Manufacturers and retailers of decorative lighting for interiors and exteriors. Includes reproduction Gothic, Tiffany, Art Deco and classic styles for table, ceiling and walls, spotlights, picture lights and lanterns.
(pp.164-5, 8, 12, 15; pp.168-9, 13, 15; p. 173, 6, 22)

Conant Custom Brass Inc.

266-270 Pine Street

Burlington

Vermont 05401

USA

TEL: (802) 658 4482

FAX: (802) 864 5914

E-MAIL:

wholesale@conantcustom
brass.com

WEB SITE:

http://www.conantcustom
brass.com

Manufacturers of a range of lighting in a choice of 16 finishes. Also custom-made commissions and brass restoration, including paint removal, nickel stripping, polishing, lacquering, gold leafing, retinning, rewiring, etc. (pp.48-9, 9, 22; pp.168-9, 11)

Forbes & Lomax Ltd

205b St John's Hill

London SW11 1TH

TEL: (0171) 738 0202

FAX: (0171) 738 9224

Manufacturers of light switches and sockets in brass, Perspex, including "invisible" clear Perspex plates and a painted socket range. Also dimmers, fingerplates and one, two, three and four-gang switches.
(p.173, 23, 24)

Hamilton Litestat Group

R. Hamilton & Company Ltd

Quarry Industrial Estate

Mere

Wiltshire BA12 6LA

TEL: (01747) 860088

FAX: (01747) 861032

Manufacturers of decorative electrical accessories with rocker, dolly or push switches, dimmers, power sockets and connection units. (p.173, 3)

The London Architectural Salvage and Supply Co.

SEE DOORS (P. 175)

McLean Lighting Works

1207 Park Terrace

Greensboro

North Carolina 27403

USA

TEL: (910) 294 6994

FAX: (910) 294 2683

Suppliers of antique and reproduction 18th- and 19th-century lamps, lanterns, postlights, chandeliers and foyer lights.

Metro Lighting & Crafts

2216 San Pablo Avenue

Berkeley

California 94702

USA

TEL: (510) 540 0509

FAX: (510) 540 0549

Makers of hand-crafted lamps and fixtures in the Arts and Crafts and Art Nouveau style. Includes sconces, chandeliers and table lamps in solid copper or brass.

Newstamp Lighting Company (Division of N. E. Stamping & Fabricating Works Inc.)

227 Bay Road

PO Box 189

North Easton

Massachusetts 02356

USA

TEL: (508) 238 7071

FAX: (508) 230 8312

Manufacturers of all types of light fixtures in metal, glass and plastic. Reproductions, rewiring and new fixtures made by skilled craftsmen.

Olivers Lighting Company

Udimore Workshops

Udimore

Rye TN31 6AS

TEL/FAX: (01797) 225166

Makers of a unique range of quality reproduction electric switches, sockets and accessories. Backplates crafted by hand in a choice of timbers and finishes, including antique mahogany and oak. Available by mail order only.
(p.173, 1, 2)

The Saltbox

3004 Columbia Avenue

Lancaster

Pennsylvania 17603

USA

TEL: (717) 392 5649

Manufacturers of authentic reproduction North American period chandeliers, hall lanterns and postlights. Pieces are hand-crafted in heavy copper, solid brass, tin and pewter. Many are exact copies of original designs from the 18th century onward.

Smithbrook Iron Lighting

Smithbrook

Nr Cranleigh

Surrey GU6 8LH

TEL: (01483) 272744

FAX: (01483) 267863

Manufacturers of traditional hand-made metal lighting, created and finished by crafts-men. Most notable are their chandeliers bearing from two to twenty simulated wax candles and available in a range of finishes, including black, verdigris, black gold and aged gold, and in a range of traditional styles.

Stiffkey Lampshop

Stiffkey

Wells-Next-Sea

Norfolk NR23 1AJ

TEL: (01328) 830460

FAX: (01328) 830005

Suppliers of unusual and antique lamps and shades, from elegant library lamps to Victorian gasoliers and ornate candelabrum. Include reproduction polished-brass table, wall and ceiling lamps.
(pp.164-5, 14)

Victorian Lighting Works

251 S. Pennsylvania Avenue

PO Box 469

Centre Hall

Pennsylvania 16828

USA

Tel: (814) 364 9577

Web Site:

http://www.vlworks.com

Manufacturers of polished or lacquered solid brass light fittings, including chandeliers, wall lights, pendants and back-plates and glass lamp shades.

EXTERIORS

Architectural Heritage Ltd

Taddington Manor

Taddington

Cheltenham

Gloucestershire

GL54 5RY

Tel: (01386) 584414

Fax: (01386) 584236

Stockists of one of the widest ranges of antique garden ornament, statuary, urns, fountains and seats. On display in the grounds of a 16th-century manor. Also specialize in antique panelled rooms and period chimney pieces.

(pp.50-1, 5; pp.120-1, 2)

Architectural Iron Company Inc.

PO Box 126

104 Ironwood court

Milford

Pennsylvania 18337

USA

Tel: (717) 296 7722

or: (800) 442 4766

Fax: (717) 296 4766

Restorers of cast and wrought iron, from gates, railings and seats to architectural decoration. Also make and supply new iron crestings, finials, newel posts and caps, ornaments and firebacks.

Baileys Home and Garden

SEE DOORS

(P.174)

Chilstone

Victoria Park

Fordcombe Road

Langton Green

Kent

TN3 0RD

Tel: (01892) 740866

Fax: (01892) 740867

E-Mail:

chilstone@hndl.demon.co.uk

Web Site:

http://www.greatbritain.co.uk/chilstone

Specialists in stone building and features for house exteriors and gardens. Includes porticos, pilasters, urns, seats, sundial plates, statues.

(pp.50-1, 4; pp.52-3, 9)

Cinder Whit & Co.

SEE STAIRCASES (P.180)

Doverhay Forge Studios

SEE DOORS (P.174))

Haddonstone Ltd

The Forge House

East Haddon

Northamptonshire

NN6 8DB

Tel: (01604) 770711

Fax: (01604) 770027

Designers and suppliers of reconstructed stoneware for garden, interior and architectural decoration, including balustrades, temples and pavilions, porticos, columns and pilasters and garden urns.

Jacksons Fine Fencing

Stowting Common

Nr Ashford

Kent

TN25 6BN

Tel: (01233) 750393

Fax: (01233) 750403

Gates and fencing specialists. All timber products are treated with a unique double-life protection. Includes ornamental galvanized steel gates, wood gates, garden arbours, arches and other features.

Joseph Tipper (Hardware) Ltd

Century Works

Moat Street

Willenham

West Midlands

WV13 1FZ

Tel: (01902) 608444

Fax: (01902) 608445

SEE DOORS

(P. 174)

Knight & Gibbins Ltd

Windham Road

Sudbury

Suffolk CO10 6XD

Tel: (01787) 377264

Fax: (01787) 378258

Designers of traditional house bells in late-Georgian/early-Victorian style. Hand-cast brass bells with a choice of solid and veneer mahogany or oak mounts. Mains run.

(pp.48-9, 23)

The London Architectural Salvage and Supply Co.

SEE DOORS (P. 175)

Samuel Heath & Sons Plc.

SEE DOORS (P. 175)

Solopark Ltd

SEE DOORS (P. 175)

Stuart Interiors

SEE WALLS (P 179)

Vande Hey's Roofing Tile Co. Inc.

1565 Bohm Drive

Little Chute

Wisconsin 54140-2533

USA

Tel: (414) 766 0156

Designers, manufacturers and installers of roof tiles in eight styles and 60 standard colours. They can custom-colour to match tiles for restoration work on period properties. Hand-crafted floor tiles and patio pavings also produced in any design and surface finish.

Weller Patents Developments

SEE STAIRCASES (P.180)

OTHER USEFUL ADDRESSES

Acanthus Associated Architectural Practices Ltd

Voysey House

Barley Mow Passage

Chiswick

London

W4 4PN

Tel: (0181) 995 1232

Fax: (0181) 747 5013

Consultancy on listed buildings and conservation areas; historic building surveys and analysis; feasibility studies on uses for old buildings; programmes of maintenance and repair; conservation of sculpture and murals. Also offer expertise on landscape architecture.

Ancient and Historic Monuments in Wales

Edleston House

Queens Road

Aberystwyth

Dyfed

Tel: (01970) 621233

Answers queries from the public concerning the age, type and function of buildings.

Architectural Salvage

Nestley House

Gomshall

Guildford

Surrey GU5 9QA

Tel: (01483) 203221

Maintains an index of all kinds of architectural items. For a fee, will put buyers in touch with appropriate sellers.

Arts Workers Guild

6 Queen Square

London WC1N 3AR

Tel: (0171) 837 3474

Guilds of artists, architects, craftsmen and others engaged in the design and practice of the arts.

British Decorators Association

32 Coton Road

Nuneaton CV11 5TW

Tel: (01203) 353776

Over 1,000 members who specialize in the decoration of period homes.

British Wood Preserving Association

Building No 6

The Office Village

4 Romford Road

Stratford

London E15 4EA

Tel: (0181) 519 2588

A free and impartial advisory service on all problems concerning timber preservation and damp-proofing. Produces publications dealing with practical problems.

Chartered Institution of Building Services Engineers (CIBSE)

Delta House

222 Balham High Road

London SW12 9BS

Tel: (0181) 675 5211

Fax: (0181) 675 5449

Advice on plumbing, heating, ventilation, etc.

Church Farm House Museum

Greyhound Hill

London

NW4 4JR

TEL: (0181) 203 0130

FAX: (0181) 359 2666

A collection consisting mainly of 19th-century domestic material. Two period furnished rooms: the kitchen set at c.1820 and the dining room at c.1850.

Civic Trust

17 Carlton House Terrace

London SW1Y 5AW

TEL: (0171) 930 0914

Encourages the protection and improvement of the environment.

English Heritage

Fortress House

23 Savile Road

London W1X 1AB

TEL: (0171) 973 3000

FAX: (0171) 973 3001

Largest independent organization responsible for heritage conservation. Provides technical advice on conservation and repairs to historic buildings. Also responsible for the preservation and the presentation of some 700 historic properties in England.

The Georgian Group

6 Fitzroy Square

London

W1P 6DX

TEL: (0171) 387 1720

FAX: (0171) 387 1721

Gives advice on repair and restoration to owners of Georgian buildings.

The Guild of Master Craftsmen

Castleplace

166 High Street

Lewes

East Sussex

BN7 1XU

TEL: (01273) 477374

FAX: (01273) 478606

Trade association helping to put prospective clients in touch with experienced craftsmen and craftswomen able to carry restoration and other work.

The Historic Buildings Company

Chertsey Road

Cobham

Surrey

GU24 8JD

TEL: (01276) 856128

Publishers of the Period Property Register, *a publication devoted solely to the marketing, maintenance and improvement of period properties.*

Historic Homes of Britain

21 Pembroke Square

London

W8 6PB

TEL: (0171) 937 2402

Historic Houses Association

2 Chester Street

London

SW1X 7BB

TEL: (0171) 259 5688

FAX: (0171) 259 5590

National Federation of Building Trades Employers

Hales Road

Leeds OS12 4PW

TEL: (0113) 2630607

Recommends stonemasons, painters and decorators, etc.

The National Trust

36 Queen Anne's Gate

London SW1

TEL: (0171) 222 9251

The National Trust for Scotland

5 Charlotte Square

Edinburgh

EH2 4DU

TEL: (0131) 226 5922

Paint Research Association

Waldegrave Road

Teddington

Middlesex

TW11 8LD

TEL: (0181) 614 4800

Publishers of the Paint and Pretreatment Products Directory.

Royal Commission on Royal Incorporation of Architects in Scotland

15 Rutland Square

Edinburgh

EH1 2BE

TEL: (0131) 229 7545

Royal Institute of British Architects (RIBA)

66 Portland Place

London

W1N 4AD

TEL: (0171) 580 5533

Royal Institute of Chartered Surveyors (RICS)

12 Great George Street

Parliament Square

London

SW1P 3AD

TEL: (0171) 222 7000

The Victorian Society

1 Priory Gardens

Bedford Park

London

W4 1TT

TEL: (0181) 994 1019

A conservation amenity group dedicated to the preservation of Victorian and Edwardian buildings.

OF SPECIAL NOTE

Stephen Mack

Stephen P. Mack Associates

Chase Hill Farm

Ashaway

Rhode Island 02804

USA

TEL: (401) 377 8041

Stephen P. Mack is a nationally renowned architectural and interior designer and expert in the restoration and reconstruction of 17th- and 18th-century structures and their environments. (pp.88, 2; pp.122, 4, 5; pp. 128, 2, 3; pp.152)

GLOSSARY

acanthus Foliage ornament based on the serrated leaves of the *Acanthus spinosus* plant, native to the Mediterranean. Often used for *scrolling foliage.

Adam style *See* pp.16–17.

aedicule An opening or niche framed by two columns or *pilasters carrying an *entablature and *pediment.

aegricanes Heads or skulls of rams or goats, sometimes hung in *swags-and-tails in Greek and Roman ornament.

anthemia Floral motifs based on the flower of the *acanthus, or the flowers and leaves of the honeysuckle.

arabesques Stylized, interlaced foliage patterns of Near Eastern origin, based on laurel leaves. In Western ornament often combined with *strapwork.

arcading A range of arches supported on *pilasters or columns.

architrave Lowest part of an *entablature. Also a collective term for the mouldings around a window, door, panel or niche.

Art Nouveau *See* p.33.

Arts and Crafts *See* pp.30–1.

balusters Small posts or colonnetes used in rows to support a handrail. Together they form a **balustrade** (as on the side of a staircase or a terrace).

bargeboard A flat wooden board, often carved, that seals the space between the roof and wall on a *gable end.

Baronial style Late-19th-century mock *Gothic style of architecture based on *medieval designs of eccelesti-astical buildings and castles.

Baroque *See* pp.10–11.

bead moulding A moulding consisting of rows of small, convex or semi-circular (bead-like) shapes.

bead-and-reel A moulding comprising alternating, bead-like and cylindrical shapes.

Beaux Arts A strand of late-19th- and early 20th-century *classicism, particularly prevalent in America and based on the teachings of the influential *École des Beaux Arts* in Paris.

brattished Topped with an ornamental cresting, usually of leaf or floral forms, or miniature battlements.

broken pediment *See* *pediment.

bucrania Skulls of oxen or bulls, hung with garlands; like *aegricanes*, often incorporated into *swags-and-tails.

cantilevered A method of supporting a horizontal projection, such as a step(s), balcony, beam or canopy, with a downward force at only one end – usually through a wall into which the one end is keyed.

capital The top or head of a column or *pilaster (*see* *Orders).

cartouche A decorative panel consisting of a round, oval or scroll-shaped frame with either a plain or decorated centre.

casements *See* pp.68–9.

castellated Topped or crested with battlement-like, alternating projections and indents.

caulicolae The *fluted stalks of *acanthus leaves.

chamfered Cut or planed to an approximately 45 degree angle.

chequer pattern A geometric "counterchange" pattern consisting of regularly spaced squares of alternating colour.

chimney breast The part of a wall that contains the fireplace and projects into a room.

chinoiserie Western adaptations of Chinese furnishings, artefacts and styles of ornament.

classicism Post-*medieval revivals of the principles and forms of ancient Greek and Roman architecture and ornament.

closed-string A staircase in which the sides of the the steps are covered by a sloping member (a string) which supports the *balusters.

Coade stone An artificial cast stone made in London from the 1770s onward.

coffered ceiling A ceiling that has been divided into compartments (coffers) by exposed beams or by plaster mouldings.

Colonial Revival A late-19th- and early 20th-century revival of *Colonial-style architecture and decoration.

Colonial style *See* pp.14–15

consoles Ornamental brackets in the form of scrolls or *volutes.

corbel A stone or timber block projecting from the top of a wall and used to support a beam or part of the ceiling.

Corinthian A Classical *Order.

cornice A plain or decorative moulding used to cover the join between the walls and the ceiling.

crockets Small leaf carvings used in *Gothic architecture.

cyma recta An S-shaped moulding.

cyma reversa An S-shaped moulding in reverse.

dado Lower section of a wall (*see* pp.116–17).

dentils Decorative mouldings made up of regularly spaced, square-shaped blocks.

diaper patterns Collective term for patterns used in Western and oriental decoration, consisting of a geometric framework (such as *latticework or *trelliswork), often embellished with decorative motifs.

dog grate A metal basket used in a hearth for burning coals.

dog-leg A type of staircase (*see* p.77).

Doric A Classical *Order.

"drab" A brownish-grayish-green paint popular during the first half of the 18th century.

egg-and-dart A moulding comprising alternating egg and arrow shapes.

Empire style *See* pp.18–19.

encaustic tiles Earthenware tiles patterned with inlays of coloured clays.

en suite Designed or decorated to match other objects, surfaces or materials.

entablature The top of an *Order, made up of an *architrave, a *frieze and a *cornice.

fanlight *See* pp.40–1.

faux marbre French for "fake marble". A technique for simulating the appearance of marble using paints and glazes.

Federal style *See* pp.18–19.

field The centre section of a wall (*see* pp.114–15).

fielded A raised centre part of a panel.

finial A carved, cast or moulded ornament on top of a spire, gable or post. Also used on furniture and curtain rod ends. Typical forms include acorns, arrowheads and pine cones.

fireback A fixed or freestanding iron plate at the back of a hearth, protecting the wall and reflecting heat into the room.

fire-dogs Pairs of raised metal bars used to support burning logs in a hearth.

flat-painted A surface covered with one or more uniform, opaque coats of paint.

fleur-de-lis A stylized three-, or five-, petal lily motif, widely used since the early Middle Ages.

flocked wallpaper A type of wallpaper with a raised, textured pattern formed by sprinkling fine particles of wool (or other fibres) over the paper.

floorcloth A floor covering made from linseed-oil-stiffened canvas, and then painted or stencilled with patterns.

fluting A row of parallel, vertical, concave grooves.

"flying" stairs A staircase in which the flight or flights of stairs are *cantilevered from the wall(s) of the stairwell, and have no *newel.

foliate Leaf-like.

fretwork Carved or painted geometric patterns (such as *Greek key patterns) consisting of bands of horizontal and vertical lines.

frieze The section of wall from the ceiling or *cornice down to the top of the *field.

gable The part triangular-shaped section of a wall directly under the end of a sloping roof.

girandole A convex mirror.

Gothic *See* pp.8–9.

Gothic Revival A 19th-century revival of *medieval Gothic architecture, ornament and decoration.

gougework Patterns and motifs chiselled into wooden surfaces.

Graeco-Roman Collective term for the classical architecture, ornament and decoration of ancient Greece and Rome.

Greek key A pattern of regularly repeated, interlocking right-angled and vertical lines. Used as a border ornament, and originating in classical Greek architecture.

grisaille A monochromatic, *trompe l'oeil* technique in which figures and patterns are rendered three-dimensionally in shades of black, gray and white.

grotesques Decorations based on ancient Roman wall paintings. Typical motifs include animals, birds and fishes, set within *foliate scrolls or panels.

guilloche A form of decoration or ornament made up of interlacing curved bands, sometimes forming circles embellished with floral motifs.

herringbone Geometric pattern consisting of alternating diagonal lines, and resembling the spinal and rib structure of the herring fish.

Italianate A 19th-century style of architecture based on the rural buildings of northern Italy and the palaces of the Italian *Renaissance, typified by low roofs, bracketed overhanging eaves, entrance towers, *arcaded porches and *balustrated balconies.

Ionic A Classical *Order.

Jacobean An historical period embracing the reigns of James I and Charles I of England

jambs The straight, vertical sides of a doorway, an arch or a fireplace – in the latter, flanking the hearth and sometimes in the form of *pilasters.

key stone The central stone in the curve of an arch.

lath-and-plaster A network of thin slips of wood (laths) covered with layers of flat plaster.

latticework A grid pattern of open diamond shapes used for leading in late-16th-century glazed windows. Also worked in stone or wood as an architectural and furniture embellishment, and used as a pattern on ceramics, fabrics, wallpapers and metalwares.

limewash An early form of paint, made from lime putty, water, linseed oil and pigments.

linenfold A carved pattern resembling vertical folds in linen, and mostly applied to wall panelling and doors.

marquetry *See* pp.90–1.

medallions Circular or oval decorative devices, often bearing a portrait or other motifs and imagery.

medieval *See* pp.8–9.

Middle Ages Historical period extending from the fall of the Western Roman Empire in the 5th century A.D. to the beginning of the Renaissance in the 15th century. The *Medieval period.

millefleurs A dense floral pattern (French for "a thousand flowers"), originally used on medieval pictorial tapestries. Favoured flowers, naturalistically depicted, include roses, anemones, pinks, columbines and violas.

modillions Projecting, bracket-like ornaments used in a *cornice, and similar in appearance to small *corbels.

mortised-and-tenoned A method of joining two pieces of wood, in which a hole (a mortise) is cut into one piece to house a projection (a tenon) shaped in the other.

mosaic A pattern constructed from small pieces of coloured stone, ceramic or glass, much used in Roman and oriental architecture.

mouldings Decoratively contoured strips of wood, plaster or stone.

mullions Vertical bars (of stone or wood) used to divide windows and other openings. Also fixed or hinged, vertically divided windows.

neo-classical A style of architecture, ornament and decoration that began in the mid-18th century, and based on interpretations of classical Greek and Roman precedents. *See* pp.16–23.

newel Post at the end of a staircase, often attached to the handrail and string (*see* *open-string). On circular staircases, the central post around which stairs curve, and which supports the narrow side of the steps.

ogival arch Pointed arch formed by pairs of serpentine-shaped reversed curves.

open-string A staircase in which the side or sides of the treads and steps are not enclosed by a string (*see* *closed-string), and are thus visible.

Orders The architectural components that constitute the basis of classical Greek and Roman architecture. Each Order consists of a *column, usually rising from a *pedestal or *plinth, topped by a *capital, and supporting an *entablature. The original Greek and Roman Orders are Doric, Ionic, Corinthian, Composite and Tuscan.

oriental Collective term used in the West for Eastern artefacts and styles of decoration and ornament. Includes Arabian, Chinese, Indian, Japanese, Persian and Turkish.

overmantel The decorative treatment of the area of wall above a fireplace, often incorporating a painting or mirror.

parquetry *See* pp.90–1.

paterae An oval or circular motif based on dishes used in religious ceremonies – often with a central flower and/or *fluting. Similar to *rosettes.

pedestal The supporting base for a column, or an artefact such as a statue or vase.

pediment A low-pitched (triangular-shaped) *gable across the top of a *portico, door, window or fireplace. When the top of the triangular shape is omitted, or left open, it is called a *broken pediment.

pelmet Fabric-covered wooden fitting, or a stiffened section of fabric, fixed above a window and designed to conceal the curtain pole and the tops of the curtains.

piano nobile The principal floor of a large house or villa, containing the reception rooms.

picture rail A *moulding on upper part of a wall, sometimes defining the top of the *field or the bottom of the *frieze, and used to hang pictures.

pier glass A tall, narrow, often ornately framed mirror traditionally hung between two windows.

pilaster A flat, rectangular classical column fixed to a wall. Often used to frame a doorway, or as the *jambs of a fireplace.

plinth A square block supporting the base of a column or *pilaster.

polychrome Multi-coloured.

Pompeiian A style of architecture, ornament and decoration found in, and inspired by, the ancient Roman town of Pompeii, re-discovered in southern Italy through archaeological digs starting in the mid-18th century.

porphyry A hard, fine-grained rock, usually dark red or purple, but sometimes gray or green, and flecked with white crystals.

portico A roofed entrance, usually supported by columns.

portières Curtain designed to be hung over an archway or door.

purlins Horizontal members of the wooden framework of a roof.

quarries Panes of diamond-shaped glass, supported by *latticework leading, in 16th-century glazed windows.

quarry tile An unglazed floor tile made from fired clay.

rectilinear In a straight line, or lines, and bounded by straight lines.

Regency *See* pp.20–1.

Renaissance A term used to describe the movement in art, architecture, design and ornament that originated in Italy in the late 14th century and spread across Europe during the next 200 years. At its heart lay a revival (and re-interpretation) of the architecture and ornament of ancient Greece and Rome.

rosettes Circular, formalized floral ornament. *See* *paterae*.

roundels Circular shaped ornament, either plain or containing decorative motifs.

sash window A window formed with sashes – glazed wooden frames which slide up and down in grooves by means of counterbalanced weights. The standard type has two sashes, and is known as a "double-hung" sash.

scrolling foliage A pattern or form of ornament consisting of scrolling, curving or trailing plant forms, such as grapevines or *acanthus.

side lights Panes of glass on either side of a door.

skirting boards The wooden boards fixed to the base of an internal wall at the junction of the floor and the wall; often moulded or chamfered along the top.

slips The fascia panels often installed between the opening of a hearth and the *jambs and the *frieze or *lintel of a mantelpiece.

spandrels The approximately triangular-shaped spaces between an arched opening and any linear *mouldings surrounding it.

stencilling A technique for applying patterns to a surface by dabbing paints, glazes or dyes through cutouts made in a stencil – a thin card often made of oiled paper, but sometimes wood, metal or plastic.

strapwork Form of ornament consisting of twisted and interlaced bands (similar to strips of leather or ribbons). Sometimes combined with *grotesques, and often studded with *rosettes, or faceted, jewel-like forms – the latter known as jewelled strapwork.

stucco A fine cement or plaster made from sand, slaked lime and gypsum. Mostly applied to walls and mouldings. From the 19th century, generally known as render.

swagged-and-tailed Lengths of fabrics, or strips of carved, moulded or painted motifs (of flowers, fruits, vegetables, leaves or shells), hung in horizontal loops (swags), and allowed to hang or trail down at the ends (tails).

tongue-and-groove A method of jointing wooden boards, in which the edge of one board has a tongue, or lip, that fits into a groove cut into the edge of the adjacent board.

tracery An ornamental arrangement of intersecting ribwork, forming a pierced pattern. Often employed in the upper part of *Gothic windows.

transom The horizontal component running across the top or middle of doors or windows.

trelliswork A criss-cross support for plants, and geometric patterns based on this botanical accessory. Popular in *Medieval, *Regency and *Arts and Crafts decoration.

trompe l'oeil French for "trick of the eye". A decorative technique in which paints are applied to a flat surface to create the appearance of three-dimensional scenes or objects. *See* *grisaille*.

Tudorbethan A late-19th- and early 20th-century hybrid style of architecture, combining elements of English Tudor and Jacobean prototypes.

vaulted Arched, as in an arch-shaped roof or ceiling.

Venetian window A window with an arch-top centre section flanked by two narrower rectangular sections. Also known as a *serliana*.

volute A spiral, scrolling form, shaped like a ram's horn.

wainscoting Alternative name for wooden wall panelling.

wall-strings Diagonal or inclined timbers attached to the wall of a stairwell, into which one or both sides of the steps of a staircase are secured.

wattle-and-daub An early method of wall construction in which thin branches or *laths (wattles) are fixed to a timber frame and roughly plastered over with mud or clay (daub).

wavescrolls Undulating, linear, wave-like patterns.

weatherboarding Overlapping wooden boards applied as the external covering to timber-framed walls.

winding stairs *See* *spiral stairs.

INDEX

ACKNOWLEDGMENTS

I would very much like to thank the team at Mitchell Beazley for all the long hours, dedication and skill they have committed to this book: to Julia North for running the project, and for procuring and sifting myriad examples of period fixtures and fittings from numerous manufacturers; Christopher Sparks for the substantial and complex task of hands-on layout and design; Suzanne Woloszynska for contributing; Judith More and Janis Utton for overseeing, respectively, content and design; Karen Farquhar for production control; Bruce Darlaston for US rights; and, last but by no means least, Arlene Sobel for the expertise of her text editing and American "translation", and her unflagging patience and good humour. Thank you.

Together with the publisher, I would like to thank the numerous manufacturers of reproduction architectural fixtures and fittings on both sides of the Atlantic for supplying us with so many examples of their products. You will find their names and addresses in the Directory, on pages 174-187.

Together with the publisher, I also wish to thank all the homeowners, architects, interior designers, museums, trustees and architectural salvage companies who so kindly opened their doors to our photographers.